青銅
鑑容

Bronze Luminescence

Bronze Mirror Collections from the Present-Past Dwelling
「今昔居」青銅藏鏡鑑賞與文化研究

Dominic Cheung◎張錯 著
With the assistance of Alexandria Yen

臺北醫學大學人文暨社會科學院人文藝術中心 協同印行

The author wishes to thank Dr. Yun Yen, M. D., President of the Taipei Medical University, who not only appointed him the honor of an Endowed Chair Professorship at TMU but also provided immense support for the publication of this monograph. The writing and completion of this book was funded by the "Humanities in Medicine Project" at the Taipei Medical University. 感謝臺北醫學大學贊助出版

Table of Contents 目錄

Mirrors 鏡種

Chapter 5 | Yuan, Ming and Qing
第五章 | 元、明、清

Mirrors 鏡種

Appendix 附錄

Preface

Bronze Luminescence: Make up, Put on Caps and Gowns

Bronze Mirror Collections from the Present-Past Dwellings

In high antiquity, when there were no mirrors, people used ceramic or bronze washbasins to contain water and reflect their images to dress up and apply makeup. Such basins are called "*jian*"（監）, with two homophones 鑑 and 鑒 indicating utensils either made of ceramics or with bronze metals. In *jinwen*（金文）, or bronze script, the character *jian* ![glyph] consists of a person ![glyph], an eye ![glyph], and a clay washbasin ![glyph], which is the pictograph of a person bending over a full basin of still water watching his or her own reflection.

While examining the bronze vessels excavated from Sanmenxia（三門峽）, Guo Moruo（郭沫若）points out that "Ancient Chinese used water as a mirror, which they contained in a washbasin to reflect their images. This type of washbasin is called "*jian*"（監）, sometimes written with a different character "*jian*" 鑒 if made of bronze. The pictograph resembles the image of a person standing beside a basin looking down into the water..... Commoners used ceramic basins, while aristocrats used bronze ; a bronze basin could reflect images without water if it was polished very shiny."[1] Such is the imagery of the character *jian* displayed in the bronze script.

The character "*jing*"（鏡）appeared only after the Spring and Autumn and the Warring States periods. In *zhuanwen*（篆文）, or seal script, *jing* ![glyph] combines the radical *jin* ![glyph]（金, metal）and *jing* ![glyph]（竟, indicating both the pronunciation and the image, meaning ultimate）, which connotes metals of such supreme qualities that once polished and gleamed, they reflect the true images of the world. The ability of bronze mirrors to create reflections of humans was marveled at by ancient Chinese people.

Taking the bronze basin as a mirror, the poem "Dang"（蕩 Immensity）in the "Greater Elegance"（大雅）of the *Classic of Odes*（詩經）recites, "The reflective lesson（*jian*）for the Yin dynasty is not far away ; one just has to look at the

Water basin（jian）of Lord Fu Chai of the Wu State 吳夫差鑑

1　Guo Moruo, "Sanmenxia chutu tongqi ersan shi" (A few remarks on the excavated bronze vessels at Sanmenxia), *Wenwu* 1, 1959, 13. 郭沫若，「三門峽出土銅器二三事」，《文物》1, 1959, 頁 13.

kings of the Xia dynasty" (殷鑒不遠，在夏後之世). The *jian* of the Yin, therefore, are Yin-Shang (殷商) mirrors used as metaphor for "reflective lessons".

Chapter "Dechongfu" (德充符 Virtue-infused Talisman) in *Zhuangzi* (莊子) mentions, "Confucius said, 'One should not take flowing water as a mirror; instead, take still water as a mirror' ". It implies that only through the stillness of the calm mind-heart (*xin*) can an

Bronze water basin of King Southern Yue in West Han 西漢南越王墓銅鑒

image be captured and reflected truthfully, and the mind should stay as still water; otherwise, once the mind moves as flowing water, there is no way to distinguish truth. In this sense, *jian* means more than an ordinary mirror but also functions as a vehicle to reflect reality of the society.

The external chapters of *Zhuangzi* parallel the mind of a "*zhiren*" (至人 the ultimate person) or sage with a bright mirror:

"The ultimate person uses his mind as a mirror: the mind neither conducts nor anticipates; it responds, but does not retain; hence it can bear all things without being harmed".

"The mind of the sage is still, it is the reflection of heaven and earth, and it is the mirror of ten thousand things".

"For those who were born beautiful, one has to provide them with mirrors, otherwise they would not know of their own beauty".

Mozi (墨子) claims in "Feigong" (非攻 Condemnation of offensive wars) that "A noble person does not use water but people as his mirror. Using water as the mirror, he sees only the appearance of his face; using people as the mirror, he comprehends fortunes and misfortunes." Mozi was more pragmatic than Zhuangzi because he applied the mirror to the public, whereas Song Yu (宋玉) in the "Nine Arguments" (九辯) limits the function of the mirror to mere personal adornment — "Dressing up and glancing at the mirror today, one might yet hide and conceal〔his ambitions〕tomorrow".

In the 14th year of the Reign of Qianlong in the Qing dynasty (1749A.D.), Liang Shizheng (梁詩正), Grand Scholar and Chancellor of the Board of Offices, was commissioned along with other court officials by imperial decree to compile a catalog of the 1,529 pieces of ancient bronze *ding*-tripods and yi wine vessels in the collection of the imperial court. In addition to a fine illustration of its shape and form, each item has been recorded for its inscription and seal, dimension, capacity, and weight. The catalog contains 93 pieces of bronze mirrors, which are referred to as "*jian*" instead of "*jing*", and the same character "*jian*"（鑑）is also adopted in the title of the catalog, *Xiqing gujian*（西清古鑑 Examination and Evaluation of the Antiquities in the Imperial Studio of Western Purity）, and in its sequel *Xiqing gujian yibian*（西清續鑑乙編 Second Extension to the Examination and Evaluation of the Antiquities in the Imperial Studio of Western Purity）[2]. The sequel lists a total of 910 bronze vessels from the Shang, the Zhou, the Han, and the Tang dynasties including 100 mirrors（which are referred to as "*jian*", suggesting a consensus of the interchangeability of "*jing*" and "*jian*"）. Even though the compilers of the catalogs were erudite scholars of the highest literary capacity and knowledge of history, they mistakenly identify the sea lions and grapevine mirror（*Haishou putao jing* 海獸葡萄鏡）of the Tang dynasty to be of the Han, which is a tragic flaw of the catalogs.

Modern scholar Liang Shangchun（梁上椿）has proposed an outline of the historical process of the development from washbasins to bronze mirrors:

Still water → still water in the washbasin → polished bronze basin without water → polished bronze plate → bronze plate with a knob at the back → mirror with a plain back → plain ground with color paints → color paints with engravings of pictorial or decorative patterns → inscriptions.[3]

According to Liang's proposal, the bronze mirror evolved from the bronze washbasin. Bronze refers to a certain type of alloy made of copper, tin, and lead（sometimes also with a small amount of zinc）. Because pure copper is quite soft, it needs the addition of tin to improve luster and increase hardness, but too much tin makes it brittle and easily breakable. On the other hand, lead not only brings down the melting point of the alloy from above 1,000℃ to around 800℃, but also shows high stability and compatibility with the liquefied copper alloy since it does not generate air bubbles during the melting of the alloy and leaves no flaws once the mirror cools down. The "*Kaogongji*"（考工記 Record of Craftsmanship）records the ratios of the metal components in different alloys and for different vessels, for instance, "one portion of copper and a half portion of tin makes the formula for *jiansui*-mirrors"（金錫半謂之鑒燧之劑）. Without the assistance of any surveying or measuring apparatus, ancient craftsmen cast the mirrors based purely on their work experience and the transmission of such experience；this is a great achievement indeed.

Aside from bronze mirrors, ancient Chinese also used flint mirrors called *yangsui*（陽燧）to reflect and concentrate sunrays to make fire. In Cui Bao（崔豹）'s *Gujinzhu*（古今注 Commentaries on things past and present）, the seventh chapter of the "Miscellaneous Commentary"（雜註第七）states, "A *yangsui* is made of bronze in the shape of a mirror held towards the sun to generate fire；to place Artemisia underneath will obtain fire". Cui Bao lived in the Western Jin dynasty, and his commentaries record and comment on past and present things. The comments are not completely reliable, but at least they inform of certain shared functionalities of both the mirror（*jing*）and the flint mirror（*sui*）, even though no flint mirrors from the early Xia and Shang dynasties have been excavated until now.

The two hypotheses that the bronze washbasin and the flint mirror are proto-mirrors remain questionable due to the lack of direct archaeological evidence. A modern bronze mirror scholar He Tangkun（何堂坤）proposes a third hypothesis. He contends that if mirrors did come from bronze basins, such basins must have existed prior to the two early bronze mirrors of Qijia Culture（齊家文化 2400-1900B.C.）— one plain mirror excavated at Qijiaping in Gansu（甘肅齊家坪）, in 1975, and one seven-pointed star

Triangular design mirror of Qijia Culture Period 齊家文化時期三角紋鏡

mirror at Duomatai in the Guinan County of Qinghai（青海貴南縣朵馬台）, in 1976. However, current excavated bronze vessels of or parallel to Qijia Culture are only common small-scale craft tools and daily utensils without a trace of water containers or basins, whereas the bronze basins we see today came from the Spring and Autumn and Warring States periods, which could not have been the prototype of bronze mirrors.[4]

Tang square flint mirror with lions design
唐代獅子紋方型陽燧

The hypothesis that bronze mirrors came from flint mirrors is also problematic. The *yangsui* that have been excavated so far date from the Western Zhou（1027-771B.C.）, the Tang（618-907A.D.）, or the Song（960-1279A.D.）dynasties, which include:（1）a Western Zhou mirror, 9.9cm in diameter, excavated in 1975 from a wooden casket tomb at Baifucun in the Changping District of Beijing（北京昌平區白浮村西周木槨墓）;（2）a Warring States（475-221B.C.）mirror, 3.6cm in diameter, excavated in 1981 at the foot of the western Lion Mountains in Potang Communities in

2　Modern reprint of both catalogs are published by Jiangsu guangling guji keyinshe in 1992. 此兩書均由江蘇廣陵古籍刻印社影印發行，1992.

3　Liang Shangchun, "Gujing yanjiu zonglun"（General discussions on the study of ancient mirrors）*Dalu zazhi* vol. 5, issue 5, 1952, 190. 梁上椿〈古鏡研究總論〉《大陸雜誌》5卷 5期，1952，頁 190.

4　See He Tangkun, *Zhongguo gudai tongjing de jishu yanjiu*（A technological study on Chinese ancient bronze mirrors）（Beijing: Zijincheng chubanshe, 1999）, 317-321. 何堂坤《中國古代銅鏡的技術研究》，北京，紫禁城出版社，1999, 頁 317-321。

Shaoxing, Zhejiang（浙江省紹興市坡塘公社獅子西麓）；(3) a Tang lion-patterned square mirror, 14.4cm per side, donated by Chen Danian to the National Museum of China in 1959；and (4) a Song mirror in imitation of a Han sunlight condenser, 18.5cm in diameter, discovered and retrieved by the Beijing Cultural Relics Research Team from a recycling center.

When compared with those of Qijia Culture mentioned earlier, these mirrors are at least 800 to 1,000 years late.

He Tangkun holds that mirrors came neither from bronze basins nor flint mirrors, but were instead "inspired by the reflections from sabers, axes, rings, bullet primers, and various early types of metal objects which reflect things on polished surfaces." He supports this hypothesis with the instances of "qudao weijing"（屈刀為鏡 bending saber to make a mirror）and "daojian quhuo"（刀劍取火 to make fire from saber and sword）from later documents.

But this hypothesis also has certain flaws. The "later documents" he cited, such as Cui Hu's（崔護）"Qudao weijing fu"（Rhapsody on bending saber to make mirror）in the Tang dynasty, refers to Tang sabers that came out several thousand years later than the mirrors of Qijia Culture. Isn't the association between the two too far-stretched? In the case of "to make fire from saber and sword", he again refers to Wang Chong's（王充） *Lunheng*（論衡 On balance）of the Han dynasty, in which chapter "Shuaixing"（率性篇 Being at will）says, "In ignorance, people of the day rub and polish the moon-shaped hook blade until it turns shining bright, then hold it against the sun to make fire. The moon-shaped hook is not a flint mirror, and the reason why it can make fire is because of the constant rubbing and polishing." Therefore, He Tangkun has misinterpreted the meaning of "to make fire from saber and sword" and mistakenly drawn upon this instance out of its original context.[5]

Wang Chong's point is on the true and false approaches to the "Way of Heaven"（天道 tiandao）. True approaches naturally correspond with Heaven, while false ones can also be conducted through knowledge or wisdom which is no different from true approaches. Holding a *yangsui* or flint mirror towards the sun to produce fire is the true method of fire making, but fire can also be produced by rubbing the moon-shaped hook blade or sabers and swords and place them against the sun. The moon-shaped hook blade is not a *yangsui* or flint mirror, and it can make fire because the shining bright surface reflects the sun.[6] Wang Chong then follows, "For people of evil nature these days, if they can be put together with the people of good nature, and be encouraged to become good. Even they are of a different kind, they can still be instructed to learn to change like the Daoists making jade, Marquis Sui making glass beads, or those who make fire by rubbing the moon-shaped hook blade. Instructing people with learning to accumulate virtue, they will gradually attain the conduct of benevolence and righteousness."

Thus, to make fire with saber and sword is simply an analogy between the particular method of fire making and the cultivation of good human nature. For people of good or evil nature, there is always a way towards hope and brightness. The real saber and sword have nothing to do with the origins of bronze mirror or flint mirror.

Due to the mirror's light reflecting and refracting function, and aside from being used for personal dress up and make up, bronze mirrors also bear religious significance to ward off evil spirits and propitiating the gods. Regretfully however, modern scholarship mostly focuses on the periodization and typology of bronze mirrors with few approaches from the perspectives of

Concentric mirror of Shang Dynasty 商代同心紋鏡

culture, art, and literature. Shen Congwen（沈從文）while working in the History Museum in Beijing, and organizing Chinese antique bronze mirrors had the following lament:

.....Especially for the mirrors, a legacy of a series of excellent artworks have remained, which allow us to study the different shapes, forms, and the evolution of the decorative designs and patterns, and to see how they reflect in various ways the social reality in terms of other superstructures of social life, how they can be connected with literature, poetry, music, art, and religious belief. They help us to achieve a deeper level of apprehension of the development of each of the compartments above-mentioned and mutual influences among one another. We therefore come to understand that nothing is absolutely isolated, and that there is no single product remained uninfluenced and in turn influences one another. As to the mirrors, for example, what about the position they deserve to be in the craftsmanship of Chinese bronze and in sculpture of Fine Arts history？There is social formation background, artistic

---

5 | Cui Hu's "Qudao weijing fu"（Rhapsody on bending saber to make a mirror） chants, "Though sabers and mirrors differ in name, they share the property of firmness and strength in substance. Great is the touching of the numinous and celestial hand；nuanced is the working of the intricate and witting heart. Upon unsheathing the sharp blade, one bends it close to make a circle；once the bright mirror is formed, one wipes it in fear and the light emits." 崔護〈屈刀為鏡賦〉內云「惟刀鏡之異名，共堅剛以為質，懿靈仙之手澤，得微妙之心術。銛鋒始拔，乍盤屈以規圓；朗鑒俄成，駭拂拭而光溢。」

6 | 王充《論衡》〈率性篇〉「今妄以刀劍之鉤月摩拭朗白，仰以向日，亦得火焉。夫鉤月，非陽燧也，所以耐取火者，摩拭之所致也。」

Tang double phoenix with ribbons mirror annotated by Shen Tsung-wen
沈從文先生筆註唐代雙鸞啣綬鏡（內治雙鸞鳳作成的雙鸞鳳不壞。能放大成
一寸二大小，效果會很好。）

Painted sword fight scene mirror of King Souther Yue of West Han
（partial）西漢南越王墓彩繪觀鬥劍鏡（下圖為局部）

formation background to be considered as well. If we need to deepen our discussion on these mirrors, we need to consider simultaneously various aspects of the achievement and development of the mirrors, so that our observations will not be lopsided or partial. [7]

"Nothing is absolutely isolated", we can thus say that from the evolution of the bronze basins to the mirrors, a text of the bronze mirror is formed. From each dynasty and time period, there were different shapes, forms, decorative designs and patterns representing various discourses of religion, literature and art. Looking from the angle of cultural studies, these discourses had been tightly woven with the life and ideology of the aristocrats and commoners in the society of those times.

Archaeological excavations indicate that the bronze mirrors of the Warring States and the Han-Wei period (206B.C.-265A.D.) were usually found among the funerary objects of the tombs of aristocrats. Entering Tang dynasty, the decorative *suanni* sea lions（狻猊）and grapevines patterns from Central Asia with high reliefs, gold and silver inlaid, conch and sea shell embedded in lacquer all look glamorous and magnificent that they quickly captivated the fondness of both aristocrats and commoners alike. Obviously, the Warring States, the Western and Eastern Han, and the Sui-Tang

7 | Shen Congwen, "Cong xinchutu tongjing dedaode renshi"（A few thoughts on the newly excavated bronze mirrors）, *Tongjing shihua*（Talking about the history of bronze mirrors）（Shenyang: Wanjuan chuban gongsi, 2004）, 203. 沈從文〈從新出土銅鏡得到的認識〉《銅鏡史話》，沈陽萬卷出版公司，2004，頁203。

Tang mirror with grapes amd auspicous sea lions 唐代海獸葡萄鏡

are the three historical periods that epitomize the most splendid representational stages of the bronze mirror history.

In the second year of the Jingkang Reign（靖康二年）in the Northern Song（1127A.D.）, Jin armies came down from the north and abducted Emperor Huizong and Emperor Qinzong, which marked the demise of the Northern Song dynasty. Later, Emperor Gaozong ascended the throne, moved south, and set up a new capital at Lin'an（臨安 , Hangzhou 杭州）, which was Southern Song（1127-1279A.D.）. In early Northern Song, due to the long-term confrontation between the Song regime and the Khitan-Liao（916-1125A.D.）in the north

【金銀平脫鸞鳥啣綬鏡】

張錯（2002／06／15 聯合報）

因為相信昔日情愛
有如黃金永不褪色
詩人遂以此為名
並在八月初五的千秋節日
舉國歡騰，群臣各獻甘露壽酒後
分別攜回一面面盤龍葵花鏡或
銀背鎏金鳥獸菱花鏡。
然而這張金銀平脫四鸞啣綬鏡
從圓鈕開始
是三張銀光閃閃蒲團荷葉
有如鑲嵌螺鈿一般晶瑩明亮
荷葉內圈各擁三座小蓮蓬
呼應著鈕座內區一圈金絲同心結。
主旨仍是四隻口啣飄動綬帶
以金箔剪裁錘脫成彩光熠熠
展翅伸足的環飛鸞鳥，
鸞鳳和鳴之餘
自是喻指綬壽同音
夫妻祥和相愛，共偕白首；
鸞鳥間各飾一朵銀白菊花
更是地久天長之意。
可是天地有愛時光無情
千年之後
內外區兩圈同心結已開始脫落
就像昔日那些金色詩句
以及耳邊喃呢的海誓山盟
隨著光陰而無法自圓其說──
因為同心只有一生
共壽亦只有一世；
除此以外，只能有過許多曾經美麗的心
黏貼在鏡背渾厚漆地裡
像無垠長夜碧海青天
不斷見證著開元天寶的絢麗。

Tang mirror conch and sea shells inlaid with gold and silver phoenix on a lacquered base 唐代錯金錯銀平脫鸞鳳啣綬鏡

and the constant warfare against the Xixia (1038-1227A.D.) in the northwest, the minerals for producing bronze was scarce, and the mirror quality was far inferior to their Tang forerunners. When Southern Song moved its court to the south, a large population exodus migrated from north to south, and the economic center also shifted southward. Silk, porcelain, printing, smelting, papermaking, and other industries all entered a time of unprecedented growth and prosperity. The bronze mirrors manufactured in Huzhou (Wuxing 吳興), Kuaiji (會稽，Shaoxing 紹興), Raozhou (饒州，Boyang in Jiangxi 江西鄱陽), Jizhou (吉州，Ji'an 吉安), Jiankang (建康，Nanjing 南京), Lin'an, Chengdu (成都), and Suzhou (蘇州) gained nationwide fames, while the mirrors of Huzhou became the most acclaimed and valued. Even Southern Song was a stage of deterioration in the history of bronze mirrors, but mirrors took a more pragmatic turn, looked less fancy, and became lighter in weight and slender in form. They displayed the splendor and charm of the simple, the pure, and the unadorned, which can be regarded as a reactionary or subversive force to the previous art styles. The mirrors made by Second Uncle Nien of the Shi Family in Huzhou gained such popularity for a time that the brand became one of the bestsellers. Because the pure and clear water of the canals were especially suitable for polishing mirrors, Huzhou emerged as one of the national mirror manufacturing centers whose dominance continued until the late Qing, when the rise of glass mirrors imported from the West led to its gradual decline. The mirror workshops of Huzhou at the time

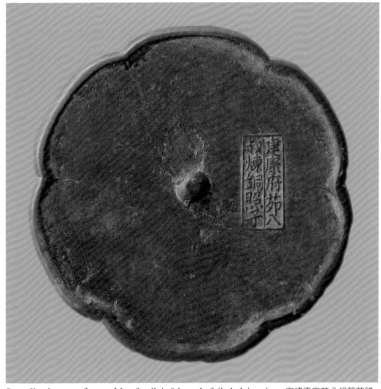

Song Jian kang prefecture Mao family's 8th uncle foiled plain mirror 宋建康府茆八叔葵花鏡

were all located around the Yifeng Bridge（儀鳳橋）at the pier of grain transport, where the most renowned crafters came from the Xue（薛）and the Shi（石）families.

As far as casting technology is concerned, the bronze mirrors manufactured in the Yuan（1279-1368A. D.）and the Ming（1368-1644A.D.）dynasties should have been more technically advanced than those of the Song, the Liao, and the Jin. But as mentioned above, the Northern and the Southern Song suffered from continual military operations and incessant warfare, and the casting of weaponry consumed a large amount of copper. This led to the extreme dearth of copper in the manufacture of bronze utensils and other artifacts, including bronze mirrors. In the Yuan, the Mongols' iron-hand control of the trading and private manufacturing of bronze was even more conspicuous—

Song golden mirror stand with a rhinocero gazing back at the moon 宋代鎏金犀牛望月鏡座

the "Basic Annals of Shizu" in the *Yuanshi*（元史·世祖本紀 *Official history of the Yuan*）mentions the bans on private manufacture of bronze vessels and on the use of gold, silver, and copper coins as currencies in self-organized overseas trading. In the meantime, for a stringent control on the excavation and casting of copper and bronze, the Yuan court also established official bronze bureaus and workshops, while the casting technology started to wane.

The Ming started with great prosperity and peace and lasted for almost three hundred years, which should have allowed the mirror industry to shine and flourish, only that the timing was wrong. On the practical level, Western imports entered China via maritime trade, bringing in the knowledge of optics and large and bright glass mirrors which eclipsed local bronze mirrors. On the level of industrial and artistic design, tens of thousands of blue-and-white and other types of porcelains were exported via the Sea Silk Route, which became the artery of Ming economy, and artisans were more concerned about the crafting, kilning, and design of porcelains, but not on mirrors any more. For these reasons, Ming mirrors lacked freshness of idea in design, and even the high-quality "cloud dragon mirror"（yunlongjing 雲龍鏡）with grotesque-looking cloud dragons of bared teeth and swinging claws remind one only of the cloud-dragon patterns on the thickly and sumptuously painted *wucai*（五彩 five-colored）porcelain of the Ming. Hence there were a particularly large number of archaic mirrors produced in the Ming, which were modeled after Han and Tang mirrors and engraved with the name and title of the artisan and the character "*zao*"（造 manufacture）, such as "Li zao"（李造 manufactured by Li）and "Zhangjia zao"（張家造 manufactured by the Zhang family）.

On the other hand, Ming mirrors by and large broke away from the early mysticism of the Han and the exoticism of the Tang, and turned to supplement its content by auspicious words of blessing, such as "zhuangyuan jidi"（狀元及第 Top candidate chosen in the Imperial Examination）, "changming fugui"（長命富貴 longevity, wealth, and fame）, or "wuzi dengke"（五子登科 five sons going in officialdom）and other large-character inscriptions. The inclusion of such auspicious inscriptions further developed in the Qing and became a hallmark of Qing bronze mirrors.

Just as one cannot regard Tang poetry, Song lyrics, and Yuan drama as the only genre of literature in its respective dynasties, it has been conceived in the beginning of writing this book to try to break away from the conventional classification of mirrors by dynasties. Therefore, each chapter preceding the typology of mirrors in this book focuses on a particular theme to introduce the characteristics of the mirrors of corresponding dynasties, while the chapters on Yuan, Ming, and Qing（1644-1911A.D.）mirrors remain absent, which signifies the lack of a thematic style of the mirrors of these three dynasties.

The four characters of the book title, *Bronze Luminescence（qingtong jianrong,*青銅鑑容）came from the inscription of a pear-shaped Song mirror, which are here adopted as the title of the catalog and cultural studies of the bronze mirror collections from the *Present-Past Dwellings*（今昔居）. The phrase "bronze reflections" has an origin of profound meaning. Emperor Taizong of the Tang dynasty was known to

Ming Hongwu 22nd year reign cloud dragon mirror 明洪武廿二年雲龍鏡　　Qing mirror with 「san yuan ji di」 inscriptions 清三元及第鏡

have complimented his loyal minister Wei Zheng（魏徵）with a famous analogy about mirrors. When Wei Zheng died of illness, the mournful Emperor Taizong said to his entourage, "Using bronze as a mirror, one beautifies his appearance; using the past as a mirror, one discerns the rises and falls of dynasties; using people as a mirror, one apprehends his own virtues and vices. Now with the death of Wei Zheng, I have lost a mirror!" Thus we can see the rich symbolism associated with mirrors and the importance of taking people as "mirrors".

This book has selected more than one hundred bronze mirrors from the collection of the *Present-Past Dwellings'* owner. Like firefly flickering lights, they cannot be compared to the full moon of much grandeur collections in museums or other eminent private collectors. Nevertheless, the process of collecting each and every one of these hundred mirrors is quite Buddhist, leading to the understanding of illusory life like "a flower in the mirror, a moon in the water." The completion of this book arouses myriad threads of thoughts and recollections. First I have to thank Dr. Yun Yen, M. D., President of the Taipei Medical University, who not only appointed me the honor of an Endowed Chair at TMU but also provided me immense support. The writing and completion of this book was funded by the "Humanities in Medicine Project" at the TMU and by the Faculty Research Fund at the University of Southern California, with which I was able to enlist the help of a number of assistants, most notably Alexandria Yen, who helped to process the images with Photoshop and draft the contents of the mirror entries. My other assistants, Di Luo and Jingyu Xue, helped to complete the chapters on bronze mirrors, for whom I am grateful.

Lillian Lan-ying Tseng, a former colleague at USC（now Associate Professor of East Asian Art and Archaeology at the Institute for the Study of the Ancient World, New York University）, has inspired me by her study on the TLV mirrors. The book, Moriya Kozo's *Hokaku kiku shijinkyo zuroku* (Pictorial Catalog of the TLV four-spiritual-beasts mirrors) she gave me many years ago remains an important reference source at hand. It was also through Lillian that I got access to the library copies at the Fu Sinian Library of the Academia Sinica in Taiwan of the 1950s-60s China mainland's publications on the bronze mirrors excavated

Qing mirror with「Five Sons in Officialdom」incriptions 清五子登科鏡

in the provinces of Shaanxi, Zhejiang, and Sichuan. Professor Yin Cheng at the Chinese Culture University in Taiwan, who specializes in material and visual culture, also helped immensely to collect bronze mirror information from various sources and make mirror cases with Taiwanese Paulownia wood. I am deeply indebted to both of them.

My colleague Sonya Lee, Associate Professor of Art History and East Asian Languages and Cultures at USC, has been a close friend and rich resource of art historical information since I encroached into the territory of Chinese art history. I still recall that one summer she accompanied Professor Lothar von Falkenhausen of the Department of Archaeology at UCLA to my office, where the three of us carefully scrutinized the images of the bronze mirrors of the Cotsen collection ready to be published. We had a pleasant and exciting talk that day ; later, UCLA held a two-day symposium on the Cotsen mirrors attended

Song peach mirror with 「qing tong jian rong」 inscriptions 宋青銅鑑容桃心鏡

by a great many Chinese and Western scholars and experts, which made me realize even more deeply the importance of bronze mirrors to the fields of art history, culture, history, literature, and archaeology. It is my hope that the publication of *Bronze Luminescence* will give us another chance or angle to research and testify to the relationship between material evidence and cultural issues.

Dominic Cheung

University of Southern California, 2015

序言 青銅鑑容・以正衣冠

「今昔居藏鏡」

　　上古未有鏡子時，多用盛水陶盆或銅盆借水的光影修飾儀容，這種容器稱為「監」，銅製容器稱為「鑑」或「鑒」。「監」字在金文寫法是 ![字]＝ 人（人）＋ 目（目）＋ 皿（皿，陶製水盆），就是人俯首在陶盆靜止的水面上反觀自己影像。

　　郭沫若在考証三門峽出土銅器曾指出，「古人以水為監，即以盆盛水而照容，此種水盆即稱為監，以銅為之則作鑑，監字即像一人立於水盆俯視之形……普通人用陶器盛水，貴族用銅盆盛水，銅器如打磨得很潔淨，即無水也可以鑒容。」[8] 這就是「鑒」字在金文表現出來的意象。

　　「鏡」字要到春秋戰國後才出現，篆文 ![字]＝ 金（金，金屬）＋ 竟（竟字是聲旁也是形旁，終極之意），引申為極品金屬，利用銅盤光亮表面反映真實投影；銅盤能照出人影，古人以此為神奇。

　　以鑒為鏡，《詩經》〈大雅・蕩〉內稱「殷鑒不遠，在夏後之世。」殷鑒，就是殷商的鏡子。《莊子》〈德充符〉內謂「仲尼曰：人莫鑒於流水，而鑒於止水。」引申為心的靜止才能反影迴照，所謂心如止水；心的流動如水，便無從鑑別真相了。因此鑒雖是鏡子，卻有引申反映社會現實功能載體的涵義。

　　莊子〈外章〉數篇均提到至人或聖人之心，有如明鏡，「至人之用心若鏡，不將不迎，應而不藏，故能勝物而不傷」，「聖人之心，靜乎天地之鑒也，萬物之鏡也」，「生而美者，人與之鑒，不告則不知其美於人也」。墨子在〈非攻〉內則稱，「君子不鏡於水而鏡於人。鏡於水，見面之容；鏡於人，則知吉與凶」，他比莊子更務實，把鏡子用在群眾，不像宋玉在〈九辯〉裡僅限於個人修飾，「今修飾而窺鏡兮，後尚可以竄藏。」

　　清乾隆 14 年（1749AD），大學士吏部尚書梁詩正等人奉旨編撰著錄清宮所藏古鼎彝尊 1529 件，每件皆摹繪圖形、款識、記錄尺寸，容量和重量等，內含銅鏡 93 面，不稱鏡而稱鑑，書名亦稱《西清古鑑》，後又繼刊《西清續鑒乙編》[9]，錄清宮藏商、周、漢、唐四朝銅器 910 件，內含銅鏡 100 面，亦稱為鑑，可見鏡、鑑二者已有同識，但是儘管編纂這些古器的大學士們滿腹經綸，在書中居然把唐代的海獸葡萄鏡訂為漢鏡，美中不足。

　　近人梁上椿曾把從鑒到銅鏡的發展過程列出以下公式：

　　止水 → 鑒盆中靜水 → 無水光鑒 → 光面銅片 → 銅片背面加鈕 → 素背鏡 → 素地加繪彩 → 改繪彩加鑄圖文 → 加鑄字銘。[10]

　　根據梁說，所謂青銅鏡，就是由銅製的鑒盆進化而成。那是一種包括銅、錫、鉛的合金鑄成（有時也有小量的鋅）的鏡子，因為純銅較軟，需要加錫以增其光澤及硬度，然錫太多則易脆裂，加鉛則可以降

8　郭沫若，「三門峽出土銅器二三事」，《文物》，1959，1 期。
9　此兩書均由江蘇廣陵古籍刻印社影印發行，1992。
10　梁上椿〈古鏡研究總論〉《大陸雜誌》5 卷 5 期，1952。

低熔點在攝氏 800 度左右（一般多要在 1000 度以上），而且對青銅合金的溶液較有包容性與穩定性，不會因合金溶解時產生氣泡，成為鏡子冷卻後的瑕疵。至於《考工記》內記載不同合金在不同器物內的比例，「金錫半謂之鑒燧之劑」，古代工匠靠經驗傳承，能夠在無任何合金測量儀器下鑄鏡成功，已屬難得可貴。

　　於是我們知道，除鑒之外，古人借陽光反射引燃火種，還有聚光取火的陽燧。崔豹《古今注》〈雜註第七〉內云「陽燧以銅為之，形如鏡，向日則火生，以艾承之則得火也。」。崔豹為晉朝人，《古今注》是一本對古代及當今事物解說注釋的著作，雖不可盡信，但至少指出鏡燧功能一致，即使至今尚未有出土有夏商早期的青銅陽燧。

　　以上用鑒、燧作為銅鏡前身的說法，均因未有直接出土考古証據使人信服。近人何堂坤提出第三種看法，他認為如果鏡自鑒來，那麼一定存有比目前出土的兩面「齊家文化」時期銅鏡（1975 年在甘肅齊家坪出土的素鏡及 1976 年青海貴南縣朵馬台出土的七角星紋鏡）更早的銅鑒出土，但迄今為止，所有齊家或同期系列出土銅器都是一般小型手工業工具及一生活用器，未曾見過水鑒容器。目前看到的銅鑒都屬於春秋戰國時期，自然不可能是銅鏡的前身。

　　至於鏡自燧來亦有疑問，目前出土的陽燧均屬西周或唐宋時期，包括（1）1975 年北京昌平區白浮村西周木槨墓中出土直徑 9.9cm 的陽燧，（2）1981 年浙江省紹興市坡塘公社獅子西麓出土直徑 3.6cm 的戰國陽燧，（3）1959 年陳大年捐贈國家博物館的一面唐代獅紋方型陽燧，長、寬各 14.4cm，（4）北京市文物工作隊在廢品收購站揀選出一面 18.5cm 宋仿漢陽燧。

　　若與上面「齊家文化」銅鏡比較，最少晚了 800 到 1000 年時間。

　　何堂坤認為鏡非自鑒來，亦非自燧來，「而是受到了刀、斧、指環、銅泡等多種早期金屬器光潔表面映像事的啟發後，才發明出來的。」他指出後世文獻常有「屈刀為鏡」或「刀劍取火」之說。[11]

　　但此說亦有瑕疵，他引用的「後世文獻」，譬如唐代崔護〈屈刀為鏡賦〉，崔護之屈刀，自是唐代之刀，與「齊家文化」之鏡，相差何止十萬八千里？至於「刀劍取火」之說，他又引用漢代王充《論衡》〈率性篇〉內所謂「今妄以刀劍之鉤月摩拭朗白，仰以向日，亦得火焉。夫鉤月，非陽燧也，所以耐取火者，摩拭之所致也。」之句，表示刀劍亦可取火，其實亦僅是斷章取義而已。

　　王充指的是天道有真偽。真者固自與天相應，偽者亦可加以知識機智來開導，看來亦與真者無異。就像取火的陽燧，向著太陽火就來了，這是真正取火方法。但是今天隨便用摩拭雪亮刀劍或月牙鉤對著太陽，亦可得火。月牙鉤不是陽燧，能取火，就是摩拭雪亮得到太陽反映所引致。王充跟著又說，「今夫性惡之人，使與性善者同類乎，可率勉之，令其為善，使之異類乎，亦可令與道人之所鑄玉，隨侯之所作珠，人之所摩刀劍鉤月焉。教導以學，漸積以德，亦將日有仁義之操。」那就是說，現今若要使性惡的人與性善的人同類，可以引導和勉勵他們向善，即使他們不同類，亦可去學習道人鑄玉，隨侯作珠，以德行去逐漸

11　崔護〈屈刀為鏡賦〉內云「惟刀鏡之異名，共堅剛以為質，既靈仙之手澤，得微妙之心術。銛鋒始拔，乍盤屈以規圓；朗鑒俄成，驟拂拭而光溢。」
　　王充《論衡》〈率性篇〉「今妄以刀劍之鉤月摩拭朗白，仰以向日，亦得火焉。夫鉤月，非陽燧也，所以耐取火者，摩拭之所致也。」
　　何堂坤《中國古代銅鏡的技術研究》，北京，紫禁城出版社，1999，317-321頁。

感化他們去具備仁義的操行。

　　由此可知，刀劍取火，亦不過用來與陽燧打個比方，說明取火的另一種方法，正如性善性惡的人，都有方法走向光明的所在。刀劍與鏡子或陽燧的來源無關。

　　由於鏡子能折光反射，它的功能從儀容修飾進展入辟邪、敬神等宗教方面，可惜近人研究銅鏡多在於分期或分類，極少從文化、藝術、文學等入手。沈從文先生早年在歷史博物館整理戰國入漢唐青銅鏡時曾發出以下的感嘆。他說：

　　…特別是鏡子，留下了一系列優秀作品，我們可以從不同形制和圖案花紋發展中，看出它對於社會現實的種種不同反映，和社會上層建築中的文學、詩歌、音樂、美術及宗教信仰的種種聯繫。幫助我們更深入一層理解如上各部門的發展過程，彼此之間的關係和影響。並藉此明白，沒有一種事物是完全孤立的，沒有一種生產不受其他影響而又影響其他。而鏡子本身的問題，譬如它在中國青銅工藝和雕刻美術史上應有的地位，及形成的社會背景，藝術形式背景，我們想深入一些來談它時，也就勢必需要同時從各方面的成就與發展研究，才不致於顧此失彼，孤立片面。[12]

　　「沒有一種事物是完全孤立的」，我們可以這樣說，從鑒到鏡，已經形成了一個青銅鏡子文本。每一朝代時期不同形制和圖案花紋，都代表著每一朝代時期的宗教、文學、藝術等等的話語（discourse）。從文化角度來看，這些話語緊密連接著當時社會裡貴族或人民的生活意識型態。

　　出土文物顯示，戰國漢魏銅鏡多見於貴族陪葬品，到了唐代，西域而來的狻猊葡萄圖案紋飾，弧面浮雕、錯金錯銀、螺鈿鑲嵌、金銀平脫，瑰麗華貴，擄獲每個宮廷貴族或平常百姓攬鏡臨照的青睞。事實上很明顯，戰國、兩漢、隋唐這三個歷史時期的鏡子代表了銅鏡發展史最輝煌而具代表性的時代。

　　北宋靖康二年（1127A.D.），金兵南下，徽宗、欽宗二帝被擄，北宋滅亡。後高宗即位南渡定都臨安（杭州），史稱南宋。宋初由於北方與契丹政權長期對峙，西北又與西夏連年用兵，銅料缺乏，質量甚遜唐鏡。南宋偏安江南後，北方大量人口南遷，經濟重心也隨著南移；絲織、瓷器、印刷、冶煉、造紙等手工業也得到空前發展，其中湖州（吳興）、會稽（紹興）、饒州（江西鄱陽）、吉州（吉安）、建康（南京）、臨安府、成都、蘇州等地所產銅鏡遠近馳名，湖州銅鏡更是個中翹楚。南宋雖為銅鏡史的衰退期，但鏡子轉趨實用，不尚花俏，鏡身輕巧薄細，頗有反璞歸真、素面相見之意，那是藝術風格的另一種反動力，湖州石家念二銅鏡，風靡一時，成為暢銷品牌鏡子。由於運河水系水質清冽適於磨鏡，湖州就是全國鑄鏡中心之一，延續到晚清，直至西洋玻璃鏡興起，才轉趨衰落，當時鏡店均位於漕糧運輸碼頭儀鳳橋一帶，以薛家、石家等鏡匠名聞天下。

　　就以鑄造技術而言，元、明兩代的銅鏡製作應比宋、遼、金進步，但如上所述，南北兩宋連年用兵，戰亂繁頻，兵器鑄製又需大量銅料，因而銅製生活器具匱缺，銅鏡正是最受影響工藝品之一。到了元代，蒙古人鐵腕拑制銅料買賣私製更是明顯，《元史‧世祖本紀 8,11,14》內均有載禁止私造銅器及用金銀銅錢私相越海互市，並設有嚴格控制銅料資料開採與鑄造的官管銅局及作坊，銅鏡工藝開始退步。

　　本來明代開國鼎盛，社會安定，國祚長近三百年，銅鏡工藝應可大放光芒，然而時機（timing）錯失。

實用方面，西方海上貿易進入中國，攜入光學知識以及玻璃鏡，碩大明亮，青銅鏡相對失色。工藝美術設計方面，明代海上絲綢之路（Sea Silk Route）出口青花及其他各要瓷器數以萬計，為國家主要經濟脈動，工匠心力多用在瓷器燒製及設計，而非銅鏡。因此明代銅鏡設計缺乏新意，即使高品質的雲龍鏡，雲龍張牙舞爪的怪異（grotesque）形態，亦僅能讓人聯想起明代瓷器濃重鮮艷的五彩（wucai）雲龍紋飾。因此明代仿古鏡特多，多為仿漢、唐鏡，並在鏡上冠以工匠名號及「造」字，譬如「李造」或「張家造」。

此外，明代銅鏡已大部分脫離漢、唐早期神話或異國情調，轉以祈福的吉祥語代替，譬如「狀元及第」、「長命富貴」或「五子登科」等大字銘文。這種吉祥銘文鏡一直發展入清代，而成為清代銅鏡的特色。

本書當初構思，就是企圖打破以朝代劃分鏡種的觀念，猶如不可視唐詩、宋詞、元曲為朝代獨一文類代表。因此書內各章均以特別主題引介其朝代鏡種特色，而元、明、清一章則付諸闕如，正是代表這三個朝代銅鏡主題風格的稀薄孱弱。

「青銅鑑容」四字來自一面宋代桃型「青銅鑑容」青銅鏡銘文，現用作「今昔居藏鏡」目錄與文化研究文集書名，其中頗有深意焉。唐太宗有名句以鏡稱許忠臣魏徵，魏徵病逝，太宗悲慟之極，謂侍臣：「人以銅為鏡，可以正衣冠，以古為鏡，可以見興替，以人為鏡，可以知得失。魏徵歿，朕亡一鏡矣！」可見鏡子的豐富象徵與人鏡的重要。

此書選出一百多面鏡子，為今昔居主人所藏部分，螢火之光，不足與典藏大家或博物館皓月之輝比美，然收集過程，得失拿捏，可謂「鏡花水月，借鏡人生」，千種點滴心頭的人生開悟，自非區區百多面鏡子所能反映於萬一。

本書完成，千頭萬緒，首先要感謝臺北醫學大學校長閻雲博士，我自被北醫聘任為講座教授，除了無上榮譽，他給予支持援助是龐大的，銅鏡一書進行完成，也是多得臺北醫學大學的「人文醫學計畫」特別經費（Humanities in Medicine Project）與南加州大學的教授研究基金（Faculty Research Fund）協助聘用助理人員，其中 Alexandria Yen 貢獻傑出，她不但利用 photo-shop 技術修繕圖像底色，同時協助撰寫條目內容，功不可沒。其他助理尚有羅迪、薛京玉協助完成銅鏡章回，至是感謝。

南加州大學前同事曾藍瑩教授（現為美國紐約大學古代世界研究所東亞藝術副教授）當年研究 TLV 博局鏡對我有啟發作用，她送我京都國立博物館出版的《守屋孝藏蒐集方格規矩四神鏡圖錄》至今仍是手頭參考書。此外，中國大陸早期編印一九五、六十年代陝西省、浙江省及四川省出土銅鏡的幾本書也是藉藍瑩在台灣「中研院傅斯年圖書館」的版本借我影印。此外，我也得台灣中國文化大學中文系鄭穎副教授研究中國文學詠物傳統及物質文化專業之便，多方協助搜集銅鏡資料及製作台灣桐木鏡匣，深深感激。

南加州大學藝術史系東亞藝術副教授 Sonya Lee 是我多年由文入藝的知音對話者，猶記得有年夏天她和加州大學洛杉磯分校（UCLA）考古系的 Lothar von Falkenhausen 教授來訪，在我研究室細鑑準備出版的 Cotsen 氏藏鏡圖片，縱論古今，後來 UCLA 更以 Cotsen 氏藏鏡召開兩天研討會，中外專家學者雲集，讓我感到青銅鏡在藝術、文化、歷史、文學、考古領域的重要位置，希望《青銅鑑容》的出版，也能帶來一個實物與理論的研討印證機會。

 序於 2015 年南加州大學

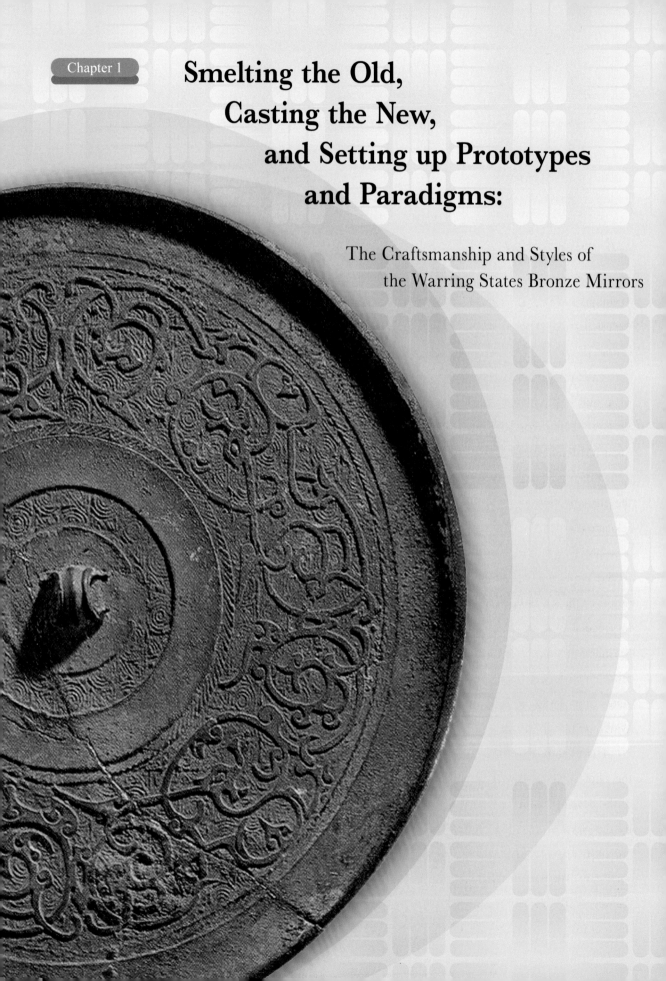

Chapter 1

Smelting the Old,
Casting the New,
and Setting up Prototypes
and Paradigms:

The Craftsmanship and Styles of
the Warring States Bronze Mirrors

Warring States Period

I. Breakthroughs in Craftsmanship and Technology

The emergence of bronze mirrors in the Warring States, together with the formation of a distinct developmental stage in the history of bronze mirrors, is no coincidence but a process building upon past experience and opening up future advancements. In a broader sense, it represents the interaction between the overall progress of craftsmanship and the holistic cultural reformation of the specific era.

The Spring and Autumn and the subsequent Warring States period started with the decline of the Zhou royal house. In 770 BC, on the pretext that the decadence and corruption of the court was induced by Bao Si（褒姒）, the favorite concubine of the King You（幽王）of Western Zhou, Marquis Shen（申侯, the state of Shen locates in modern-day Henan, in the County of Yang 陽縣）allied with Marquis Lu（呂侯）, Marquis Zeng（曾侯）, and the Western barbarian Quanrong（犬戎）to attack the royal capital Gaojing（鎬京）, capturing the city and slaying the king in Lintong（臨潼）. King Ping（平王）, upon his enthronement, was forced to relocate his capital eastward to Luoyi（洛邑）, hence the beginning of the Eastern Zhou dynasty when the king was forever at the mercy of his overpowering vassals. As a consequence, the Zhou sovereignty weakened day by day while the vassals of the various states assumed superiority one after another. The "successive rise to power of the states of Qin, Jin, Qi, and Chu," as observed in the *Records of the Grand Historian*（*Shiji* 史記）, the decentralization and division of royal power which became well established in the political arena of the Spring and Autumn, a 291-year period spanning from 772 to 481 BC. The following centuries witnessed the tense coexistence, fierce competitions, shifting alliances, and incessant warfare among the most powerful states until the Qin unification of China. The 259 years between 480 and 222 BC came to be known as the Warring States period.

Historically termed as the "Pre-Qin Era", this period of time marks the time when the central power of the Zhou royal house disintegrated as regional authorities all over China aroused and flourished. In terms of the development of craftsmanship, it represents the liberation of a rigid style which, originally restrained by the Northern sovereignty, was at this time able to transform into artistic vogues rejuvenated by the creativities of all different regions, and the powerful state of Chu in the south was most distinguished for such new tastes. The manufactured bronzes decreased significantly in number at the royal house, while the vassals were instead casting at an accelerating rate, producing a great many artifacts remarkable for their distinct local styles. Some of the most celebrated pieces include food vessel（*gui* 簋）and bell（*bo* 鎛）of Duke

Qin, and square vase (*fang hu* 方壺) made by Marquis Zhongyoufu of Zeng (曾仲游父), all exemplary of their exquisite shapes and forms, ingenious designs, and resplendent patterns and decorations.

Coming to the Warring States period, the tomb of Marquis Yi of Zeng (曾侯乙) in the County of Sui (隨縣) in Hubei yields a great variety of bronze vessels, notably, a set of sixty-four chime bells (編鐘) having a wide breadth of pitches, a multi-layered openwork mat weight (*duishi* 堆飾) of coiling dragons (*pan-hui* 蟠螭), bronze beakers and plates surrounded by coiling dragons with horns and hornless, and huge wine vessels (*fou jian* 缶鑑) for cooling and heating wine. Spectacular and stunning, these vessels also testify to the groundbreaking artistic and technological advances brought by the Warring States bronzes.

Many scholars and experts have acknowledged that this innovation of style reflects the ideological change mainly ensued from the aforementioned historical and political factors. Especially in the middle of the Warring States, with the decline of the ritual function of the royal house and the expansion of the ruling power of the vassals, the line between aristocracy and the commoners gradually diminished, bringing in a great number of utensils, tools and paraphernalia for daily use including bronze mirrors, belt hooks (*daigou* 帶鉤), and bronze lamps—each requiring handcrafting skills and ingenuity of design. For example, copper and turquoise became embedded in the vessels, gold and silver inlaid was added, gilding and exuberant decoration were adopted, and even a special bird-shaped seal script was applied for inscription in the state of Chu. All these innovations formed a confluence in the tide of "visual revolutions" of the Pre-Qin inscribed bronzes.

To use a modern critical term from the West, a revolutionary innovation against the orthodox norm or decorum is a "subversion" or "transgression". In other words, from the Spring and Autumn to the Warring States period, the rise of the gentry-warrior class (*shi* 士) and the prosperity of culture propelled the transformation of the styles of art and artifacts. Concomitant with the decentralization of royal power and the liberation from the orthodoxy, there also existed in each state an aspiration for political autonomy and artistic distinctiveness.

However, any essential progress in craftsmanship and style in a certain era has to rely upon the continual advances and breakthroughs in technology. Starting from the 875-kilogram *Simuwu Ding* (cauldron 司母戊鼎)—made in the late Shang dynasty as a food container and the biggest and heaviest bronze cauldron extant—the casting technique of bronzes has made constant progresses and achieved great accomplishments. Bronze is an alloy of copper, tin and lead ; a mastery of the proper percentage of each element is a prerequisite for successfully casting vessels of varying degrees of hardness. In the case of *Simuwu Ding*, modern scientific examination discloses that it contains 84.77% of copper, 11.64% of tin and 2.79% of lead, aptly in accordance with the formula for casting bells and cauldrons given by the "Record of Craftsmanship (*Kaogongji* 考工記)" *in the Rites of Zhou* (周禮). This formula belongs to a total of six formulae for copper alloys: "There are six formulae of copper alloys. Taking six portions of copper and one portion of tin make an alloy for bells and cauldrons." Comparing this to the 6 to 1 ratio revealed by modern scientific examination, one realizes that Chinese craftsmen had already acquired the correct proportion for casting bronzes by the Shang dynasty. The other five types of copper alloys include a 5 to 1 ratio of copper and tin for making axes, 4 to 1 for dagger-axes and halberds, 3 to 1 for broadswords, 5 to 2 for sheaths and arrows, and 2 to 1 for *jiansui* flint mirrors（鑒燧）. The *jiansui* mirror is a concave mirror which makes fire by facing the sun and condensing the sunbeams. It is a composite of two different layers "reflector" (*jian* 鑒) as a mirror to reflect images and "receptive flint" (*sui* 燧) as a condenser to gather sunlight and make fire. Both are in fact mirrors ; in the case of *sui*, the receptive flint, since it requires a silvery white surface for ideal reflection and collection of sunlight, it contains a higher proportion of tin—hence resulting in the 2 to 1 ratio of copper and tin—which makes it rigid and brittle. The Warring States mirrors that came afterward, however, adopted a different ratio for the alloy. In *Chinese Ancient Bronze Mirrors*（中國古代銅鏡）, Kong Xiangxing and Liu Yiman（孔祥星、劉一曼）have listed a total of ten Warring States mirrors tested in Chinese and Japanese laboratories. Two of the ten mirrors derived from Chu tombs in Hunan, while the other eight pieces were circulated into Japan. The data of the lab tests indicate the ratio of copper and tin for most pieces to be 3 to 1.[1] This probably explains why the Warring States mirrors could remain so unbelievably slim and slender while bearing such exuberant decorations and intricate patterns. The makeup of the bronze alloy more or less imparts the hardness of the mirror and the level of pressure it could endure in the casting procedure.

As a matter of fact, the greatest breakthrough in the casting technique of bronzes from the Shang to the Warring States lies in the renovation of the casting mould and the smelting furnace. The renovation covers three major casting techniques of ancient China, namely, clay-mould（泥範 or earthenware-mould, if after firing and baking）casting, iron-mould（鐵範）casting, and melting-mould casting (also known as the lost-wax 失蠟法 or extracted-wax method 撥蠟法）. The *Simuwu Ding* mentioned above was cast by piecing together multiple earthenware plates into a mould. The evolution from clay to metal moulds allows repeated usage of moulds and faster cooling, which considerably benefited the production of iron and the manufacturing of agricultural implements and hand tools. The lost-wax method starts with the crafting of a model using a specially concocted wax compound, upon which clay is applied and let dry ; the model is then heated to melt the wax inside and placed into furnace to be baked, and molten bronze is poured into it while still in high temperature. The three casting techniques began to develop in the Shang dynasty ; the lost-wax method, though earlier evidence deduced its application to first appear in the Han dynasty, the excavation of the tomb of Marquis Yi of Zeng soon demonstrates that it had been adopted back in the Spring and Autumn and the

---

1 | Kong Xiangxing, Liu Yiman. *Zhongguo gudai tongjing*（Ancient Chinese Bronze Mirrors）. Beijing: Beijing *wenwu chubanshe*, 1984. Kong and Liu divide the development of bronze mirrors into six periods ; mirrors of the Qijia culture and the Shang and Zhou belong to the first period, the "early period", and mirrors of the Spring and Autumn and the Warring States belong to the second, the "developing and prevailing period". This book was republished in 1994 by the Taipei *yishu tushu* Inc. under the name of *Zhongguo gu tongjing*（Old Chinese Bronze Mirrors）, but since the reprint contains a mixture of traditional and simplified Chinese characters and omits the number of all images, it is very difficult to identify the image with the text.

Warring States period.

Similar techniques have been applied to making moulds for mirrors, but in a smaller scale. The Warring States mirrors commonly adopted clay-mould casting, yet people tend to overlook the highly challenging artistic task behind the technological accomplishment of mould production, and that is the crafting of the model. The model (*mo* 模) comes first and the mould (*fan* 範) second. The first stage of mirror making is to craft not the mould, but a piece of original clay model with all the reliefs and patterns. The caster is a technician responsible for moulding, pouring of molten bronze , and post-casting procedures such as residue cleaning, sanding and polishing (Chapter "Xiuwu xun" in *Huainanzi* 淮南子〈修務訓〉mentions, "to powder by dark tin and polish by white felt," 粉以玄錫‧磨以白旃 which means to apply quicksilver to the surface of the mirror and polish it by a cloth of white felt), while the original model is by and large crafted by a skilled local artisan who sculpts the model and its various patterns before delivering it to the caster. Indeed the mirrors have become the best testimony to the virtuosity and styles of popular art! Of course, such situation changed when the Han court followed Qin to establish the *shangfang* (尚方) bureau, the official foundry which became the gathering place of all skilled modelers and casters.

The master model is but a circular clay mirror that needs to be placed inside a rectangular wooden box framed with wooden panels on four sides, into which a compound of clay and water is poured. A female (depressed) model (陰模) is thus created and is taken to be baked to reach a greater firmness. Then, the procedure is repeated to make yet another male (raised) model (陽模). While the female model serves as the master copy for the making of endless secondary, male models, it on the other hand becomes the template for making moulds and casting mirrors.

Curator Dong Yawei (董亞魏) of the City Museum of E-zhou (鄂州) in Hubei has experimented for many years the techniques of moulding and casting in the actual production of bronzes. Retrieving and adopting the ancient bronze-casting methods, he was able to mass produce bronzes in order to test and verify many ancient crafting skills. In *Zhongguo gudai tongjing gongyi jishu yanjiu* (*The Craftsmanship and Technology of the Ancient Chinese Bronze Mirrors* 中國古代銅鏡工藝技術研究), a self-published book in China, he has detailed the procedure of making models and moulds:

⋯In most cases, the casters did not have the skill of crafting the original model. Instead, the original model was provided by modelers specialized in clay crafting and then used by casters in their own casting system to make female models. The inscription on the backside of the mirror was inscribed by the casters after a female model was produced. Naturally, the characters should be reversed when inscribed and they would be un-reversed again with the making of the male model. The clay moulds were made after the male model, during which process the inscription would be reversed just as the one on the female model, and the reversed inscription (反字) would be restored to proper characters (正字) once the mirror was cast. However, since the degree of literacy varied among casters, it is not uncommon to see missing, incorrect, or reversed characters and blanks in the inscriptions on some of the mirrors (109).

This passage indicates that the emergence of certain patterns on the backside of the mirror is closely associated with the individual design of the modeler. Other probable factors include: (1) the demands and tastes of the aristocrats, (2) the predilection of the caster for particular patterns, who instructed the modeler to craft in a certain way, and (3) folklores and vogue, which turned the mirrors into consumables possessing a high commercial value. The above factors all make one believe that the emergence of the multifarious pictorial motifs on the Warring States bronze mirrors—such as whorls, lozenges, and the totemic coiling dragons—unmistakably relates to the interaction between cultural concepts and popular craftsmanship of the time. The same interaction becomes especially salient for the *shenshou* (divine beast 神獸) mirror, *zhaoming* (linked arc 昭明、連弧) mirror, and TLV (博局) mirror in the Han dynasty. The fact that the inscription was inscribed on the female model by the casters with "a varying degrees of literacy and illiteracy" explains why there are often reversed and incorrect characters, whether in the seal or the clerical script, on the mirror.

II. *Formation of Style*

If we look at art and artifacts from a new angle—to determine the period of a certain object by style but not by history—we realize that throughout the course of the development of bronzes from the Shang onward, no other artifacts can match the Warring States mirrors in their ostensible display of the startling discrepancies between different styles in different periods. As a particular species of bronzes, the Warring States mirrors, just as the Hundred Schools, coalesced ritual traditions of the Shang and Zhou and cast unique styles and features suitable for the new era. The 1976 excavation of the tomb no.5 of the tomb of Fu Hao (婦好) in the Yin Ruins of Anyang (安陽殷墟), Henan, which derived several bronze mirrors, together with other finds in several tombs of Qijia (齊家) culture in Qinghai and Gansu in the same year, including a piece of "seven-point star mirror" (七角星紋鏡) frequently referred to by bronze mirror studies, has pushed the beginning of the use of bronze mirrors to no later than Late Shang or even further to 2000 BC, when primordial communal societies just started to disintegrate.

Fragmentary historical evidence is incapable of reconstructing the era of bronze mirrors. We can even say that while time turns into history, art creates history. The bronze mirrors of the efflorescent Warring States period, in terms of the scale of mass production and the range of distribution, has progressed from the technical basis to a stage of style formation, when prototypes and paradigms took shape and canonical forms and standardized formulae were set up, giving birth to a unique era.

Based on the varying intricate pictorial patterns and decorations, Chinese and Japanese scholars, such as Umehara Sueji (梅原末治) and Liang Shangchun (梁上椿), have classified the Warring States bronze mirrors into more than ten types. However, as the standards of classification differ, these scholars often come to different conclusions. Kong Xiangxing and Liu Yiman have selectively adopted and synthesized these conclusions and consequently classified the Warring States mirrors into thirteen types: (1) plain mirror, (2) patterned-ground mirror, (3) floral-and-leaf mirror, (4) *shan*-character (山字) mirror, (5) lozenge mirror, (6) fowl-and-beast mirror, (7) coiling-dragon mirror, (8) feather-and-scale mirror, (9) linked-arc mirror, (10) painted mirror, (11) double-tier mirror, (12) gold-and silver-inlaid mirror, and (13) multiple-knob mirror.[2]

Among these types, the following ones possess the most distinct styles and features and have become the most celebrated throughout generations:

(1) Patterned-ground mirror using the motif of feather-hooks or whorls (羽鉤). The so-called "patterned-ground" (地、底紋) refers to the ground pattern, similar to the ground color (地色) in Chinese porcelain design. For instance, a yellow-ground blue-and-white porcelain plate with a pattern of plucked branches of flowers and fruits produced in the Zhengde period of Ming Dynasty uses yellow glaze as ground color, hence the name "yellow-ground" (黃地). A feather-hook or whorl mirror means that such a motif is applied as the ground pattern of the mirror. The feather-hook is a swirl drawn in a half circle, which is fairly common. The whorl starts with a single fine line drawn in the counterclockwise direction to form a complete circle of swirl, which is known as the cloud motif (雲紋)；then, together with two crisscrossing oblique triangles known as the thunder motif (雷紋), these elements are combined together and become the cloud-and-thunder, or whorl motif (雲雷紋). A patterned-ground mirror (純地紋鏡) uses exclusively the combination of the cloud and thunder motifs as the ground pattern.

(2) *Shan* (mountain 山) character mirror using three to six characters of *shan* as the decorative pattern.

Warring States mirror with feather hooks 戰國羽鉤葉紋鏡

Warring States mirror with whorl patterns 戰國純雷雲地紋鏡

A three-*shan* mirror has three fluted knobs and has three deer (or two deer and a hound) distributed between the three characters. A six-*shan* mirror is extremely rare and is much greater in volume than its three-*shan* counterpart. The six-*shan* mirror excavated from the tomb of King of Southern Yue of the Western Han dynasty (西漢南越王墓) in Guangzhou reaches 21cm in diameter, almost as large as a Tang mirror, which contains three fluted knobs, two knob-bases, and six *shan*-characters engraved on a feather-hook ground. The six characters occupy much space and are therefore engraved askew and arranged tightly in pairs ; the strokes are slenderer and appear more graceful. There are six floral petals outside the knob-bases, each pointing to the bottom of the adjacent character, and six more petals between the characters and the rim of the mirror, amounting to a total of twelve petals. Such a petal pattern greatly influenced the style of the grass-leaf mirror of the Han dynasty. Ever since the discovery of the *shan*-character mirrors, the Chinese and Western scholars have been hotly debating the provenance of this peculiar pattern. Max Loehr contends that "*shan*" originates from the decorative motif of the Shang ritual vessels, whereas Bernhard Karlgren argues that it comes from the transmission between the Shang and the Zhou bronzes. William Watson believes the T-shaped "s*han*" character to be a variation of the bronze script "s*han*" , and that the significance of this character is recorded in *Shuowen* (*Explanation of Characters* 説文), which instructs that "*shan* means suitable ; it signifies the suitability of dispersing the spiritual energy and engender the myriad things." The Japanese scholar Komai Kazuchika (駒井和愛) concurred with this hypothesis, who agrees that the character shan has an auspicious implication and should not be conceived upside down as a "T" shape. In his Research on Ancient Chinese Mirrors (Japan: Iwanami, 1953, pp.72-76), he publishes the results of his study on the *shan*-character and points out that though the three-halberd pattern, similar to the *shan*-character, appeared on the Warring States roof tiles (wa dan), it does not indicate that the "*shan*" on bronze mirrors evolved from this pictograph.[3]

(3) Lozenge mirror (菱花紋鏡) applying geometric designs. This type of mirror uses the folding, symmetrical lozenges to divide the surface into nine subdivisions, with each subdivision (including the knob-base as the central subdivision) containing one round pistil and four petals unfolding into a

Warring States with 3 shan (mountain) characters mirror 戰國三山鏡

2 | Ibid
3 | All the above opinions are derived from Diane M. O'Donoghue, *Reflection and Reception: The Origins of the Mirror in Bronze Age China* (Museum of Far Eastern Antiquities, Stockholm Bulletin, v.62, 1990), 84.

Warring States with lozenges design mirror 戰國菱花紋鏡

cruciform. In recent years, some scholars have pointed out that the lozenge mirror should be actually regarded as the "cup-pattern mirror"（杯紋鏡）,[4] because the so-called lozenge is in fact the prevailing pattern found on lacquered ear cups in the Warring States. The lacquered ear cup is a wine cup with two ears, one on each side, and several such cups from the Warring States and the early Western Han have been excavated from the Jiudian tomb（九店楚墓）in Jiangling in Hubei（湖北江陵）and the Mawangdui tomb（馬王堆漢墓）in Changsha in Hunan（湖南長沙）. The double-ear cup later evolved into a prevailing pattern in the Warring States and appeared on the fabrics of the state of Chu known as the lozenge "cup-pattern gauze"（杯文綺）. The silk gauzes derived from the Mawangdui tomb no.1 include cup-pattern gauzes of smoke-color, crimson, and vermillion. Moreover, since the state of Chu was beside many rivers, it by and large adopted the lotus flower for the cup pattern, thus the round pistil and the four petals are not some simple flower-and-tendril motif but the pictorialized lotus flower and its seedpod.

(4) Coiling dragon mirror using the pattern of *panchi*. As a combined word in Chinese, *pan* is a dragon but also means to coil and twine, while *chi* is a dragon with one horn or no horn at all. There are also small snake-like reptiles of *hui*（虺）, which, like *panchi*, are characteristic of the Warring States mirrors and fraught with cultural and mythological implications. Obviously, *panchi* is a dragon totem of ancient China charged with forceful auspicious and tutelary power. This type of mirror uses three fluted knobs if small in diameter, while a bigger one may have an extremely exquisite chased knob. The coiling dragons intertwine with each other, sometimes head to tail or otherwise tail to tail; they are intricately interlinked, with eyes bulged, tongues stuck out, teeth bared and the three-toe claws stretched, appearing and disappearing on the mirror. Big or small, long or short, the dragons shoot to the sky and plummet into the sea; among rolling clouds and rain they gallop and undulate, changing in tens of thousands of ways.

There is also the three-*kui*-dragon mirror（三夔龍鏡）, the *kui*-dragon having a lozenge-shaped body with its single foot stepping on the knob-base（The one-footed *kui* is recorded in Chinese antique archives and, like *taotie*（饕餮）, is a common motif used on Shang and Zhou bronze vessels）. Ju Hsi Chou, Curator

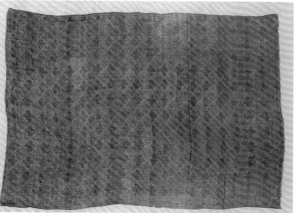

Warring States gauze with lozenge patterns from Mawangdui tombs 戰國絳色綺羅（馬王堆）

Lacquered ear cup from Mawangdui 漆耳杯（馬王堆）

of the Department of Chinese Art in the Cleveland Museum of Art, has emphasized in her monograph that this particular design—the one-footed dragon stepping on the knob-base with its long tail unfolding and spiraling inward—conveys a "centripetal" tension.[5] The rim of the mirror is either plain or decorated by eleven linked arcs, the composition of linked arcs also belonging to a newly invented design pattern of the Warring States mirrors which was transmitted to and inherited by the linked-arc-with-resplendent-sunlight mirror, the linked-arc-with-grass-leaf mirror, and the multiple-concentric-circle mirror of the Western Han.

(5) The double-tier mirror（透雕鏡）is a composite mirror putting together one frontal piece and one back piece that are cast individually. The frontal piece is a reflective surface, and the back piece has patterns in high relief. The double-tier mirrors that we usually see today include the four-tiger-biting-the-loop mirror（四虎咬環透紋鏡 the loop is the round knob-base）and the four-coiling-dragon-biting-the-loop mirror.

The best method to discern and differentiate the styles and types of the Warring States bronze mirrors is by antiquarian identification, because demonstrative evidence for such identification often depends on the consistency in the style of the antique objects in question. The means by which experts of the bronze mirrors make identifications, as a matter of fact, has to first rely upon formal features, casting techniques, and decorative themes of the object, and then upon the examination of miscellaneous factors such as the historical background, the socio-economical context, and various cultural implications. Qiu Shijing（裘士京）has proposed a six-step method of identifying a bronze mirror, which incorporates the observation and synthetic analysis of form, the knob, the knob-base, the rim, decoration, and inscription（including the location, the script used, and the content of the inscription）.[6] When applying this method to the identification of a Warring

4 | Fu Juyou, "On the Cup-Pattern Mirrors of Chu", in *Zhongguo wenwu shijie*（World of Chinese Antiques）144（1997）: 59-73. His proposal is quite inspiring and applicable, but it seems too far-stretched to argue that the coiling dragon（panchi）motif evolved and transformed into a pattern of "coiling-dragon cup-pattern mirror".

5 | Ju-hsi Chou, *Circles of Reflection: The Carter Collection of Chinese Bronze Mirrors*（The Cleveland Museum of Art, 2000）, 29.

6 | Qiu Shijing, *Tongjing*（Bronze Mirrors）（Huangshan shushe, 1995）, 47.

Warring States mirror with coiling dragons 戰國蟠螭紋鏡

States bronze mirror, assisted by a subjective evaluation of its quality and a discrimination of the authenticity of its verdigris encrustation and "black lacquer antique"（黑漆古）, we can reach the following conclusion:

The mirrors in the early Spring and Autumn period were mainly small-sized plain mirrors and patterned-ground mirrors. When it comes to the Warring States with the advent of *shan*-character mirrors and lozenge mirrors, the size of the mirror increased and the decorative patterns became refined and more sophisticated, reflecting not only the ingenuity of the artisans but also the fruition of the highly developed mirror industry. The Warring States mirrors were slim and lightweight, measuring 0.1 to 0.2cm in thickness and 10 to 15cm in diameter, which is in direct contrast to the thick and heavy Han mirrors weighing between 10 to 300 grams and susceptible to cracking and breaking. The only exception is the aforementioned bronze mirror excavated from the tomb of King of Southern Yue in Guangzhou, which is a large-sized, painted linked-arc mirror measuring 42cm in diameter.

Attention should also be paid to different types of knobs characteristic of the Warring States mirrors, which include the bow-shaped knob, triple fluted knobs, and the half-loop knob, all usually small in size. Among these types, the triple fluted knobs are the most popular and apply to 80-90% of mirrors, and hence should not be overlooked. The rim of the mirror is usually simply protruded from the surface with little decoration, and it is not until the Han that mirrors started to apply the plain broad rim or use patterns of the floating cloud, the rippling wave cloud, the triangular saw-tooth, or the Tang twirling floral to decorate the rim. Of all vassal states, the state of Chu yielded the largest quantity of mirrors. The so-called Huai-mirror（淮式鏡）, Changsha-mirror, and Qin-mirror referred to by early scholars such as Umehara Sueji, O. J. Todd, and R. W. Swallow in their monographs respectively published in Tokyo, Beijing, and Shanghai, should all in fact be categorized as Warring States mirrors.[7]

7 │ See Umehara Sueji, *Kan izen no Kokyo no kenkyu*（Study on the Pre-Han Ancient Mirrors）（Kyoto: Toho bunka gakuin kyoto kenkyujo, 1936）. R. W. Swallow, *Ancient Chinese Bronze Mirrors*（Peiping: Henri Vetch, 1937）. Milan Rupert and O. J. Todd, *Chinese Bronze Mirrors: A Study Based on the Todd Collection of 1000 Bronze Mirrors Found in the Five Northern Provinces of Suiyuan, Shensi, Shansi, Honan, and Hopei, China.*（Peiping: San Yu Press, 1935）.

第一章

融舊鑄新，開宗立範

戰國銅鏡的工藝與風格

《歷史文物》月刊，
歷史博物館，台北，
2002，5，106期，30-39頁。

一·工藝技術突破

戰國銅鏡之出現，以及能在銅鏡發展史自成體系，繼往開來，自非偶然。宏觀而言，可以代表著一個時代整體工藝演進與文化變革兩個層面相互配合。

所謂春秋戰國時期，實是指周室衰微，西元前 770 年，西周幽王妃子褒姒縈亂朝政，申侯（申國在今河南陽縣）聯合呂侯、曾侯及西夷犬戎攻陷鎬京，殺幽王於臨潼。後來平王繼位，被迫東遷洛邑，是為東周，並仰息於眾諸侯。自後周室日益微弱，各國諸侯相繼坐大，《史記》所謂「秦、晉、齊、楚代興」，即指業已形成的春秋割據局面，從西元前 772 年到西元前 481 年，共二百四十年。及至後來群雄並存，互競長短，合縱連橫，戰禍連綿。從東周滅亡至秦統一中國為止（西元前 480 至西元前 222），凡二百五十九年，稱戰國時期。

這一段史稱「先秦時期」的五百年，代表著周室中央集權瓦解，以及全國地方勢力蓬勃興起。從工藝發展史而言，更代表著從北方君主集權統一拘謹風格，解放入全國各地創意盎然的藝術采風，其中尤以南方強大楚國最具特色。就銅器製作來看，周王室鑄器已大量減少，各國諸侯鑄治卻相繼增加，許多具備獨特地方風格器物，譬如春秋時期的秦公簋、秦公鎛、曾仲游父壺或三輪車盤，不是形態構思奇巧，就是紋飾綺麗堂皇。

到了戰國時期，湖北隨縣曾侯乙墓出土所呈現各類銅器，如六十四件具備不同音域編鐘、多層縷空蟠虺紋堆飾，四周蟠龍環繞青銅尊盤、或是用來冰酒溫酒巨型缶鑑。除了令人嘆為觀止，更認定戰國銅器已具備劃時代意義。

因此許多學者專家認為這種風格創新，是一種意識形態反映，主要來自上述歷史政治因素，尤其是戰國中期，王室祭祀禮器衰落，各國諸侯君權擴張之餘，氏族與庶民界限日漸消失，帶來大量民生飲食器皿及用具，包括銅鏡、帶鉤或銅燈等手工藝需求與設計巧思。例如在器皿上鑲嵌紅銅，綠松石或錯金錯銀、鎏金或繁縟紋飾，甚至楚國改用鳥篆書體銘文，都給先秦金文銅器帶來圖象革命。

套用一句現代批評術語，那是一種「顛覆」。也就是說，從春秋進入戰國時代，武人階級與文化的興起，牽動了文物風格變化。除了對皇室正朔的離心，更有意落實戰國本土城邦的自主性與特徵。

但是一個時代工藝風格演變，關鍵還是技術層面的有恆突破進步。從商代晚期用作坎器器鼎、目前為最大最重，達八百七十五公斤的司母戊鼎開始，青銅鑄造在技術演進，一直獲得輝煌成績。青銅是紅銅、錫及鉛等元素的合金，必須掌握到這些元素正確分配比例，才能得心應手，以治煉出不同硬度銅器。就以司母戊鼎為例，據後來科學鑑測，成份是含銅 84.77%，錫 11.64%，鉛 2.79%，恰好符合《周禮考工記》上卷載，六種青銅合金第一種用來製造鐘鼎的溶劑。這種銅錫溶劑比例是：「**金有六劑。六份其金而錫居一，謂之鐘鼎之劑。**」

金指青銅，看到上面科學鑑測鐘鼎六份之一成份，就知道商代早已準確掌握劑料配方。其他五種銅錫比例，包括五比一製斧斤，四比一製戈戟，三比一製大刃，五比二製削、殺、矢，以及二比一製鑒燧。

鑒燧就是用來面對太陽，聚光取火的曲面鏡子。有人解釋為兩種不同物件，鑒，就是照容貌鏡子；燧，才是聚光取火銅鏡。其實都是鏡子之義，尤其後者的陽燧，因要磨製成銀白光亮用來面光聚映，所以含錫量高而犯剛脆之忌，才有二比一的銅錫比例。後來的戰國銅鏡，合金比例就不一樣。孔祥星、劉一曼在《中國古代銅鏡》一書內列出中國及日本曾對十面戰國銅鏡，進行化驗分析結果，十鏡中二面是湖南楚墓所出，八面是流傳入日本的戰國鏡，得來數據，銅錫比例大多數是三比一。[1]也許就解釋了戰國鏡厚度，為何如斯輕巧纖薄，卻又能負擔繁複的紋飾布局圖案。鏡子合金成份軟硬，多少提供出鑄治過程所能承擔的忍受程度。

其實青銅器從殷商到戰國，鑄治最大技術突破，還是在於鑄範（casting mould）和溶爐的改進演變。那就是稱為古代三大鑄造技術的泥範（焙燒後就稱陶範）鑄造、鐵範鑄造、及熔模鑄造（又稱失蠟法或撥蠟法）。前面提到的司母戊鼎，就是用多塊陶泥合範接鑄而成。從泥範進展入金屬鐵範，更可一範重複使用，快速冷卻，對生產鑄鐵，用來製造農具及手工器具甚有裨助。失蠟法是用調製好的油蠟料做模，再外敷泥料做型，模型乾後，加熱溶掉裡面蠟模，再入窯燒焙泥型，成陶胚後便可趁熱澆銅汁在溶模內鑄造。以上這三種鑄造技術，從商代開始發展，本來脫蠟法推論要到漢代才使用，但曾侯乙墓出土文物後，隨即證實春秋戰國時期，已經具備這種技術條件。

鏡範製作亦大同小異，只不過規模較小，尤其戰國銅鏡多用泥範鑄法。但是許多人忽略了製範只是技術成就，隱藏在泥範背後，還有高度藝術挑戰的鏡模雕塑。所謂模範，就是先有了模，後才有範。銅鏡製作最初階段不是造範，而是造一塊雕塑圖案的原始泥模，鑄鏡師只是技術工匠，只負責製範澆鑄及後期製作如去泥、打磨、拋光（《淮南子‧修務訓》內所謂「粉以玄錫，磨以白旃」就是塗上水銀，用一塊白氈團在鏡面打磨拋光）。一般原始模多另由民間巧匠藝人造型，雕塑好各類圖案模型後，再由鑄鏡師選用。那真是民間雕塑藝術風格成就的最大見證！當然入漢後政府遵秦制成立官家作坊的「尚方」，集天下巧匠精工於一爐，又另當別論。

母模或原始模只是圓型泥鏡，還需把它放在一塊木板，四周用木框好後填入泥料及水，複製成另一塊陰模，再拿去燒製成堅強度較高的陶模。重複這一程序，便可複製出另一面泥版陽模。陶版陰模便成母版（mastercopy），可以翻製成無數片再版陽模，陽模有如版印（template），便可成範，再合範澆鑄合金溶劑，便可成鏡。

湖北鄂州市博物館的董亞巍先生，經過長期青銅範鑄生產實踐，採用古代青銅鑄治技術還原，進行長期批量生產後，証實了許多古代工藝技術。他在《中國古代銅鏡工藝技術研究》（自費出版並無發行）一書內曾敘述製作模範細節，並指出：

…鑄鏡師們大都沒有雕塑原始模的技能，而是由專門從事泥雕的工匠提供原始模，然後由鑄鏡工匠自己設置澆鑄系統後翻製陰模，銅鏡背面的銘文是鑄鏡師翻出陰模以後才刻上去的。在陰模上刻銘時須刻反字，翻成陽模以後自然成為正字；製範只用陽模，當在陽模上翻出泥範後，泥範上的銘文與陰模上的銘文一樣是反字，鑄成銅鏡後，反銘又被還原成正字了。但由於鑄鏡師們的文化水平參差不齊，所以，造成一些銅鏡銘文缺字短句、錯字、反字及局部空白等現象的發生。（109 頁）

上面這段話，說明了鏡背圖案的產生，與工匠個人泥雕設計有密切關係。但其他因素也可能包括有（1）貴族要求及喜好，（2）鑄鏡師對母模某種圖案偏愛，並授意泥雕工匠刻製，或（3）民間流傳信仰及時尚，使成為消費品的鏡子更具商業價值。以上三種因素，都令人覺得戰國銅鏡各類圖案題旨（motif）呈現，譬如鏡背的雲雷、幾何菱形或蟠螭圖騰，都牽涉著當時文化觀念與民間工藝的互動。這種現象尤以入漢後的神獸鏡、昭明鏡或博局鏡最為顯著。也因為銘文是鑄鏡師在陰模上自己加刻，而且「文化水平參差不齊」，說明了鏡上篆隸銘文經常有反寫及錯字的原因。

二・風格的定型

假如我們採用一種新的角度來看藝術——以風格決定時代，而非以歷史決定時代。則銅器發展史自殷商以降，沒有器物能有如戰國銅鏡，如此明顯顯露時代風格的懸殊。就以一個特殊獨立銅器品種而言，戰國銅鏡有如諸子百家，融匯商周舊禮傳統，鑄治時代獨新風貌。雖然一九七六年河南安陽殷墟婦好五號墓發掘出的幾面銅鏡，以及同年在甘肅青海等地，分別在齊家文化墓葬中，出土數面銅鏡，包括其中一面經常被書籍引用的「七角星紋鏡」，把銅鏡使用歷史起碼推前到殷商晚期，甚至是西元前二千多年的原始公社解體時期。

零碎歷史證據，無法建立一個銅鏡時代。我們甚至可以說，時間可以變成歷史，但藝術可以創造歷史。銅鏡史一直到多姿多采的戰國時期，無論從數量生產或使用分布地區，都從技術本位進展入風格定型，開宗立範，形成了一定規範體制形式，才成一個獨特的時代。

戰國銅鏡紋飾圖案細膩繁複，中、日學者如梅原末治，梁上椿按類型分成十多大類。但由於彼此對劃分類型標準不同，結論可謂人言言殊。孔祥星、劉一曼則採擷綜合，分為以下十三類。即是：（1）素鏡類，（2）純地紋鏡類，（3）花葉鏡類，（4）山字鏡類，（5）菱紋鏡類，（6）禽獸紋鏡類，（7）蟠螭紋鏡類，（8）羽鱗紋鏡類，（9）連弧紋鏡類，（10）彩繪鏡類，（11）透雕鏡類，（12）金銀錯紋鏡類，（13）多鈕鏡類。[2]

以上種類，又以下列諸鏡，風貌特殊，傳世最盛：

（一）羽鉤（feather-hooks）或雲雷（whorls）之「純地紋鏡類」，所謂地紋，有如陶瓷底色設計，譬如明正德黃地青花折枝花果紋盤，即是以黃釉作基本底色，故稱「黃地」。羽鉤或雲雷作地紋就指用這種圖案做底紋。羽鉤紋飾為勾半圈漩渦，非常普通。雲雷紋飾以單細線反時鐘方向勾勒，成整體圓圈渦紋

---

1 ｜ 孔祥星、劉一曼著，《中國古代銅鏡》北京文物出版社，1984；孔劉二位把銅期發展分為六個時期，齊家文化及商周銅鏡為第一期「早期」，春秋戰國銅鏡為第二期的「發展與流行期」。此書後為台北藝術圖書公司於 1994出版，改名《中國古鏡》，惟因重排，繁簡字體交雜，圖片亦未標出書內指出之號碼，甚難辨認。

2 ｜ 仝上。

和兩個相錯斜三角紋組成，圓渦為雲紋，斜三角方紋為雷紋，合稱雲雷紋。純地紋鏡就是純粹以這兩大類地紋組成整體圖案的鏡子。

（二）由三個至六個「山」紋飾組成的「山字鏡類」，其中「三山鏡」為三絃鈕（flutedknob），三個山字之間分布有三隻鹿或二鹿一犬。「六山鏡」至為稀少，體積也較三山大得多，廣州西漢南越王墓出土的「六山鏡」直徑達 21 公分，幾與唐鏡面積相若，三弦鈕，雙鈕座，羽鉤地紋，上刻六個山字。因為多山佔積，字形傾斜對配排列，字體較為瘦長，更顯清秀。鈕座外有六瓣花葉，分別指向山字底座，另有六瓣花葉在山字與鏡緣之間，合共十二花葉。這種花瓣圖案，強烈影響漢代「草葉紋鏡」的風格。山字銅鏡出土後，中外學者一直為「山」字爭辯不休，羅樾（Max Loehr）認為出於商代禮器紋飾，高本漢（Bernhard Karlgren）則謂是商周銅器的傳承。William Watson 則認為 T 狀的山字，實為古代金文山字演而成，更兼《説文》有載：「山，宜也，謂宜散氣生萬物也。」此「文字説」得到日本學者駒井和愛支持，同意山字蘊含吉祥之意，絕對有「山」意而非「T」型。但在他《中國古鏡的研究》（日本岩波，1953，pp.72-76）內對「山」字研究結果，指出戰國瓦當雖有三戟圖象，作為山的圖案，但並不等於鏡內之山，就是象形文字演變而成。[3]

（三）幾何圖形（geometricdesigns）的「菱花紋鏡類」，這種鏡子以折疊式對稱的菱紋（lozenges），把鏡面分成九個菱形地區，每區（包括鈕座為正中區）內各有一圓形花蕊，四瓣花朵，作十字形展開。近年也有人指出這類菱紋鏡子正確應稱為「杯紋鏡」。[4] 因為一般所謂的菱花紋，其實是戰國流行的漆耳酒杯紋。所謂漆耳杯，就是兩側有耳的酒杯，湖北江陵九店楚墓及湖南長沙馬王堆漢墓，分別出土有戰國及西漢初期漆耳杯。後來雙耳杯發展成戰國流行圖案，出現在楚國絲織品上，成為菱狀形的「杯文綺」。馬王堆一號漢墓出土的絲織綺羅圖案，即有煙色杯紋綺、絳色杯紋綺、朱色杯紋綺。更因楚國位在水鄉，杯紋多以芙蓉花（荷花）為紋飾，所以這圓形花蕊和四瓣花朵，不是花葉紋，而是圖象化的蓮蓬和荷花。

（四）蟠螭類的龍蛇紋飾，蟠，就是盤曲纏繞；螭，是無角之龍，有時則帶獨角；其他還有小蛇形狀的虺，都是戰國銅鏡特色，還牽涉文化及神話因素。因為非常明顯，蟠螭是古代中國龍形圖騰，帶著強烈吉祥與保護神意味。這類銅鏡除了直徑細小而用三弦鈕外，面積較大的也會有極其精緻的透雕巨鈕（chased knob）。蟠螭圖案互相糾纏，有時首尾相連或是尾尾相交，枝蔓交錯，張目吐舌，伸牙舞爪，足多作三趾，時隱時現，能大能小，縮短修長，上天下海，翻雲覆雨，奔騰起伏，千變萬化。

另外又有三夔龍紋鏡，軀體呈菱狀，單足踏於鈕座（古籍有謂「夔一足」，與饕餮常見於商周銅器），美國克利夫蘭藝術博物館中國藝術部門主任周汝式女士，在其專著內強調，這種單足踏鈕，長尾伸展倒捲的形態設計，具有「向心」（centripedal）張力。[5] 鏡緣以素邊或十一連弧（linked arcs）組成，連弧構圖亦為戰國鏡之創新工藝設計，傳承入西漢的連弧日光昭明鏡、連弧草葉鏡或多層連弧紋（concentric circles）鏡。

3 ｜ 以上諸家見解，均採自 Diane M. O' Donoghue, *Reflection and Reception: The Origins of the Mirror in Bronze Age China* 一書，Museum of Far Eastern Antiquities, Stockholm Bulletin, v.62, 1990, p.84.

4 ｜ 傅舉有，「論杯文楚鏡」，《中國文物世界》，144期，1997，香港，59-73頁。這種見解頗為新穎，也有可取之處，但如把蟠螭圖形申引為變形杯紋的「蟠龍杯紋鏡」，卻未免以偏概全了。

5 ｜ Ju-hsi Chou, *Circles of Reflection: The Carter Collection of Chinese Bronze Mirrors*, The Cleveland Museum of Art, 2000, p.29.

（五）「透雕鏡類」是鏡面與鏡背分別鑄冶，再二合為一（double-tier）的合成（composite）鏡子。也就是正面是平面照人的鏡面，另一背面是浮雕（high relief）圖案的鏡背，現今常見有四虎咬環透紋鏡（環指圓型鈕座而言）或四蟠螭咬環透紋鏡。

去辨識戰國銅鏡風格種類，最好方法還是從文物鑒定下手。因為鑒定的有力證據，往往是文物風格上的一貫性（consistency）。銅鏡專家提出鑒證方法，其實都是根據器物型製特徵、鑄冶技術及主題紋飾等特色，再配合當時歷史背境、社會民生、文化內涵——種種因素，才下定論。裘士京先

Warring States mirror with openwork 4 tigers biting a ring 戰國四虎咬環透雕紋鏡

生曾提出六種銅鏡鑒定方法，就是從鏡型、鏡鈕、鈕座、鏡緣、紋飾及鏡銘（包括銘文位置、字型及內容）多方面的觀察而進行綜合分析。[6] 如果把這些方法應用在戰國銅鏡，再加上對鏡子品相的主觀評價，銅綠鏽及黑漆古的真偽判斷，我們便可得到下面的結論。

早期春秋鏡以小型素鏡或純地紋為主，但發展入戰國時期的山字鏡及菱紋鏡，體積便較大，而且圖形清淅精細，不止工匠巧思，還見高水平整體作業成果。鏡厚度薄而輕巧，一般在 0.1 到 0.2 公分之間，直徑在 10 至 15 公分上下，與漢鏡之厚重寬闊恰好相反，重量多為數十至三百公克左右，所以也較易裂破。除非如前述廣州南越國王墓出土銅鏡，有大型連弧彩繪畫鏡，直徑達 42 公分。

其他還需注意尚有戰國鏡特徵的弓形鈕、三弦鈕，以及半環形鈕，大都細小，其中尤以三弦鈕最為流行，佔十之八九，不可掉以輕心。鏡緣多凸起為素捲邊，甚少紋飾，要到漢鏡才有寬素緣或流雲紋、水波雲紋、三角鋸齒紋或唐草紋飾鏡邊。戰國銅鏡又以楚國鏡數量最為大宗，早期學者包括梅原末治、O. J. Todd 及 R. W. Swallow 等人在分別在東京、北平、上海出版專書內所稱之「淮式鏡」、「長沙鏡」或「秦式鏡」，其實均應歸納為戰國銅鏡範疇。[7]

6　裘士京，《銅鏡》，黃山書社，1995，47頁。

7　See 梅原末治，《漢以前古鏡之研究》，內外出版印刷株式會社，1935。
　　R. W. Swallow, *Ancient Chinese Bronze Mirrors*, Henri Vetch, Peiping, 1937.
　　Milan Rupert and O. J. Todd, *Chinese Bronze Mirrors: A Study Based on the Todd Collection of 1000 Bronze Mirrors Found in the Five Northern Provinces of Suiyuan, Shensi, Shansi, Honan, and Hopei, China*. San Yu Press, Peiping, 1935.

1. Mirror with coiling dragons 戰國蟠螭鏡

Warring States（475-221 BC）   Diameter：9.7cm

Our first mirror showcases a *panchi*, or coiling dragon motif. Cast in low relief, long serpentine beasts weave and interlock with one another to creating a multi-layered, coiling and curling effect. Smaller arrow-like points and curls protrude from beasts' linear bodies and create further intricacy in the decorative form. This motif is offset over a fine, circular whorl pattern in the background, which creates two embellished surfaces on the mirror. Various concentric rings frame all of this: two thin bands are carved into the mirror's surface restricting either side of the *panchi* pattern；they bound the ornamentation into single, circular, wide register. An undecorated slightly, beveled border frames the edge of the piece. A pair of rings, one in the same whorled ground pattern, then a thick undecorated ring, frame the mirror's small, central triple-fluted knob. Save for small encrustations on the knob and rim, the preservation and production quality of the piece is unmatched.

2. Mirror with feather-hook patterns 戰國羽狀鏡

Warring States (475-221 BC)　　Diameter : 8.5cm

Here we see another decorative motif characteristic of the Warring States era. A plain, concentric border frames a mirror whose entire surface is covered in an intricate ground pattern. The design consists of rows of modular rectangles, and each unit is made of four wave-like "feathers" curling centripetally inwards towards a lozenge in the middle. Unlike the previous piece, the ground pattern has no other decorative overlay save the border and a plain, raised ring that surrounds the mirror's central knob. The eye's focus is entirely on this elaborate, repetitive design.

3. Mirror with whorl patterns 戰國雲雷鏡

Warring States（475-221 BC） Diameter : 13.5cm

This piece is made entirely of concentric rings in different shapes and sizes. including its ground pattern. The first set of rings form the rim of the mirror. The raised rim gently bevels inward into a wide, undecorated border. Then a thin, concentric ring, and hachured band frame the wide, main register, decorated with a repetitive ground pattern. The motif consists of a whorl, or concentric swirl, and two triangular shapes stacked on top of each other and buttress each circular curl. This whorl-triangle design repeats and creates multiple horizontal rows across the mirror. Echoing the border, another set of concentric rings overlays the decoration and restricts a flat, half-loop central knob set in an undecorated circle. The entire mirror is worn and badly damaged. A large crack halves the object, and some of the whorl pattern is worn with layers of green patina.

4. Warring States 4-Leaf with whorl-thunder background mirror 戰國四葉雲雷地紋鏡

Warring States（475-221 BC）　Diameter : 9.3cm

    A plain, beveled border and indented ring frame this mirror's main register. This space is inset with an intricate pattern of four pieces of foliage. The flora blossom from a ring surrounding the mirror's central, triple fluted knob set in a plain, wide circle. The stems space themselves at four opposite axes and blossom into a single leaf that droops to the left ; this creates a clockwise movement that revolves around the center. Curls that decorate the edges of the plants as well as a thick outline around the entire motif add further intricacy. The design overlays a ground-pattern of rectangular modular units, serving as an ornate backdrop . Each module consists of several interlocking, feather-like waves that coil and rotate clockwise within each small, rectangular shape. Granulations dot the spaces in between fine striations on each "feather". On the edges of the mirror there is some damage: encrustations have worn the frame of the mirror ; however, the extremely intricate embellishments in the main register remain clear and well preserved.

5. Mirror with 3 one-legged Kui dragons 戰國三夔龍鏡

Warring States（475-221 BC）　　Diameter：9cm

　　As Zhuangzi indicated in his philosophical treatise that *Kui* dragon has only one leg, there are 3 one-legged dragons revolve counterclockwise on the face of the mirror. These *Kui* dragons turn to the side, revealing lozenge-shaped bodies. Their heads and ornately, curved tails protrude from either side of the form, and each creature looks as if it bites the tail of the preceding beast. The *Kui* dragons sink their talons into a plain, central ring that frame's the mirror's worn, triple fluted knob. These three mystical animals are over a lightly etched design ground pattern of small, incised lozenges and round granulations. Framing all of this is a ring of linked arcs, which separate the main pattern from the mirror's undecorated border.

6. Mirror with openwork 4 tigers biting inner circle 戰國四虎咬內環鏡

Warring States（475-221 BC）　　Diameter : 8.8cm

Four tigers vigorously bite an inner ring at the center of the mirror, creating a centripetal motion towards the center. Inside this ring is a damaged, triple fluted knob set in a plain circle. The four beasts face one another at four opposite axes, and their bodies twist in profile as they walk in around the mirror's main register. Swirling coils decorate the surface of each creature's body. Incised lines delineate their triangular ears, eyes, and flat noses. For each tiger, front and back claws dig into the mirror's plain border, made of a thin concentric ring, and wide, undecorated rim. As the creatures pace clockwise, the back of one tiger touches the face of the next one, creating a seamless, never-ending sense of movement.

7. Mirror with openwork 4 tigers biting outer circle 戰國四虎咬外環鏡

Warring States（475-221 BC）　　Diameter：8.8cm

Here is another set of tigers, but they differ stylistically from the previous piece. This double-tiered type of casting leads to more plastically rendered, three-dimensional forms that are attached to the mirror's plain surface. Four mythical animals bite the edges of a plain, wide border and create a centrifugal movement outwards. The creatures have elongated, snake-like bodies that intertwine with one another, and each animal bites the body of the preceding beast. As they twist and tangle with one another, they each intersect once with a central concentric ring that bounds the mirror's triple-fluted knob. These "tigers" look similar to Shang *taotie*（饕餮）, mythical, zoomorphic beasts that decorated the surfaces of ancient ritual vessels. There are two types of these animals ; one set has horns on its head while the other has round, circular ears, both decorative characteristics often seen in *taotie*. Each pair of creatures is placed on opposite axes, facing away of one another. Their bodies are further intricately rendered with raised circular rings decorating their backs and small, incised lozenge shapes patterning their serpentine bodies.

8. Mirror with 3 *Shan*（Mountain）characters and 3 deer 戰國三山三鹿紋鏡

Warring States（475-221 BC）　Diameter：8.6cm

　　This mirror is a synthesis of various Warring States styles superimposed layer by layer over one another. The base layer is a repeating, feather whorl（or feather-hook）ground pattern, which often decorates the backdrop of many Warring States pieces in this collection（see mirrors 1,2）. The next layer has three deer turning their heads to the right and planting their hooves firmly on the mirror's plain border. Small petal-like spots decorate their bodies. Finally, the character *shan*（山）, which means mountains, overlays the fauna and whorl pattern. Each of the characters slants to the right and protrudes from the plain border. At the center of the mirror is a triple-fluted knob framed by a wide undecorated ring.

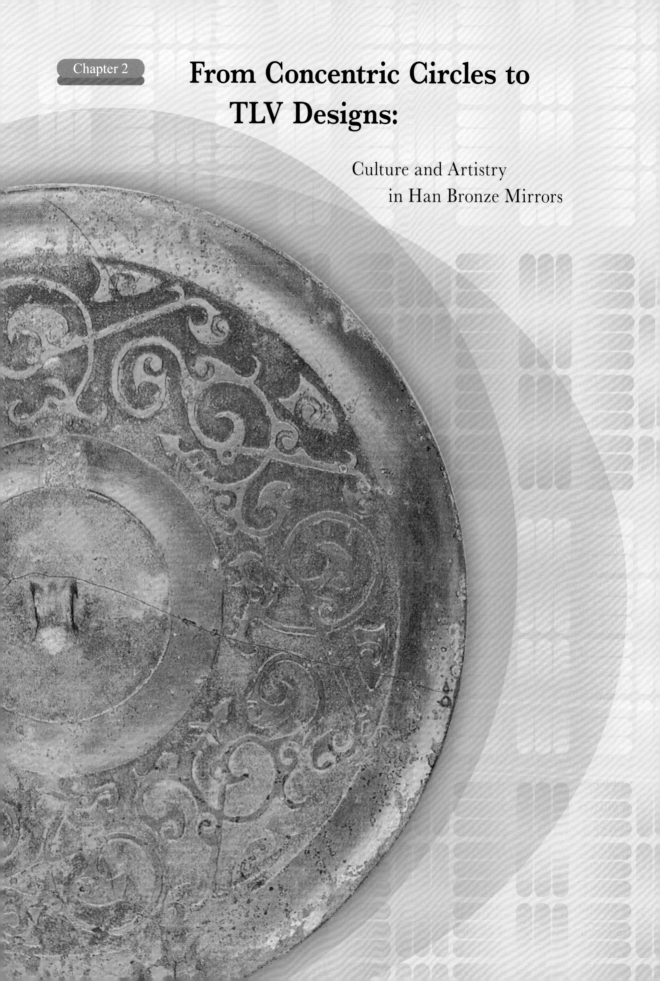

Chapter 2

From Concentric Circles to
TLV Designs:

Culture and Artistry
in Han Bronze Mirrors

Han, Wei, and Six Dynasties

I.

The emergence, culmination, and eventual diminution of a certain craft not only relates to the successes and failures of craftsmanship but is also closely connected with the historical development of its social and cultural factors. The history of Chinese ancient bronze mirrors serves as a typical example, since what matters is not our conclusion that imports of glass artifacts from the West replaced traditional mirrors in Ming and Qing China, but instead the question of why and how bronze mirrors of the Han and Tang dynasties were able to attain such splendid achievements in the overall development of Chinese mirrors. As far as Han mirrors are concerned, this success conveys at least three following historical and cultural implications.

First, as is known by many, Han porcelain reached a wider range of consumption and major technical breakthroughs which far surpassed the Shang, the Zhou, and the transitional era of the Spring and Autumn and Warring States period, and such a progress in the historical development of porcelain was made possible by the unification of the empire. A new era was manifest with the use of glaze, the innovation in porcelain types, and the rise of pragmatism. Especially notable were the Eastern Han primeval porcelain, a new type evolved from the primitive, high-temperature hard-paste porcelain, and celadon and black-glazed porcelain using iron-oxide paste in the areas of Zhejiang and Jiangsu, which not only reached a higher degree of firmness and durability of the biscuit, but were also remarkable for the tightly attached glaze which was lustrous, smooth, impermeable, and did not wear off. The porcelains produced also became multifarious in type and versatile in usage : in places where water and wine containers, cooking and eating utensils, and ritual vessels (together with the light and elegant lacquer wares prevalent in the early Warring States) had been used, porcelains gradually substituted the all-important Shang and Zhou bronzes. However, porcelain cannot substitute bronze for mirrors ; by contrast, the highly advanced Han craftsmanship made the casting of mirrors a challenging task for all artisans.

Second, the so-called "*shangfang*" (尚方 Supreme Tools Bureau) as in the well-known "*Shangfang precious sword*" (尚方寶劍) is actually the name of the official metal-casting foundry of the Han dynasty, which originated as a Qin institution administered by *Shaofu* (少府 Minor Ministry) and specialized in producing objects exclusively for the royal family, not the public. Such an institution was adopted by the Han, which was further subdivided into the Left, the Middle, and the Right *fang*, or workshops. According to the *History of the Latter Han* (*Houhanshu* 後漢書), "*Shangfang*… administers the production of handcrafted sabers, swords, and items of entertainment and interest for the royal house." The Left *Shangfang* produces bows and arrows, crossbows, and other types of weaponry ; the Middle *Shangfang* produces ornaments made of gold, silver, glass, jade, and precious stones ; and the Right *Shangfang* produces objects of daily use such as mirrors, trays, and pots and cauldrons. In the beginning of the Han, when all-under-heaven was just unified by Gaozu (高祖 August Progenitor) Liu Bang (劉邦), the political stability in real sense had not yet been fully realized. Any effort of attaining such a stability was further compromised by the regency of Empress Dowager Lu (呂后) and the infighting among the princes, and the society was settled only through the reigns of Emperor Wen and Jing (文景之治) with the assistance of capable ministers like Jia Yi (賈誼) and Chao Cuo (晁錯), paving the way for the grand enterprise of Wudi (武帝 Martial Emperor) and the peaceful reigns of Emperor Zhao and Xuan (昭宣二帝). In the meantime, the prosperity of the mirror industry gave rise to local manufacturing and private workshops which emanated peculiar glamour and excellence. Eminent mirror crafters at the time included Liu (劉氏), Wang (王氏), Long (龍氏), San-yang (三羊 three sheep, the archaic character *yang* 羊 or sheep is an abbreviation of *xiang* 祥 or luck), Qing-yang (青羊 green sheep), Huang-yang (黃羊 yellow sheep), Li (李氏), Zhu (朱氏), Du (杜氏), and others, whose products were not at all inferior to the official *shangfang* mirrors in quality. This quite resembles the situation of the Shi family in Huzhou (湖州石家) of the Southern Song dynasty, who specialized in making "*sujing*" (素鏡), or pristine plain mirrors. The ruling class in the early years of the Han did not possess a high level of cultural attainment or much experience of running the government (Liu Bang had been a *tingzhang* 亭長, a petty post much resembling today's local sheriff ; Xiao He (蕭何) and Cao Can (曹參) had been low officials ; and Fan Kuai (樊噲) had been a dog-butcher in the market, which is why many basic institutions of the former Qin dynasty became adopted by the Han, including the *shangfang* imperial workshops. For this reason, the style of the early Western Han bronze mirrors retained many distinctive characteristics of their Warring States predecessors (the short rule of Qin lasted only fifteen years). As far as the ground pattern of the mirror is concerned, the distinctive motifs of the Han mirrors—such as the whorl, the feather-hook, the water-wave, and the more developed and artistic *panchi* (蟠螭 coiling dragon), *panhui* (蟠虺 coiling snake), linked arc, grass-leaf, star-cloud, and fowl-and-beast—can all be viewed as a continuation and extension of the Warring States mirrors.

　　Third, starting in the Eastern Han, philosophical thought of the prevalent Huang-Lao Taoist School (黃老) in the Former Han was complemented by and combined with resurgent Confucianism, and the confluence of the two schools further incorporated later theories of *chenwei* (讖緯) mysticism, yin-yang, the Five Agents (五行), and the cosmological model of the consonance between heaven and humans, leading to a unique and peculiar view of life: on the one hand, life, like in a long and young night, is to seize the moment and indulge in worldly pleasures ; on the other hand, it is also to detach from the secular world and travel freely across the seas in search of the elixir of immortality. This conception created a huge impact on the manufacture of mirrors and entailed the appearance of inscription, which carried messages of wishes and blessings typical of the Han culture and unprecedented by the Warring States mirrors. Therefore, the three common aspirations of the ancient Chinese, which, as mentioned above, include the worldly aspiration for wealth and prosperity and the transcendental aspiration for longevity, immortality, and the telepathy with Heaven. These notions all became embodied in the inscription of the Han mirrors especially in the TLV mirrors of the later period. None has ever imagined that the same inscription would have later evolved into a much romantic form in the Tang dynasty, when it would carry pieces of elegant, melodious poems, or even rhapsodic palindromes engraved along the circular contour of the mirror.

II.

In *Ancient Chinese Bronze Mirrors* (*Zhongguo gudai tongjing* 中國古代銅鏡), the co-authors, Kong Xiangxing (孔祥星) and Liu Yiman (劉一曼), classify the most well-circulated Han mirrors into fifteen types, which has become the standard for the study of Han mirrors for many years.[1] The first type is the coiling-dragon patterned mirror (蟠螭紋鏡 *panchi wenjing*). It can be further divided into three subtypes according to the variations in pictorial design—the interlocking (纏繞式), the intermittent (間隔式), and the regular (規矩式 *lit.* compass and square, a.k.a. TLV) patterned mirrors. These mirrors carry the motif of "coiling dragons" or *panchi*, an auspicious totem in Chinese dragon culture, which became especially distinctive and forceful during the Han. Meanwhile, one cannot overlook how *panchi* as an artistic motif is represented；Kong in his another seminal work, *A Pictorial Compendium of Chinese Bronze Mirrors* (*Zhongguo tongjing tudian* 中國銅鏡圖典), provides the following descriptions on the shapes and forms of *panchi* of the Warring States and Han mirrors:

〔The Coiling Dragon Leaf-patterned Mirror, page 114〕… The ground pattern uses densely laid out whorls and appears rather fuzzy. The main pattern consists of three coiling dragons. The head of each dragon is at the center of the mirror, attaching to the concave ring；crooked horns grow on top of the head, the mouth opens, the body twists and makes several C-shape turns, while the four limbs curl in different ways.

〔The Coiling Dragon Leaf-patterned Mirror, page 115〕… The main pattern consists of four coiling dragons. Each dragon turns its head back, with an open mouth, huge eyes, and long, bifurcating horns growing from the back of the head. The body winds into an S shape, with swirling tendrils extruding from the two flanks；the two feet are at either side of the body, stretching widely apart.

〔The Coiling Dragon Lozenge-patterned Mirror, page 122〕… The main pattern consists of four coiling dragons in low relief. Each dragon has its head close to the rim of the mirror, raising the neck and lifting

---

1｜Kong Xiangxing and Liu Yiman. *Zhongguo gutongjing*（Chinese Ancient Bronze Mirrors）. Taipei: Yishu tushu gongsu, 1994.

Warring States Coiling Dragon Leaf-patterned Mirror 戰國蟠螭葉紋鏡，北京故宮博物館藏

the head high. It opens the mouth, bears the teeth, and sticks out the tongue ; there are horns splitting into multiple branches on top of the head, while the body interlinks and intertwines, with one limb bending backward into the shape of confronting lozenges. The head, the body, the tail, the limbs, and the claws all change in varying ways and are fully vitalized and animated by the spiritual energy and rhythm.

〔The Great-Joy Fame-and-Fortune Four-leaf Coiling Dragon Mirror, page 167〕… Locating between the two circles is the inscription ring engraved in the seal script and with the following content: "Great

Warring States Coiling Dragon Leaf-patterned Mirror 戰國蟠螭葉紋鏡，Donald Graham Jr. 藏

joy, fame and fortune；for a thousand autumns and ten thousand ages, may you have good wine and food," and the sentence ends with the graph of a fish⋯ The dragon has a small head, round eyes, and a pointed snout；at the center, toward the rim of the mirror, the two claws stretch left and right, while the body swirls and intertwines in a flowing curve, full of elegant and exuberant details.[2]

Of the above four examples, the first three come from the Warring States while the fourth, the Great-

Warring States Coiling Dragon Lozenge-patterned Mirror 戰國蟠螭菱紋鏡，上海博物館藏

Joy Fame-and-Fortune Mirror（大樂富貴鏡）, belongs to the Han. The descriptive text alone aptly evokes the animated, agile, winding dragons each lifting its head and flaunting its body vigorously, giving away to a dynamic image fraught with energy and rhythm. Herein lies the continuation as well as manifestation of the casting and sculpting traditions of the transitional period from the Warring States to the Qin-Han.

In the last example, through the short lines of inscription, we can already see that the Han people were well versed in ode-chanting and prayer-saying. These coiling-dragon or coiling-serpent mirrors（mostly

West Han Great-Joy Fame-and-Fortune Four-leaf Coiling Dragon Mirror 西漢蟠螭「大樂貴富，千秋萬歲，宜酒食魚」上海博物館藏

four-serpent mirrors) display a combination of rich images and texts；the texts, though succinct, are no less sentimental and evocative, as shown by the following exemplary inscriptions：

"The great joy has not yet receded；Miss me often, and wish we do not forget each other."

「大樂未央，長相思，願毋相忘。」

"Miss me often, and forget me not；Perpetual fortune and fame, and never-ending joy."

「常相思，毋相忘，常富貴，樂未央。」

West Han Great-Joy Fame-and-Fortune Four-leaf Coiling Dragon Mirror 西漢蟠螭「大樂貴富，得所好，千秋萬歲，延年益壽」博局鏡，
Donald Graham Jr. 藏，另一面在河北滿城中山靖王妻竇綰墓出土

"Always with you, my lord, we make each other joyful and delight；forget me not, and look not afar in forlorn."

「常與君，相謹幸，毋相忘，莫遠望。」

Such lines, when one first reads them, sound almost like new tones from the "Music Bureau" (*yuefu* 樂府)：on the one hand, they beseech fortune, fame, food and wine, and the joy of the fleeting moment；on the other hand, the mirrors become the vehicle for sentimental expressions. Each day when one looks into the mirror, the inscription at the back earnestly pleads that the beholder today not to forget yesterday's affection.

In this way, the romantic sentiments of the Han people accompanied and traveled along with conscripts and wanderers as mirrors. Such artistic, lyrical expression had never been surpassed until the Sui-Tang period, when the four-character parallel prose and the five- or seven-character poem became incorporated into the mirror inscriptions.

III.

The linked-arc motif of the Warring States mirrors also brought the Han mirrors into a new artistic height of glamor and splendor. The so-called "linked arc"（連弧）indicates a half-circle pattern composed of curves or wide concave bands on the backside of the mirror；the usual number of arcs are six or eight, depending on the size of the mirror or the design of the pictorial composition. Linked-arc mirrors of the Warring States by and large used the motif of coiling dragon and the ground pattern of fine whorls, forming the "whorl-patterned linked-arc mirror" or "whorl-patterned coiling-dragon linked-arc mirror".

In the Han dynasty, the linked arc expanded to the outer ring, while the inner ring contained a large square surrounding the knob, adopting the scheme of "Round Heaven and Square Earth"（天圓地方）. The square usually consists of a band with a simple two- or four-character inscription on each of the four sides, e.g., "Seeing the light of the sun；The eternal joy has not yet receded；"（見日之光，長樂未央）or "Perpetual fame and fortune, and never-ending joy；Miss me often, and forget me not."（常貴富，樂未央，長相思，毋相忘）. The decorative motif of grass-and-leaf is added outside the square, which, in addition to the already mentioned linked-arc pattern (amounting to twelve to sixteen arcs due to the large size of the mirror), forms the so-called "grass-and-leaf linked-arc mirror."（草葉連弧鏡）

West Han Grass-and-leaf linked-arc mirror. 西漢「見日之明，長毋相忘」草葉連弧鏡，北京故宮

West Han Grass-and-leaf linked-arc mirror rubbing image from Chen Jie-qi collection. 西漢草葉「常貴富，樂未央，長相思，毋相忘」拓本，陳介祺藏鏡第十五面

In many cases, the pattern of nipples or TLV are also added to the grass-and-leaf pattern and the linked arcs. Combining both the round and the square, this particular scheme of decoration focuses on mutual correspondence and symmetry, thus generating the Han ideal of harmony and balance.

If the linked arcs contract inward and surround the knob-base, whereas the outer ring is inscribed by lines like "Seeing the light of the sun；Bringing great brightness to all-under-heaven"（見日之光・天下大明）or "Seeing the light of the sun；Forever forget me not,"（見日之光・長毋相忘）the mirror would be the famous "linked-arc sunlight mirror."（連弧日光鏡）. An alternative name for this type of Han mirrors is the "illuminated bright" or *zhaoming* mirror（昭明鏡）, because the inscription sometimes includes sentences like "The nature of inner purity reveals brightness（*zhaoming*），"（內清質以昭明）or even the hardly decipherable space-word "*er*"（而）… "Inner-*er*-blue-*er*-to-*er*-reveal-*er*-brightness-*er*-light-*er*-fu-*er*-sun-*er*-moon-*er*"（內而青而以而昭而明而光而夫而日而月而）. There are many subtypes of the *zhaoming* linked-arc mirror, and the naming is usually based on the first several characters of the inscription or the overall content of the text, such as the "*tonghua* linked-arc mirror"（銅華連弧紋鏡）or the "*ri-you-xi* linked-arc mirror."（日有憙連弧紋鏡）. Both names derive from their respective inscriptions: for the former, "Casting copper essence（*tonghua*），clear and bright；Making it a mirror, suitable for patterns and embellishments；Extending the year and prolonging the age, away from things inauspicious"（涷治銅華清而明・以之為鏡宜文章・延年益壽去不羊）and for the latter, "The sun is bright（*ri-you-xi*），The moon is full；… The market measures〔and benefits〕the ten thousand things."（日有憙・月有富…賈市程〔利〕萬）. While the former seems to be the mirror of a scholar, the latter is perhaps that of a merchant. A linked-arc mirror is usually heavier and bigger in size than a coiling-dragon mirror（the Warring States mirrors are remarkable for their slimness and lightness and are easy to carry and hold in the hand），which is also the characteristic of the later Han mirrors at a time when mirrors were commonly used in the households. In other words, during the Han, especially the reign of Emperor Wu in the Western Han, people enjoyed a wealthier and happier life, and the mirrors that had formerly been used exclusively by aristocrats now prevailed among commoners and merchants and were often hung in their houses.

The global fame of the Han sunlight mirrors, however, comes from its peculiar semi-transparency. When facing the sun, some of these mirrors are said to be able to project the backside image onto the ground or flat walls, as if transparent. The light penetration mirrors excavated in modern Japan have been marveled at, regarded as "magic mirrors" by some Westerners. In the Tang marvel "*Gujing ji*（古鏡記 Record of Ancient Mirrors），" the narrator Wang Du（王度）obtained an ancient mirror from a scholar Hou（侯生），which allegedly was able to protect its possessor against all kinds of evil. This mirror, "when bathed in sunlight, the text and image on the back are cast into the shadow without missing a single detail," hence it is a genuine light penetration mirror.

According to various sources, the actual reason for such semi-transparency lies in the casting process:

East Han ri-you-xi linked-arc TLV mirror 東漢日有熹博局鏡

when the hot mirror is quickly cooled, the backside pattern takes form as raised or depressed parts, developing a varying degree of thickness. The sanding and polishing afterwards reduces the difference in thickness, and the raised and depressed parts are made less apparent. Therefore, when taken to face the sun, the mirror casts a shadow of mixed degrees of brightness, and this becomes what we call as the "light penetration mirror"（透光鏡）. It is fair to say that for both linked-arc and TLV mirrors, it is precisely their pictorial composition and emergent inscription on the bronze that make them the two most distinctive mirror types of the Han.

West Han linked-arc sunlight (magic) mirror 1 西漢連弧透光鏡
上海博物館藏

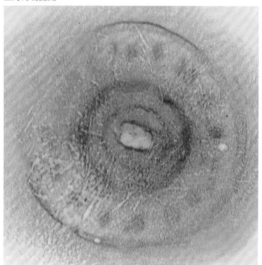

9. West Han linked-arc sunlight (magic) mirror 2 西漢連弧透光鏡
透光鏡紋

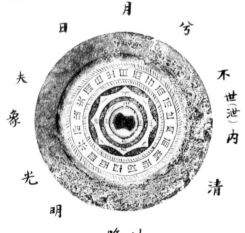

West Han linked-arc sunlight (magic) mirror 3 西漢連弧透光鏡

IV.

The essence of the art of Han mirrors is epitomized by the TLV mirror (also known as the *boju*-chessboard mirror or the *guiju* 規矩 compass-and-square mirror). The name "*boju*" (博局) is derived from an ancient table game called "*liubo* (六博 six gambles)," and the chessboard used in the game comes to serve as the ground pattern of the mirror. The chessboard is further adorned with the four spiritual animals—Azure Dragon, White Tiger, Vermilion Bird, and Black Tortoise-snake—in addition to other fowls and beasts, feathered demigods, toads, and paired birds, while both the inner ring (which surrounds the knob-base) and the outer ring include inscription bands, diagonal sunrays, saw-toothed wheels, rippling waves and clouds, or floating clouds. The composition is exquisite and sophisticated and abounds with rich cultural meanings, which makes the mirror a feast for the eyes and a joy for connoisseurship. Well-crafted TLV mirrors are marked with even more delicate, clear engravings, moderate thickness and weight, and the thousand-year-old "black lacquer antique," (黑漆古) giving a special charm of utmost glisten and luster. In particular, large-scale TLV mirrors allow an increased number of inscribed characters, evoking the grace and grandeur of the Shang-Zhou bronze vessels and also conveying the highly vivid imagination, the exquisite artistic design, and the unique cosmological ideal of the Han people.

The Han people are widely known for being fond of gambling. Early Western, Chinese, and Japanese scholars interested in the TLV mirror all focused on inquiring if the backside pattern evolved from the long lost *liubo* table game or from the graduated sundial which tells time. That the chessboard is indeed the pictorial prototype of

West Han Shangfang TLV mirror 西漢尚方作鏡四靈博局鏡

the TLV mirror has become unquestionable since the excavation of an entire *liubo* game set from Mawangdui tomb no. 3 in Changsha in 1973. Though ancient rules of gambling have been lost, we might be able to restore the game rules of *liubo* according to ancient texts and excavated objects.

In the 1950s, Lien-sheng Yang（楊聯陞）discussed the Han rules of gambling by citing the "*liubo* mnemonic tune"（六博口訣歌）recorded in *Xijing zaji*（西京雜記 *Miscellaneous Records of the Western Capital*）. His research, however, remained presumptive at the time due to the lack of archaeological finds.[3] Similarly, Lao Kan's（勞幹）article "The Evolution of *Liubo* and *Boju* Games" in the 1960s also lacked the support from

3 | See Yang, Lien-sheng. "An Additional Note on the Ancient Game Liu-bo." Harvard Journal of Asiatic Studies, vol. 15, no. 1/2 (June 1952)：124-39.

excavated objects : as the TLV pattern still remained unidentifiable, his speculation on the game rules turned out largely erroneous.[4]

In the 1980s to 1990s, scholars took up a new approach with the introduction of the study of material culture: they were not only exposed to the gambling game sets but also informed by various other materials such as the Han stone relief of *liubo*（六博漢石圖畫）, the stone weight for gambling（石博鎮）, the bronze weight in the image of gambling figurines（博戲人物銅鎮）, and the like. A good example is a set of four exquisite figurine weights made of bronze excavated in the Fujiagou Han tomb no. 1 in Lingtai, Gansu（甘肅省靈台傅家溝一號西漢墓）in 1974. Such a weight in the Han dynasty was a stone or bronze heavy object used to anchor the four corners of the chessboard, when people spread the mat and started gambling. From the four figurine weights, we can infer that the Han gambling can be played by two or four players. In the latter case,

Han liubo chess game board and chess from Mawangdui 長沙馬王堆出土六博棋盤器具

Han stone liubo chess game players 漢代六博棋戲石雕

the four players are paired into two, with one of them in the charge of tossing the dice or sticks and another player responsible for moving the chess pieces. The game must have been extremely intense and exciting, as all four figurines are vivid in countenance and posture as if yelling and applauding madly.

Thanks to the decade-long effort of the researchers, it is now clear that the TLV pattern represents the twelve available routes of the chess pieces in the gambling game. That is to say, the T, L, and V mark the location and moving direction of the chess pieces which, amounting to a number of six for each gambler, move right at the letter of "L", either left or right at "T", and left at "V". The three letters hence indicate different stops, where the two gamblers (or pairs of gamblers) each toss a dice-like ball or bamboo sticks to determine their next moves based on the numbers they cast.

Because of its intense competitiveness, the game gradually became a type of gambling. The chessboard game existed and prevailed in the Spring and Autumn and the Warring States periods, when even Confucius commented on it:

It is no easy matter for a man who always has a full stomach to put his mind to some use. Are there not such things as *po* (*bo*) and *yi*? Even playing these games is better than being idle (the *Analects*,

XVII.22）.

飽食終日，無所用心，難矣焉。不有博奕者乎，為之猶賢乎己。

The last sentence is a denouncement of idleness by Confucius, who believes that even an indulgent gambler is better than an idle and lazy man. The *liubo* game in the Han dynasty underwent further changes and was aimed at eliminating all chess pieces of the opponent（though details of the rule are still unknown）, which was embraced by joyful, tireless men and women, old and young as the best entertainment to last all night.

The TLV pattern, originally a chessboard used in the well-known gambling game, can also be used as mirror decoration, yet such appropriation does not seem to be quite in tune with the auspicious nature of the mirrors. With the discovery of the "*boju zhan*"（博局占）wooden slip from the Yinwan Han tomb no. 6 in Donghai, Jiangsu（江蘇東海尹灣六號漢墓）in 1993, the scheme of the *liubo* chessboard pattern was verified to have been used in divination, hinting at the mysterious and auspicious connotations emanated from the TLV mirror. Lillian Lan-yin Tseng（曾藍瑩）has made a major breakthrough by examining the arrangement of the "Heavenly Stems and Earthly Branches"（天干地支）and the divination texts on the Yinwan wooden slip. She compares these elements with the mnemonic tune of Xu Bochang 許博昌（a *liubo* game expert during Jingdi's 景帝 reign in the Western Han）recorded in *Xijing Zaji*, and successfully attempts to restore the moves of the chess pieces at that time.[5]

Since the TLV mirror is enshrouded in a mysterious religious atmosphere, at a time when magic, divination, and the theory of yin-yang and the Five Agents prevailed among the common folks, the emergence of the four spiritual animals on the mirror paralleled the appearance of *taotie, panchi, panhui,* and *kuifeng*（夔鳳 one-legged phoenix）in the early Warring States in a sense that they were not just auspicious animals but also helped subjugate the evil and protect the household. The four guardian animals, Azure Dragon, White Tiger, Vermilion Bird, and Black Tortoise-snake, were extremely popular in the Han and their images frequently appeared on bronze mirrors, clay roof tiles, stone sculptures, and lacquer wares to ward off evil and bring blessings. Cao Zhi's（曹植）"Rhapsody on the Numinous Tortoise（神龜賦 shengui fu）" chants,

I praise the four divine beasts for their established virtues, each of them guarding one direction:

The Azure Dragon coils at the Eastern Mountain, the White Tiger bellows at the Western Hill；

The Black Tortoise-snake stops at the Frosty Gate, the Vermilion Bird perches in the Southern Wilderness.

嘉四靈以建德，各潛位乎一方，蒼龍於東岳，白虎嘯於西崗，玄武集於寒門，朱雀栖於南方。

4 | Lao Kan. "Liubo ji boju de yanbian（The Evolution of *Liubo* and *Boju* Games）". *Lishi yuyan yanjiusuo ji*（Journal of the Research Center for History and Language）35（1964）: 15-30.

5 | Tseng, Lillian Lan-ying. "Yinwan hanmu 'bojuzhan' mudu shijie（A Tentative Interpretation of the 'Bojuzhan' Wooden Slip Excavated from the Yinwan Han tomb）." *Wenwu*（Cultural Relics）, no.8（1999）: 62-65. To explore more concept of Han cosmology, see also Tseng's *Picturing Heaven in Early China*, Harvard University Press, 2011.

The four animals between the inner and outer rings of the TLV mirror therefore symbolize the guardians of the four cardinal directions, who patrol at and protect the Eight Ultimates（八極）. There is even the appearance of the legendary "*huanlongshi*"（豢龍氏）, a dragon-raiser who holds a numinous ganoderma（*lingzhi* fungus）in the hand and stands by the side of the Azure Dragon（as mentioned in *Bronze Mirrors From Ancient China: Donald H. Graham Jr. Collection*）.[6] This is not just an evidence for the Han model of heaven-human consonance, but it also tells us the harmony and intimacy between humans and beasts（dragons）.

Coming to the inscription on the TLV mirror, we are again informed of the Han ideal of traveling and roaming with celestial beings to approach the eternal Way and pursuit longevity, or even immortality. The most frequently used inscription is:

> The Supreme Tools Bureau（or names of the artisan such as Sanyang or Wang）makes this mirror in a superb quality. In heaven, there is the celestial being who, not knowing what getting old is, drinks the jade spring when thirsty and eats the jujube when hungry, and he travels everywhere under heaven and roams above the four seas. May your years are like gold and stone and may our country is protected.

> 尚方（或工匠名字如三羊、王氏）作鏡真大好，上有仙人不知老，渴飲玉泉飢食棗，浮游天下遨四海，壽如金石為國保。

On the other hand, copper in the early Han was produced in Danyang（丹陽 modern-day Dangtu in Anhui 安徽當塗）, which later moved to Xuzhou（徐州）. In the prefecture of Danyang, there was an official post set for administering the production of copper, while the seat of the prefect was in Xuancheng（宣城）in charge of seventeen counties. For this reason, there are also such lines frequently used for inscription:

> The fine copper of the Han is produced in Danyang ; mixed with silver and tin, it becomes pure and bright. The Dragon on the left and the Tiger on the right dominate the four directions ; the Vermilion Bird and the Black Tortoise-snake mediate between yin and yang.

> 漢有善銅出丹陽，和以銀錫清且明，左龍右虎主四彭，朱爵玄武順陰陽。

The metallic combination of copper, silver, and tin mentioned in the beginning should be a combination of copper, tin, and lead in real cases, sometimes added with a small amount of zinc.

Outside the inscription band, the ground pattern is mainly composed of diagonal lines symbolizing the sun rays or saw-toothed triangles symbolizing the sun, while the rim of the mirror is usually adorned with floating clouds of the sky or sea waves. Therefore, the overall pictorial composition of the TLV mirror starts from the sky and the sea at the outermost rim, enters the four corners guarded by the four spiritual animals, and finally reaches the twists and turns of the move of chess pieces in the liubo game, as if the footsteps and traces left by humans in history, all corresponding to the harmony between heaven, earth, and humans that were always aspired to by the Han people.

---

6 | Nakano, Toru, Youhe Zeng, and Suzanne Elizabeth Cahill. *Bronze Mirrors from Ancient China: Donald H. Graham Jr. Collection.* Hawaii: Donald H. Graham, Jr., 1994, p. .

Bibliography

Books:

· Chou, Ju-hsi. *Circles of Reflection: The Carter Collection of Chinese Bronze Mirrors.* Cleveland, Ohio: The Cleveland Museum of Art, 2000.

· *Gugong tongjing xuancui*（Selected Bronze Mirrors from the Palace Museum）. Taipei: National Palace Museum, 1971.

· *Jingyue Chenghua——Xizai cangjing*（Pristine Moon, Pure Splendor: The Mirrors in the Collection of Resting Studio）. Taipei: National Museum of History, 2001.

· Kong Xiangxing and Liu Yiman. *Zhongguo gutongjing*（Chinese Ancient Bronze Mirrors）. Taipei: Yishu tushu gongsu, 1994.

· Kong Xiangxing and Liu Yiman. *Zhongguo tongjing tudian*（A Pictorial Compendium of Chinese Bronze Mirrors）. Beijing: Wenwu chubanshe, 1992.

· Li Jinyun. *Gujing jianshang*（Connoisseurship of Ancient Mirrors）. Guangxi: Lijiang chubanshe, 1995.

· *Lidai tongjing*（Bronze Mirrors of All Dynasties）. Taipei: National Museum of History, 1996.

· Nakano, Toru, Youhe Zeng, and Suzanne Elizabeth Cahill. *Bronze Mirrors from Ancient China: Donald H. Graham Jr. Collection.* Hawaii: Donald H. Graham, Jr., 1994.

· O' Donoghue, Diane M. "Reflection and Reception: The Origin of the Mirror in Bronze Age China." PhD diss., Harvard University, 1988.

· Qiu Shijing. *Tongjing*（Bronze Mirrors）. Hefei, Anhui: Huangshan shushe, 1995.

· Tian Zibing. *Zhongguo gongyi meishushi*（History of Chinese Arts and Crafts）. Taipei: Danqing tushu youxian gongsi, publishing year missing.

· *Tongjing Pian*（Bronze Mirrors）. 2 vols. Taipei: Zhonghua wuqiannian wenwuji, 1993.

· Xu Changyi. *Zhongguo gudai qingtongqi jianshang*（Connoisseurship of Chinese Ancient Bronze Vessels）. Sichuan: Sichuan University Press, 1998.

· Yu Jiming. *Zhongguo tongjing tujian*（A Pictorial Examination of Chinese Bronze Mirrors）. Zhejiang: Zhejiang University Press, 2000.

· Zhao Ming and Hong Hai. *Gudai tongjing*（Ancient Bronze Mirrors）. Beijing: Zhongguo shudian, 1997.

· *Zhongguo qingtongqi quanji*（Complete Collection of Chinese Bronze Vessels）. Vol. 16, Bronze Mirrors. Beijing: Wenwu chubanshe, 1998.

· 守屋孝藏蒐藏《方格規矩四神鏡圖錄》，日本，京都國立博物館，1969。

Journal Articles:

· Fu Juyou. "Hanzhen zhimei canlan qiangu（The Thousand-year Splendor of the Han Weights）." *Lishi wenwu*（History and Antiques）, vol. 8, no. 1（1998）: 45-55.

· Huang Maolin. "Tongjing, Liuboju shang suowei TLV/Guijuwen yu boju qudao poyi ji xiangguan wenti（On the deciphering of the TLV/*guiju* pattern and the gambling game routes on bronze mirrors and the *liubo* chessboard, together with other relevant issues）." *Yazhou wenming*（Asian Civilization）3（1995）: 97-120.

· Lao Kan. "Liubo ji boju de yanbian（The Evolution of *Liubo* and *Boju* Games）". *Lishi yuyan yanjiusuo ji*（Journal of the Research Center for History and Language）35（1964）: 15-30.

· Loewe, Michael. "TLV Mirrors and Their Significance." In *Ways to Paradise: The Chinese Quest for Immortality.* London: George Allen & Unwin, 1979: 60-87.

· Tseng, Lillian Lan-ying. "Yinwan hanmu 'bojuzhan' mudu shijie（A Tentative Interpretation of the 'Bojuzhan' Wooden Slip Excavated from the Yinwan Han tomb）." *Wenwu*（Cultural Relics）, no.8（1999）: 62-65.

· Yang, Lien-sheng. "An Additional Note on the Ancient Game Liu-bo." *Harvard Journal of Asiatic Studies*, vol. 15, no.1/2（June 1952）: 124-39.

· You Zhenqun. "Handai liubo yu boxi zhi feng（The Liubo Game and the Vogue of Gambling in the Han Dynasty）." *Gugong wenwu*（Antiques of the Palace Museum）, vol.17, no.9（1999）: 114-133.

第二章

從昭明到博局──

漢代銅鏡的文化藝術

一．

一種工藝的興起、臻達輝煌、而終趨式微，不可能只是工匠手藝的成功或挫敗，而與社會文化因素的歷史進化息息相關。中國古代銅鏡發展史是一面典型借鏡，因為我們的結論不在於明清之際，西洋琉璃傳入中國取代了傳統銅鏡，而在於銅鏡發展史裡，漢、唐兩代為何能取得如此輝煌成就？就以漢鏡而言，它的成功至少具備了下面的三種歷史文化意義。

第一，許多人都知道，在陶瓷發展史上，由於國家大一統局面，漢代陶瓷器的普及應用與技術突破，遠遠超越了由商周以降，帶入春秋戰國的變革時期。無論在釉料及器皿類型改進與實用觀點，都強烈顯示劃時代意義。尤其在東漢成功由高溫硬陶發展入的原始瓷，浙江、江蘇一帶以氧化鐵釉料燒成青瓷與黑瓷，不止胚胎堅固耐用，而胎釉緊密結合，不會剝脫，更有澤亮光滑，不吸水功能。燒出來的器類繁多，用途廣泛，在盛水或酒、烹飪及飲食器具，或甚至祭祀禮器方面（配合早在戰國便已盛行的輕便美觀漆器），都慢慢取代以商周以來一直扮演重要角色的青銅器皿。但銅鏡無法由陶瓷所代替，相反，由於漢代手工業的高度發達，鑄鏡，成了工匠的藝術挑戰。

第二，許多人都知道尚方寶劍一詞，其實尚方是漢代隸屬官金屬鑄作工坊，本來在秦代屬少府分支，專管製作供給皇家而非在民間使用物品。漢朝沿襲這項體制，分左、中、右三方，《後漢書》載：「尚方⋯掌上手工作御刀劍玩好器物。」左尚方製弓箭弩機兵器，中尚方製金銀玻璃玉石裝飾，右尚方製鏡、槃、釜民生用具。漢初自高祖劉邦一統天下，尚未大定，又經呂后及諸侯等亂，一直到文景之治，並得賈誼、晁錯的進策，天下方才篤定，成就漢武帝霸業及昭宣二帝的承平，製鏡業的興旺發達，發展入民間私人作鏡行業，大放異采，名家如劉氏、王氏、龍氏、三羊、青羊、黃羊、李氏、朱氏、杜氏等，其品質保證並不遜於官府的尚方。這方面有點像後來南宋湖州專做素鏡的石氏家族。但同時也在漢朝開國早年，因為統治階層缺乏文化素養與行政經驗（劉邦本為有如今日警察的亭長，蕭何、曹參為下級官吏，樊噲為市井屠狗輩），亡秦後，許多官方體制仍襲前朝，尚方工匠亦不例外，因此我們看到西漢早期銅鏡風格，仍然具有濃厚的戰國銅鏡（秦統一的封建王朝非常短暫，只有十五年）色彩。就以銅鏡紋飾背景來看，漢代銅鏡的雲雷紋地、羽狀或水波紋地、發展入高度藝術化的蟠螭紋、蟠虺紋、連弧紋，草葉紋、星雲紋及禽獸紋，都可視為戰國銅鏡的傳承延續。

第三，自入東漢，立國前期黃老思想與儒術復興的互補揉合，再加後期方士讖緯、陰陽五行、天人感應的宇宙觀盛行，做成了一種獨特奇異的人生

《歷史文物》月刊，歷史博物館，台北，2002，9，110期，8-17頁。

觀。一方面是長夜未央，行樂及時的入世享樂，另一方面卻是海外遊仙以求長生的出世逍遙。製鏡藝術遂而承受巨大衝擊，產生用文字入鏡的鏡銘，以表寸心，這不但在戰國鏡上前所未有，同時更是漢鏡文化特色。胡適曾指出古人三種主要求索，即是上述入世與出世的長生不老、富貴蕃昌及天人感應。這些觀念都在漢鏡銘文中有具體反映，尤其在後期博局鏡（TLV）系列。到了唐朝，鏡銘詩作幽雅纏綿，甚至利用圓型鏡背，鑄銘以蕩氣迴腸的迴文詩，更非始料所及。

二．

　　孔祥星、劉一曼合著的《中國古代銅鏡》裡，把最流傳的漢鏡款式分為十五類，已是多年來研究漢代銅鏡典範。其中第一大類，就是蟠螭紋鏡。此類又可因圖案變調而另分為纏繞式蟠螭紋，間隔式蟠螭紋，及規矩（即博局）蟠螭紋等三大類。其中以蟠螭作為中國龍文化的吉祥圖騰，極其顯著強烈。但同樣不能忽視的是以蟠螭作為主題的藝術表現，孔氏在其另一經典著作《中國銅鏡圖典》內就戰國與漢鏡裡的蟠螭形態，有以下幾段文字描述：

〔蟠螭葉紋鏡，頁114〕…地紋為細密的雲雷紋，較模糊。主紋為三蟠螭紋。蟠螭頭部居中，貼近凹面形帶，頭頂有彎角，張嘴，身軀作數個 C 字形糾結，四肢作不同形態的捲曲。

〔蟠螭葉紋鏡，頁115〕…主紋為四蟠螭紋。蟠螭回首、張口、大目、頂部向後伸出長角，角端分二岐枝，身軀作 S 形蟠曲，從腹部向兩側伸出彎捲的蔓枝，螭的二足位於身軀兩側，呈八字形外展。

〔蟠螭菱紋鏡，頁122〕…主紋為四蟠螭紋，淺浮雕。蟠螭頭近鏡緣處，引頸揚首，張嘴露齒，口吐長舌，頭上有多岐枝冠，身軀勾連交錯，一肢向後曲折作對菱形。頭、身、尾、肢、爪曲盡變化，氣韻生動。

〔大樂貴富四葉蟠螭鏡，頁167〕…兩個圓圈之間為銘文帶，銘文篆體，內容是：「大樂貴富，千秋萬歲，宜酒食」，以一魚紋結句…蟠螭頭小圓眼尖嘴，居中近鏡緣處，兩肢爪向左右伸張，身軀蟠旋糾結，曲線流轉，細膩繁縟。

　　以上四例，前三例為戰國鏡，第四例大樂貴富為西漢鏡。即使是文字，也可窺探出蟠螭呼之欲出，靈活蜿蜒，伸首弄姿，氣韻生動的動態圖象。這正是自戰國入秦漢，鑄塑藝術風格傳承與表現。

　　即使短短三句銘文在最後一例裡，我們也可看到漢人善頌善禱的一面。在這類蟠螭或蟠虺（以四虺最多）圖文並茂呈現裡，雖然文字簡潔，但也感性動人，譬如下面幾則銘文：

「大樂未央，長相思，願毋相忘。」

「常相思，毋相忘，常富貴，樂未央。」

「常與君，相護幸，毋相忘，莫遠望。」

　　驟眼讀來，幾疑是樂府新聲，一方面是富貴酒食，行樂及時，另一方面卻是借鏡抒情，藉照鏡人每日臨鏡之時，在鏡背諄諄囑咐，今日攬鏡，毋忘昨日之情。如此一來，漢人浪漫情懷，隨著征人遊子的攜鏡在懷，長隨左右。這種意境，一直要等到隋唐，以四字駢文或五、七言律絕詩歌入鏡，才能相提並論。

三．

　　戰國時期的連弧紋紋飾，亦將漢鏡帶入輝煌境界。所謂連弧，即是鏡背以弧線或凹面寬弧帶連成半圈，作為主紋，多為六弧或八弧，視鏡子本身大小或圖案設計需要而定。戰國弧形多配蟠螭或細碎雲雷紋地，而成「雲雷紋地連弧紋鏡」或「雲雷紋地蟠螭連弧紋鏡」。

到了漢代，連弧紋擴張到外圈，再在內圈圍鈕座（knob）成一大方格，做成天圓地方的格局。方格做一銘文帶圍繞，四面配上簡單兩句或四句銘文，如「見日之光，長樂未央」或「常貴富，樂未央，長相思，毋相忘」。方格外再置草葉紋飾，加上前述的外圈連弧紋（因為鏡子較大，連弧圈多達十二到十六面），而成所謂「草葉連弧鏡」，經常也有乳釘或規矩博局圖形，附加在草葉連弧上。這種方圓並存的紋飾圖案設計，由於特別講究互相呼應的對稱（symmetry），也就同時產生了和諧（harmony）與均衡（balance），這是漢代的文化理想。

如果連弧紋收縮成內圈圍繞鈕座，外圈再圍配如「見日之光，天下大明」或「見日之光，長毋相忘」的銘文，那就是著名的連弧日光鏡了。這類漢鏡有時也稱昭明鏡，因為另有銘文「內清質以昭明」的句子，或似是而非的「內而青而以而昭而明而光而夫而日而月而」。這種連弧鏡種類非常多，命名就以銘文開首數字或內面文字特色而定，譬如「銅華連弧紋鏡」或「日有熹連弧紋鏡」，都是因為銘文中有「湅治銅華清而明，以之為鏡宜文章，延年益壽去不羊。」或「日有熹，月有富…賈市程（利）萬物」。前者看來就是讀書人鏡子，後者則是商賈用的。一般的連弧鏡都比蟠螭鏡厚重，面積也較大，（戰國鏡的特性是輕與薄，便利攜帶及攬鏡而照），這也是後期漢鏡特色，代表鏡子在房舍普及功能，也就是說，到了漢代，尤其西漢武帝時期，民生富裕安樂，從前只是貴族專用的鏡子，現在已遍及百姓商賈，在家中架起或懸掛鏡子也就非常普遍了。

但是漢代日光鏡名聞中外，卻因它另有的透光功能，據說有些日光鏡只要對著光線，在地上或平壁上便會反射出鏡背圖案，有如透光一樣。因為近代日本出土有透光鏡，驚為奇物，西方人也有稱之為「魔鏡」（magic mirror）者。唐人傳奇「古鏡記」裡，便有作者王度，自汾陰奇士侯生處，獲贈古鏡一面，據云持之百邪不侵。其鏡如「櫳日照之，則背上文畫，墨入影內，纖毫無失」，這就是名符其實的透光鏡了。

其實據研究指出，所謂透光，主要是在鑄造過程中急速冷凝，使鏡背圖案在厚薄程度上產生較大凹凸度，再在平面加工磨礪，掩飾其表面較明顯凹凸不平地方，把鏡子對著日光，便會反射出明暗不同效果，這就是所謂「透光鏡」。但是我們可以這樣說，昭明鏡和博局鏡，無論在構圖或銅器上銘文重現，才是最具漢鏡特色的兩項鏡種。

四·

能顯影漢代銅鏡文化藝術精髓，就是博局鏡（有時又稱規矩鏡或 TLV 鏡）。這種取自古代博戲六博棋盤作為主要紋飾的鏡子，配以青龍、白虎、朱雀、玄武四靈獸或其他鳥獸，羽人、蟾蜍及對鳥，又在鈕座內圈及大外圈帶配以銘文，以及斜光線、鋸齒輪、水波雲紋或流雲紋。此鏡構圖繁複，內涵豐富，使人目不暇給，極耐把玩。精品博局鏡，更是刻工精細，條理清淅，厚薄重量適中，配上千年變化的黑漆古，晶瑩潔亮，光澤動人。尤其大型博局鏡，銘文字數相對增加，喚回商周青銅器高雅泱泱大度，表現了漢人高度的想像力，精巧的藝術設計，以及獨特的宇宙觀念。

漢人好博，人所共知，但早年西方及中日學者對博局鏡的興趣，還是在於推敲鏡背圖案是否即為失傳的六博棋戲，或是顯示時辰的日晷盤圖案所演變。其實自一九七三年長沙馬王堆三號漢墓出土了完整的全套六博具後，博局鏡之博戲色彩，殆無疑問。至於如今失傳的博奕方法，我們應該可以利用古籍及出土實物，重新還原六博的遊戲規則。

早在五十年代，楊聯陞先生己援引《西京雜記》內的六博口訣歌來探討漢代博戲方法，當時缺乏文物引證，仍在摸索階段。六十年代勞幹先生有〈六博及博局的演變〉一文，同樣因缺乏出土實物，根本不知TLV 為何物，因而許多有關棋戲原則均是錯誤揣測。

但自八、九十年代間，學者從介紹器物觀點入手（其實不止博具，尚有許多六博的漢石圖畫，石博鎮，博戲人物銅鎮等等可供參考）。譬如據報導，一九七四年甘肅省靈台傅家溝一號西漢墓，出土一組四件精緻博戲人物銅鎮。所謂博鎮，就是漢人舖蓆而博時，鎮壓在四隅的石或銅鎮。從這四枚人物銅鎮，我們可以看出漢代博戲，有二人相博，也有四人相博。四人博時即二人一組，一人專司投骰或箸，另一人則專管行棋。因為棋戲激烈，四人面部表情及動作均忘形狂呼，栩栩如生。

因經廿多年來學者追蹤研究，所謂 TLV 與博局遊戲內所取棋子行走的十二曲道關係，已非常清楚。也就是說，TLV 即是博奕雙方的下棋位置，每方各六棋，L 是向右方出發行棋，T 是左右兩方皆可出發行棋，V 是向左方出發行棋。也就是說，TLV 分別為彼此停棋之處，而由雙方各擲一種像骰子的小球或竹箸決定點數大小以行棋。

因為是競爭遊戲，互相搶道，而成博奕賭博。這種棋戲春秋戰國時已有，而且極為流行，夫子甚至在《論語：陽貨第十七》裡感嘆：「飽食終日，無所用心，難矣焉。不有博奕者乎，為之猶賢乎已。」最後兩句，就是說夫子痛恨那些懶惰的人，覺得兇猛賭博的人比他們還有出息。入漢後六博規則經過改良，以互吃對方棋子為鵠的（細節仍不可考），足已可令漢人作終夕之歡，男女老幼樂此不疲。

雖然是人所熟識的博局戲，用棋盤為銅鏡圖案亦無不可。然以吉祥意圖而言，卻未盡能釋然。一九九三年江蘇東海尹灣六號漢墓出土「博局占」木牘後，正式証實了六博棋局設計，也可用來作占卜吉凶之用。如此一來，不但博局鏡神祕而帶吉祥表徵呼之欲出，前美國南加州大學曾藍瑩教授，更藉尹灣博局占圖天干地支排列與木牘占卜文字，對照《西京雜記》內引述西漢景帝時，擅長六博的許博昌的口訣歌，企圖還原當日走棋方向，也是一項難得突破。

因為博局鏡同時具有宗教神道氣息，更因民間巫筮卜卦、陰陽五行的盛行，所以四靈獸出現在鏡裡，亦有如戰國早期饕餮、蟠螭、蟠虺或夔鳳等神獸，不止是吉祥瑞獸，更有鎮壓邪魔，保護家宅功能。青龍、白虎、朱雀、玄武四神或四靈在漢代辟邪求福，極為流行，無論銅鏡、瓦當、石刻、漆器都常被用作題旨（motif）。曹植的〈神龜賦〉內有曰：「嘉四靈以建德，各潛位乎一方，蒼龍蚪於東岳，白虎嘯於西崗，玄武集於寒門，朱雀棲於南方。」在博局鏡內，四獸位置在於內圈及外圈之間，即是象徵此四靈獸各霸一方，巡狩護衛於八極。四靈獸的青龍旁邊，更常有手持靈芝飼龍的「豢龍氏」出現（夏威夷 Donald Graham 銅鏡收藏集中有特別提及），足見漢人不止天人感應，人獸（龍）相安，關係密切。

再進一步看博局鏡上銘文，便知遊仙求道，長生不老，為漢人理想世界。出現最多的銘文句子為：
「尚方（或工匠名字如三羊、王氏）作鏡真大好，上有仙人不知老，渴飲玉泉飢食棗，浮遊天下遨四海，壽如金石為國保。」

　　另外，因為漢代產銅地區早期在丹陽（即今安徽當塗），後期在徐州，丹陽郡設有銅官，郡治為安徽宣城，轄十七縣，所以銘文亦常有如下句子：

「漢有善銅出丹陽，和以銀錫清且明，左龍右虎主四彭，朱爵玄武順陰陽。」

　　首兩句指出的銅、銀、錫三金，其實真正合金成份為銅錫和鉛，另外有些鏡子再加少量的鋅，善就是佳或美好之意。

　　銘文帶的外圈大部分為象徵光線的斜線帶，以及象徵太陽的三角鋸齒紋帶，鋸齒外的鏡緣則多飾以代表天空的流雲紋或海洋的海波紋。因此從整面鏡子的構圖看來，博局鏡從最外圈的藍天大海開始，到四靈獸護衛四隅，那些布滿在鏡面的 TLV 六博棋戲曲道，好像就是人類在歷史走過的痕跡，符合了漢人一直追求天地人的宇宙和諧。

書籍
· 孔祥星，劉一曼，《中國古銅鏡》，台北，藝術圖書公司，1994。
· 孔祥星，劉一曼，《中國銅鏡圖典》，北京，文物出版社，1992。
· 昭明，洪海，《古代銅鏡》，北京，中國書店，1997。
· 裘士京，《銅鏡》，安徽合肥，黃山書社，1995。
· 李縉雲，《古鏡鑒賞》，廣西，漓江出版社，1995。
· 余繼明，《中國銅鏡圖鑒》，浙江，浙江大學出版社，2000。
· 田自秉，《中國工藝美術史》，台北，丹青圖書有限公司，缺日期。
· 徐昌義，《中國古代青銅器鑒賞》，四川，四川大學出版社，1998。
· 《中國青銅器全集，16，銅鏡》，北京，文物出版社，1998。
· 《歷代銅鏡》，台北，國立歷史博物館，1996。
· 《淨月澄華—息齋藏鏡》，台北，國立歷史博物館，2001。
· 守屋孝藏蒐藏《方格規矩四神鏡圖錄》，日本，京都國立博物館，1969。
· 《銅鏡篇》，上下冊，台北，中華五千年文物集刊，1993。
· 《故宮銅鏡選萃》，台北，國立故宮博物院，1971。
· *Bronze Mirrors From Ancient China*: Donald H. Graham Jr. Collection, Hawaii, 1994.
· Diane M. O'Donoghue, *Reflection and Reception: The Origin of the Mirror in Bronze Age China*, Museum of Far Eastern Antiquities, Stockholm Bulletin, v.62, 1990.
· Ju-hsi Chou. *Circles of Reflection: The Carter Collection of Chinese Bronze Mirrors*, The Cleveland Museum of Art, 2000.

論文
· Lien-sheng Yang, "An additional Note on the Ancient Game Liu-bo," HJAS, 15, no.1/2 1952, pp.124-139.
· 勞榦，〈六博及博局的演變〉，台北《歷史語言研究所集刊》35，1964，15-30頁。
· 黃茂琳，〈銅鏡、六博局上所謂 TLV／規矩紋與博局曲道破譯及相關問題〉，《亞洲文明》第三集，安徽教育出版社，1995，97-120頁。
· 傅舉有〈漢鏡之美燦爛千古〉，台北《歷史文物》月刊，vol.8，no.1，1998，48-55頁。
· 曾藍瑩〈尹灣漢墓《博局占》木牘試解〉，《文物》，no.8，1999，62-65頁。
· 游振群〈漢代六博與博戲之風〉，台北《故宮文物》月刊，vol.17，no.9，1999，114-133頁。
· Michael Loewe, "TLV mirrors and their significance" in Ways to Paradise: The Chinese Quest for Immortality, London: George Allen & Unwin, 1979, pp.60-87.

9. West Han TLV with 4 Divine Animals Mirror 西漢四神規矩鏡

Han Dynasty（202 BC - 220 AD）   Diameter : 10.5cm

This is one example of the famous Han TLV typology, derived from the ancient *liubo* board game. A square frames the mirror's central, hemispheric knob, which sits on a flattened, blooming quatrefoil. Four T shapes protrude perpendicularly from each side of the square. Positioned parallel to these, four L shapes extend from a hachured ring bounding the edge of this decorative register. Right-angled V's protrude from the same striped band, and cinch four nipples that decorate the angles of the central square. In the interstices between these embellishments are the four divine beasts: the blue dragon, white tiger, vermillion phoenix, and black turtle-snake. They pace counter clockwise in within the interstices of this decorative band. Small curlicues and hachure add further detail and fill the remaining space. At the edge of the mirror, a plain, wide rim is inset with a double saw-toothed pattern and alternating dots. This TLV piece provides us with the clear example of the visual characteristics that manifest repeatedly in this typology. All of the mirrors in the TLV style have similar embellishments and emphasize the same harmonious connection between the heaven and "square" earth at the center. We will see different stylistic variations, but most mirrors retain similar, major decorative components.

10. West Han Mirror with 4 nipples and 4 serpents 西漢四乳四虺鏡

Han Dynasty（202 BC - 220 AD）　　Diameter : 9.75cm

Four "serpents" decorate the main register of this mirror. The creatures are abstracted into scroll-like forms with curling "tails" and small nipples each set in a raised circles separate the snakes into four, distinct spaces. The small nipples echo the large, central hemispheric knob, which is set in the same manner. Surrounding this is a concentric ring with several protruding lines, four marking the distinct axes, and small, interspersed dashes that rotate around the knob. Two hachured bands bound both sides of the decorative register, and a wide, undecorated border that frames the entire piece while creating a sinking, inner well.

11. Western Han mirror with 4 nipple grass-leaves and linked arcs 西漢四乳草葉紋鏡

Han Dynasty（202 BC - 220 AD）　Diameter：13.3cm

A set of sixteen linked-arcs decorates the mirror's rim and creates a shallow, inner well. This "sunburst" motif symbolizes the sun（or heavens） and frames a set of squares bounding the mirror's central knob. Closest to the hemispheric knob is an intricate band decorated with hatched squares at each corner. Chinese characters（two on each side） filling the remaining space and read:

See sunlight　　見日之光

Forge me not　　長毋相忘

Various grass and leaf motifs grow from this "square earth." Four bunches of grass protrude perpendicularly from the four edges the central embellishment. Between each pair of tree-like figures sits a small nipple. From each corner of the central square, teardrop-shaped leaves sprout and extend towards the linked-arcs. Other organic, leaf motifs cover the remaining interstices between the sunburst border and square modality. Viewing this piece as whole, we see symbols that depict the harmonious relationship between the heaven and earth, and the prosperous, natural bounty that results from this union.

12. Western Han TLV Mirror with "*shang-fang*" inscriptions 西漢尚方規矩鏡

Han Dynasty（202 BC - 220 AD）   Diameter : 15.2cm

This mirror is highly ornate with many, popular stylistic motifs of the Western Han. Similar to the first TLV piece（Mirror 9）, the hemispherical knob sits on a quatrefoil, surrounded by two square frames. Alternating horizontal and vertical dashes decorate the inner band, and a plain, grooved band separates the central design from its surrounding pattern.

The elaborate TLV pattern differs slightly in this piece. T that usually protrudes from each side of the central square has disintegrated into a horizontal line. Four pairs of nipples instead of four cinch both side of the letters, adding further embellishment. L and right-angled V shapes extend from an inscriptive band that bounds the outer edge of the main register. The thin band has an incomplete poem, which reads:

> What a fine mirror, Shang-fang bureau made it,
> Up above are the ageless immortals
> In thirst, they drink from the Jade Spring,
> When in hunger⋯
> 尚方作鏡真大好
> 上有仙人不知老
> 渴飲玉泉飢食⋯⋯

A thin, hachured ribbon lines this ring and the rest of the pattern, creating the final register for the inner well of the mirror.

The most elaborate decoration on this piece is undoubtedly the Four Divine Beasts. The black snake-turtle, white tiger, vermillion phoenix, and blue dragon weave between the TLV shapes, nipples, and the central square. Walking counterclockwise, they are joined by four companion beasts. To fit all eight creatures, the Divine Beasts and their companions are smaller in size than what we may see in other pieces.

Framing all of this is a highly decorated, wide border. Two concentric, saw-toothed rings frame an ornate, double-saw-toothed band cast in a deeper groove. The rim follows stylistic typology but with slight variants: many TLV mirrors usually have two bands with this motif, but we see here there are three concentric rings to add increased decoration. The mirror itself is badly damaged with two large cracks breaking the mirror into four pieces, and a third crack breaking one of the fourths into two pieces. The object is repaired ; however, the restored edges clearly show where damage was sustained, and the cracks cause some of the character in inscriptive band to be unintelligible.

13. Western Han mirror with "*jia-chang fu-gui*" characters 西漢家常富貴鏡

Han Dynasty（202 BC - 220 AD）   Diameter : 13.5cm

This mirror has three distinct, decorative zones: the rim, the main, decorative register, and the central knob area. A set of sixteen linked arcs decorates the border, their pointed corners almost touching the rim of the mirror. The interior curves of the arcs slope inward and create a well for the decorative band. Two hachured rings frame either side of the register, and the mirror seems to separate into two sets of axes with an alternating pattern. For one set, eight small circles surround four raised, nipples creating a decoration reminiscent of a flower. Two tendrils extend from the four blossoms, follow the edge of the outer hachured band, and connect the adjoining "flowers" together. Small lines also extend from the two circles at the base of each flower and overlay the inner hachured band. Between each of these decorations are four, equally spaced Chinese characters. 家常富貴 roughly translates to wishing constant good fortune onto one's household. The four characters are in two sets, with 家常 facing across from one another, and 富貴 facing one another on the opposite, perpendicular axis.

The final zone in the mirror is the central knob, whose embellishments are much like a miniature mirror. The "rim" is also made up of sixteen, linked arcs, cast in a high relief to create an inner well. Inside this, eight nipples surround a small, pointed central, similar to the floral decorative motifs, but cast more plastically. Surrounding this, another set of four nipples sits on the edge of a thin, ringed boundary, and small, slanted dashes curve counterclockwise between these. The effect of these distinct registers and patterns in different reliefs creates a sense of repetition as well as heaviness. The mirror looks to have substance and weight because of its simple but heavily defined design elements. Most of the mirror is in good condition except for the central area, which has a rusted, orange patina.

14. Western Han Mirror with 4 nipples and 4 divine beasts 西漢四乳四神鏡

Han Dynasty（202 BC - 220 AD） Diameter : 9.8cm

This piece has a simpler design that focuses on its main, decorative register. Its wide, plain rim that frames the inner well of the object, where the four directional gods, or Divine Beasts, the Dragon of the East, the Tortoise-snake of the North, the Tiger of the West, and the Bird of the South walk in a clockwise direction around the central knob. The casting technique on this mirror is extremely fine with each mythical animal carefully decorated. Four small nipples set in large circular bases separate the creatures into their respective quadrants. Two hachured bands buffer this middle register. A large hemispheric, knob sits on a circular base in the center of the mirror. Sets of dashes extend from a thin concentric ring and rotate around this central point. There is mild discoloration on the rim and some slight patina on the outer, hatched register, but overall, the mirror's design is still clear, distinct, and in good condition.

15. Eastern Han Mirror with "*jun yi gao guan*" characters 東漢君宜高官鏡

Han Dynasty（202 BC - 220 AD） Diameter : 11cm

Han mirrors often have a quatrefoil design blooming from their central knob, and this variation of the design is incredibly unique. Like the other mirrors, this object has a central hemispheric knob set on circular base. The central quatrefoil is much more intricate than usual：instead of a four leaves, blossoming from the knob, each petal has curling, sharp edges reminiscent of a curved, double-sided axe. Between each "leaf is a Chinese character that creates the phrase 君宜高官 , translated as, "may you always be in high officialdom" , when read clockwise. This is a typical example of the material wishes and hopes often written on the backs of Han mirrors. The quatrefoil leaves little room for each character to fit, and a linked-arc pattern of 8 half circles tightly frames all of this. A red-orange patina mottles a third of the thick plain rim, and there is a now-restored break that divides the mirror into two pieces.

16. Eastern Han Mirror with "*zhang yi zi-sun*" characters, #1 東漢長宜子孫鏡之一

Han Dynasty（202 BC - 220 AD） Diameter : 10cm

Again, we have a similar motif where a sunburst pattern encompasses a decorative quatrefoil and inscription. A thick plain rim decorates the edge of the piece while a grooved concentric ring separates this border from the main register. The hemispherical knob sits on a large quatrefoil. Like the previous mirror, nested in the space between each of the four leaves are the characters, 長宜子孫 , roughly translated as "may the mirror be cherished by your sons and grandsons for a long time." Eight linked arcs tightly enclose and outline the shape of the quatrefoil. This is all inset in a circle just wide enough to frame the points of each rounded arc.

17. TLV Mirror with 4 divine beasts and "*ri you xi*" inscriptions 東漢日有熹四神鏡

Han Dynasty（202 BC - 220 AD）　　Diameter : 19.5cm

Four divine beasts, the blue dragon, vermillion phoenix, white tiger, and black turtle-snake, each paired with a mythical companion beast, pace around clockwise in the in the interstices of this TLV mirror. Following the typical TLV style, the mirror's central hemispherical knob sits on a circle base, tightly bounded by a square. Around this, the twelve characters alternate with twelve, small raised nipples to create an ornate, square frame. Four T's protrude perpendicularly from the each sides of this central decoration, and two raised knobs cinch the T shapes. These eight, pointed nipples could be miniature mirrors themselves ; each one is set in a circular base and framed by a linked-arc pattern. Across from each T, right-angled L shapes protrude from an inscriptive band along with four, square V shapes at four "corners" of the mirror.

The inscriptive register restricts the central square and main, decorative space where the divine beasts walk. In an archaic script, the characters read:

The sun is bright

The moon is full

Great, nothing much to do

Time for wine and food

Live in peace

No disaster or sorrow

To be entertained by flute and zither

Our hearts are full of joy

Happiness is abundant

And will last a long while

My lord is good for officialdom.

日有熹，月有富，樂毋事，宜酒食，居必安，毋憂患，竽瑟侍，心志歡，樂已茂，固常然，君宜官。

A hachured band frames all of these decorative elements within the inner well. Around this, various bands with heavenly motifs decorate the border of the mirror. A saw-toothed ring, which commonly represents the sun, decorates the inner edge of the border, and a thick swirling cloud, mimicking the cosmos surrounds this. These all create a message of order, from the celestial heavens to the earth, as emphasized in the symmetrical, axial pattern of this mirror.

18. Eastern Han Mirror with linked arcs and "*tong-hua*" inscriptions 東漢銅華連弧紋鏡

Han Dynasty（202 BC - 220 AD)　　Diameter : 14.7cm

This mirror has two defining characteristics: a linked arc pattern radiating from the central knob and a written, inscription bounded by two hachured bands. The mirror's plain, wide rim dips to create an inner well. The first decorative register is the inscribed register. Read clockwise, the characters read:

Extract and refine copper essence, clear and bright

To make a mirror fit for character inscriptions

It will increase one's lifespan and ward off evil

And will last forever like the sun.

湅治銅華清而明

以之為鏡宜文

章延年益壽辟不羊

與天毋極如日。

This is a common inscription cast on Han mirrors. It reflects Han society's attention to both the "worldly" and " transcendental." Two dashes halve the long inscription at opposite sides of the band.

At the center of this mirror is a linked-arc pattern made of 8 half circles. The central decoration is extremely ornate ; inside the sunburst motif, a raised ring and hachured band frame twelve small circles surrounding a hemispheric knob. Small curved mounds with upright lines and small coils decorate the interstices between this central pattern and the linked arcs. These embellishments may relate to the heavens and the Han Dynasty's interest in cosmology, which would complement the last phrase in the mirror's inscription.

19. TLV Mirror with 8 fowls #1 東漢規矩八禽鏡之一

Han Dynasty（202 BC - 220 AD） Diameter : 12.1cm

This is another TLV mirror but with different decorative embellishments than the previous piece. Instead of the four divine beasts and their companions, eight fowls sit on the outer, inscriptive register. There are four pairs, and each duo turns toward one another, their beaks touching. The animals' shape is simple, with a few lines indicating the fowls' body and wings. We also see that the TLV decoration is also simplified. The V's are still in four separate corners, protruding from an inscriptive band. The L's are spaced between the V's and mirror T shapes. The small

nipples cinch either side of the letter, but the vertical line in the T has now disintegrated, leaving only a horizontal line. TLV mirrors often have ornately embellished central squares ; however, this mirror has a plain hemispherical knob set in a circular base, framed by a single, undecorated square frame.

The inscriptive register takes a few characters from the first two lines of the Shang-fang（尚方）, and TLV mirror which reads:

What a real fine mirror Shang-fang has made

On it there are ageless immortals

尚方作鏡真大好，上有仙人不知老

These characters look extremely archaic, and the inscription only has a few, sporadic characters like Shang-fang（尚方）、real（真）、old（老）。 A hachured band frames all of this, restricting it from the decorative border. Two saw-toothed bands decorate the rim of the piece. This piece is also incredibly worn, with a mottled green patina covering a large part of its surface.

20. Large TLV mirror with 4 nipples 4 divine beasts 東漢大四乳四神鏡

Han Dynasty（202 BC - 220 AD）　　Diameter : 17cm

This mirror's quality is extremely compromised, with a corroded, patina surface and eroded edges. Nevertheless, this is an excellent example of a Han piece where the decorative embellishment focuses on the four divine beasts (see also mirror 17). The black snake-turtle, vermilion phoenix, white tiger, and blue dragon pace clockwise in the main band, their feet barely touching one of the hachured rings that frame either side of the decorative register. The animals' bodies are elongated and follow the curved, circular shape of the mirror. Between each beast is a small nipple set on a circular base creating four distinct quadrants. At the center, a simple raised ring bounds the hemispherical knob on a circular base, and sets of dashes decorate the space between the knob and ring. Like other Han mirrors, the rim creates an inner well that bounds the main decoration, and a double-saw-toothed pattern is inset in the border.

21. Mirror with linked arcs and "*jian ri zhi guang*" inscriptions #1 東漢日光連弧昭明鏡之一

Han Dynasty (202 BC - 220 AD)　　Diameter : 9.5cm

The inner well's inscription and concentric decorations indicate this is an "illumination mirror", or 昭明鏡. The illumination mirrors stand out from other Han typologies due to their specific inscription. The text, read clockwise, states:

| The mirror's light shines like sun and moon | 光象夫日月 |
| Its inner clarity illuminates brightness (jiao-ming 昭明) | 內清以昭明 |

The phrase is simple, in order to embellish it further, a placeholder, "er" 而 , buffers each character. Each illumination mirrors has these two sentences inscribed on a register closest to the mirror's wide, plain rim, bounded by hachured bands on either side.

Another defining motif in this typology is the central decoration. Various grooved and inset decorations cut into a large raised circle. A linked arc pattern creates a well in the circle, and its eight corners almost touch the bounded edge. Inside of this is a raised concentric ring that restricts a small, hemispheric knob on a circular base. Small hachures, short decorative dashes, look like bending grass and decorate the space between the knob and raised ring.

22. Mirror with linked arcs and "*jian ri zhi guang*" inscriptions #2 東漢日光連弧昭明鏡之二

Han Dynasty (202 BC - 220 AD)   Diameter : 10.3cm

This is another variation of the illumination mirror. Most of its stylistic qualities, the plain rim, and central linked-arc decoration remain the same, but the inscription differs slightly. The placeholder, "er" 而 , inconsistently inserts itself in the writing, unlike the uniform buffering seen in the previous mirror. Furthermore, the script in this mirror looks more archaic. The character 以 has disintegrated into a curved vertical line with a short dash attached to a circle next to it. Other characters are also simplified, creating an older form version of the 夫日昭明 inscription. There are a few other differences, instead of eight linked arcs, there are now twelve arcs carved into the central raised circle. Furthermore, this mirror is very badly damaged. A fissure bisects the mirror in half, and another crack creates a third broken shard. The surface is mottled in a dark brown and green patina, and encrustations coat the remaining, undecorated surface.

23. Mirror with linked arcs and "*jian ri zhi guang*" inscriptions #3 東漢日光連弧昭明鏡之三

Han Dynasty（202 BC - 220 AD）　　Diameter : 10.1cm

This shows further stylistic deviations that can occur within the illumination typology. This mirror has a thinner, undecorated border and inclines more gently into the inner well. The script in outermost register is even more archaic, with angular shapes such as "ri" 日 softening into an oval with a horizontal line inside. Each character is rounder and more fluid, and there is greater space between each word. The central decoration also has some stylistic differences. There are fewer hachures between the raised ring and central knob ; single dashes now separate the space into four quadrants. The linked arc pattern has eight curved lines connected together, and small swirls decorate the interstices of every other corner.

24. Mirror with "*san-yang*" inscriptions and 4 nipples, 4 divine beasts 漢三羊四乳四靈鏡

Han Dynasty（202 BC - 220 AD）　Diameter : 11.5cm

This piece is in impeccable condition, allowing us to clearly identify various stylistic elements of the Han dynasty. At the center of the piece is the hemispherical knob, and a bead pattern that restricts the mirror's handle. This decorative border is slightly unusual since similar granulated patterns are more prevalent in the Sui-Tang dynasty. In the largest, main register, the four divine beasts, the vermillion phoenix, white tiger, black snake-turtle, and blue dragon, are cast in incredible detail. There are striations and spots on the turtle snake, hachures to denote tiger stripes, and thin strokes that detail the wings and skin of the phoenix and dragon. Each beast walks counterclockwise, and their feet touching the edges of a thin inscriptive border that reads:

How magnificent! San-Yang made such mirror!　三羊作竟真大好

On the surface there is an immortal ageless.　上有仙人不知老

These are the first two lines of an unfinished poem that was a popular inscription on Han TLV mirrors. Each character is far apart from one another leaving ample space in a very thin, concentric ring. This mirror lacks the inclined edge that usually creates a defined well and raised border ; instead, the plain, narrow border bevels slightly inward. A hachured band still bounds the inscription and main register, indicating where the inset would have been. The "border" has a narrow saw-toothed ring, surrounded by another decorative band. Its scroll-like motif is possibly an adaptation of the usual cloud design that evokes the heavens.

25. Mirror with 4 nipples and 4 serpents 漢四乳四虺鏡

Han Dynasty（202 BC - 220 AD）　　Diameter : 9.75cm

Similar to mirror 13, four serpents, each with a unique head, turn to their right and hiss at the next beast, as they prance in a counterclockwise fashion. Small raised striations and granulations decorate each serpent's bodies. Four nipples separate the creatures from one another, and small tendrils and coils embellish the undecorated space in the register. A striped band and incised ring frame the outermost edge of the mirror. At the edge, the mirror bevels outward and creates a rim with two, inset saw-toothed rings.

26. TLV mirror in New Han Dynasty by Wang Mang, The Second Year of the Xinfeng Reign, Xin Dynasty（15AD）王莽新漢鏡

Han Dynasty（202 BC - 220 AD）   Diameter : 21cm

This mirror is one of very few rare pieces cast in the short reign of Wang Mang who usurped the throne briefly and established the Xin Dynasty. It starts with a round knob in the center and the inner region with a square indicating the cosmic notion of a round heaven and a square earth. There are 12 nipples in the inner square around the 4 sides, with 3 spaces on each side of the square. Altogether there are 12 spaces indicating the zodiac series of twelve hours of the day. In addition to the regular TLV designs with 4 spiritual animals guarding 4 spheres of the earth, there are also the presence of toads and "feather-wing-flying mortals".

The inscription reads as follows:

"It was a nice mirror made in the 2nd year of the Tienfeng reign. We wish our emperor long happiness and good fortune. Our parents and wives are well protected, and we advance to high officialdom throughout generations till no end."

「始建國天鳳二年作好鏡，常樂富貴莊君上，長保二親及妻子，為吏高遷位公卿，世世封傳于毋窮。」

27. Wei-Jin Dynasties Mirror with Deities #1 魏晉神人鏡之一

Three Kingdoms；Wei-Jin Dynasties（220-581 AD）　　Diameter：12.5cm

This Wei-Jin mirror reflects great stylistic changes in mirror production during this time period. Han mirrors often have plain, undecorated rims, but this piece has an intricately decorated surface. In the inner well, twelve raised squares alternate with twelve raised semicircles to frame an even more ornate decoration. The central register has a new figural style where human forms decorate the main register. Four divine animals, pixie creatures（辟邪）, are holding small scrolls in their mouth. Their bodies are difficult to discern, and only their heads are clearly defined. Between each creature is a triad of individuals sitting at four, opposite quadrants of the mirror. A fourth figure may have been present, but the mirror's surface has worn part of the decoration, making it indiscernible. Nevertheless, the typology indicates these individuals would be Queen Mother of the West（西王母）and Lord of the East（東王公）.

For further information of Queen Mother of the West, consult Suzanne Cahill, *Transcendence and Divine Passion: The Queen Mother of the West in Medieval China*, Stanford University Press, 1993.

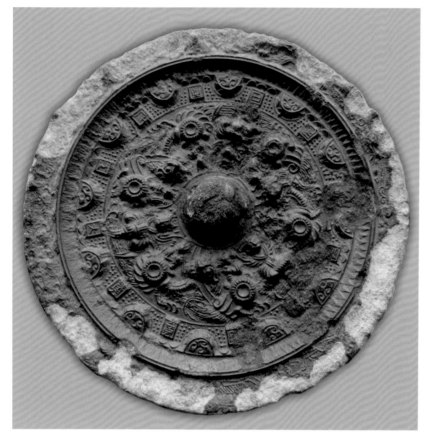

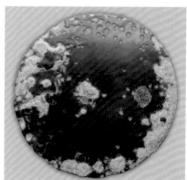

28. Wei-Jin Dynasties Mirror with Deities #2 魏晉神人鏡之二

Three Kingdoms：Wei-Jin Dynasties（220-581 AD）   Diameter: 12cm

This piece has the same motif as the previous mirror, with the Queen Mother of the West and Lord of the East, sitting on palanquins flanked by pixies. Raised circles flank either side of the figures and denote the coiled bodies of the eight mythical creatures. All of this radiates from the mirrors' central, hemispheric knob. Framing the outer edge of this register, alternating semicircles and squares protrude from opposite sides of a decorate band. A scalloped design further decorates the edge of the plastically rendered half-circles, and each square has an inscribed character. Since the mirror is quite erodea, these characters are partially legible, one sentence read: "It is good to make this mirror" （作鏡真大好）. Small granulations further speckle the interstices between the squares and semicircles.

The edge begins with a saw-toothed ring, which then bevels outward into an intricate rim. The border is heavily damaged with encrustations, but the entire piece, with its central figural motif and decorative bands all suggest rim would have had a similar motif to the other Wei-Jin mirror with deities（see mirror 27）. These two pieces could have easily been case from the same mold as seen by their identical designs.

One Mirror or Five Mirrors？

A Study of the Tang *Chuanqi*
"Record of an Ancient Mirror"

Sui, Tang Dynasties

"Record of an Ancient Mirror" (hereafter referred as "*gujing ji*" 古鏡記) is a tale of marvels (傳奇 *chuanqi*) written by Wang Du (王度) who flourished during the turn of the Sui and Tang dynasties. With its extraordinary subject matter, ornate language, intricate story, and profound meanings, it is often deemed one of the earliest masterpieces of the *chuanqi* genre. In this tale, Wang Du acquired from a certain scholar Hou an ancient mirror that can repel evil for whoever was in possession of it. The mirror grew dull and dim during lunar and solar eclipses, and regained its brilliance after the eclipse. When held up to the sun, the designs on the back can be penetrated by sunlight and projected on the wall. According to a Buddhist monk from the western regions of China, the mirror can reflect a person's inner organs after being cleansed and polished with certain magical potions. Wang Du once lent the mirror to his brother Wang Ji upon the latter's long journey. As Wang Ji traveled through mountains and rivers, forests and wilderness, the mirror warded off evil spirits of all kinds and tamed various demons for him along the way. When a scholar of profound erudition warned him that the mirror was a magical object and therefore would not remain in the midst of men for long, Wang Ji immediately took it back to his brother. After several months, a mournful sound escaped from the case where the mirror was kept. It grew in intensity until it was like the roar of dragons and the growl of tigers. When Wang Du opened the case to look, the mirror had already vanished.

Wang Du indicates at the beginning of the tale that his sense of loss and lamentation at the disturbed times has prompted him to record the twelve marvels that the mirror has wrought. He writes:

"Now these are disturbed times and I have been deeply saddened by events ; the empire is aflame with strife and there is no place where one can live in peace. And on top of all these troubles I have, alas! Just lost my mirror. I shall, therefore, set below all the marvels connected with it, so that those who come by it in future generations may know its origin."

From his words, we know that this tale revolves around the marvels connected to the ancient mirror, showing its different magical properties through a series of marvelous events. It appears to be a tale about one mirror, yet as the mirror changes with the different situation of each event, it develops into a fascinating account of the characteristics of several mirrors. There are always particular patterns on the back of bronze mirrors. The designs of bronze mirrors vary across each dynasty, each bearing its own distinct cultural, mythological, religious, literary, and aesthetic meanings. Besides providing a detailed textual description of the mirror's characteristics, through a wide array of rich textual images, the author of "*gujing ji*" also invokes the visual images of actual mirrors, which overlap, interchange, interplay and reciprocate within the story, engendering a peculiar form of visual text. This paper offers an experience of the visual text, as well as a discussion of its definition. It also explores the origins of the historical and cultural significance of the different types of bronze mirrors portrayed in the story.

1. Han Mirror — Four Deities with Twelve Zodiac Beasts（四神十二生肖鏡）

In "*gujing ji*", when scholar Hou gave the ancient mirror to Wang Du, he intimated that its possession can fend off all evil spirits. Wang Du describes the mirror as follows:

"It was eight inches in diameter, with a knob in the form of a crouching *qilin*. Around the knob were ranged four symbolic animals—the tortoise-snake, the dragon, the phoenix and the tiger—each in its proper quarter. Outside there were the Eight Diagrams and beyond these the twelve zodiacal beasts. At the outermost periphery were twenty-four characters which resembled in style the Li script but which could not be found in any of the dictionaries. According to scholar Hou they symbolized the twenty-four solar periods."

From this description we can infer that the mirror is a "Four Deities with Twelve Zodiac Beasts Mirror" from the Han, Wei, and Six Dynasties period. During the Sui and early Tang dynasty, this type of mirror gained tremendous popularity, but soon evolved into an "Auspicious Sea-lions with a band of inscriptions" Tang mirror（狻猊瑞獸銘帶鏡）. Except for the design of the patterns, the calligraphy style of the inscription is the most important characteristic that distinguishes the Han mirrors from their Sui and Tang counterparts. Han mirrors are often engraved with small characters in the simple, unadorned seal (*zhuan* 篆) or clerical (*li* 隸) script, while Sui and Tang mirrors with large characters in the more refined, elegant standard (*kai* 楷) script.

In the above quoted passage, the twenty-four

Han four dieties with twelve zodiac beasts mirror 四神十二生肖鏡

characters at the outer periphery of the mirror that resemble the *li* script should be the small ones, similar in style to the small character inscription in seal script of the TLV mirrors of the Han dynasty. Typical "Four Deities with Twelve Zodiac Beasts Mirror", "Auspicious Sea-lions with a band of inscriptions Mirror" or "Auspicious animals with Blossoms（瑞獸團花鏡）of the Sui and Tang dynasty are often engraved with an inscription of 32 characters. There are only three types of mirrors that have a 24-character inscription. The fewer number of characters allows for the larger size of each character within the limited space of the inscription band. One type is the "Light flows like a True Moon Mirror"（光流素月鏡）, prevalent between the Wude（武德）and Gaozong（高宗）reign of the Tang dynasty. Most of them are "Auspicious Sea-lions with a band of inscriptions" type. The inscription reads:

Sui-Tang auspicious sea-lions with a band of inscriptions mirror
狻猊瑞獸銘帶鏡

> *This mirror's light flows like a clear moon*
> *It is with the essence of dark mystery*
> *With clarity it reflects like water*
> *Its refraction is clear tranquility*
> *Lasting into eternity, it brightens the mind.*

The other two types of mirrors are the Tang "Watching her make-up Mirror"（窺莊〔妝〕鏡）and the "Full Round Mirror"（團圓鏡）of the Sui Dynasty. The inscription of the former reads:

> *I peep at her make-up in bright charms*
> *There are Mandarin ducks dancing in tunes*
> *This mirror will last for many thousand years*
> *And be kept for a thousand generations*
> *It brightens and reflects, and fits our descendants.*

The inscription of the latter reads:

> *This is a full round precious mirror,*
> *Bright as the moon arising*
> *I see phoenixes dancing by themselves*
> *When the sun shines on the mirror, flowers bloom*
> *When it faces the pond, the moon is full*
> *I see my beauty's countenance approaching.*

Since Wang Du lived during the late Sui and

Sui-Tang auspicous animals with blossoms mirror 瑞獸團花鏡

early Tang dynasty, it is highly probable that the

ancient mirror in "*gujing ji*" is modeled on the latter two types of mirrors that have a 24-character inscription. Although the story claims that the inscription on the ancient mirror is in the clerical script, it may just be a pretense by the author, because the pictographic quality of the clerical script helps to foreground Mr. Hou's claim that the 24 characters "symbolize the twenty-four solar periods".

In a "Four Deities with Twelve Zodiac Beasts Mirror", the "four deities" are four celestial animals that represent the four cardinal directions: the green dragon, the white tiger, the vermilion bird, and the dark warrior（an entwined tortoise and snake）. They are engraved around the central knob in the same layout as the TLV mirrors of the Han dynasty. "The tortoise, the dragon, the phoenix and the tiger" on the ancient mirror described in the quote above are none other than the four spirits of the a "Four Deities with Twelve Zodiac Beasts Mirror". Besides the first sentence, "the mirror made by the *shangfang* (the imperial workshop or supreme bureau) is truly fine", typical inscriptions on the TLV mirrors of the Han dynasty often include some reference to the four deities that can repel the evil. For example, "the dragon on the left and the tiger on the right dispel what is unlucky ; the vermilion bird and the dark warrior put yin and yang forces into harmonious order."

The twelve zodiac animals are rat, ox, tiger, rabbit, dragon, snake, horse, ram, monkey, rooster, dog, and boar, each assigned to one of the twelve earthly branches, *zi, chou, yin, mao, chen, si, wu, wei, shen, you, xu, and hai,* （子、丑、寅、卯、辰、巳、午、未、申、酉、戌、亥）respectively. It is a common folk belief during the Sui and Tang dynasty to take the twelve zodiac animals as talismans to bring good luck and protection. The twelve zodiac animals later became deities in religious Daoism. For example, the deities of the twelve zodiac animals are pictured on the Daoist murals in the Yongle Palace of the Yuan dynasty in Shanxi Province, along with the gods of the eight trigrams, the gods of the twenty-eight constellations, and the thirty-two heavenly gods. Pottery figurines of the four deities and twelve earthly branches can also be found in the Tang tombs. They are a series of tomb guardians that include the figurines of the twelve zodiac animals, and either a pair of figurines of one civilian and one military official, or figurines of a pair of heavenly gods.

There is almost always a knob in the center at the back of a bronze mirror, through which is passed a silk or cloth cord. The majority of the a "Four Deities with Twelve Zodiac Beasts Mirror" during the Six Dynasties period have rotund knobs, different from the fluted knobs of the bronze mirrors of the Warring States period, or the round knobs of the "TLV Mirror with Spiritual Animals"（神獸規矩鏡）of the Han dynasty. In "*gujing ji*", the knob of the ancient mirror "in the form of a crouching *qilin*（麒麟）" should be similar to the large chased knob of the mirrors of the Warring States period, but made in the shape of a crouching *qilin* to serve as a talisman. This round *qilin* knob is set on a square knob base, surrounded by the four spirits—green dragon, white tiger, vermilion bird, and black warrior. Beyond the four spirits are the eight trigrams. The knob, the four spirits and eight trigrams form the inner circle of the mirror. Outside the eight trigrams is the outer band, which is divided into twelve panels, with one zodiac animal in each panel, in their proper order.

2. Han "Magic Mirror" (Light Penetration Mirror 透光鏡)

In "*gujing ji*", the description of the "Four Deities with Twelve Zodiac Beasts Mirror" is followed by the quote below:

"When held up to the sun, the designs and characters on the back appeared distinctly in the reflection : when tapped, the mirror gave out a resonant note that reverberated all day."

At this point, the ancient mirror has changed from the "Four Deities with Twelve Zodiac Beasts Mirror" to a light-penetration mirror of the Han dynasty, which is known to the West as a "magic mirror". When aimed at the sun, the mirror can reflect the designs on its back from its polished face, as if it could be penetrated by the sunlight, and hence it got its name. The majority of this type of mirrors are "Linked Arcs and Concentric Circles Mirror" (連弧紋鏡), the most common ones being the small sized light-penetration mirrors "Sunlight Linked Arcs and Concentric Circles Mirror" (日光連弧紋鏡) or "By the Light of Sun Linked Arcs and Concentric Circles Mirror" (見日之光連弧紋鏡), such as "Sunlight Grass Leaves Mirror" (見日之 光草葉連弧紋鏡). Sunlight or "*riguang* 日光" and illumination or "*zhaoming* 昭明" are both from the standard inscription on these mirrors, which is in *bafen* (八分) script, a calligraphy style that is in between the seal and clerical script. Chinese written language underwent significant changes and evolutions since the Qin dynasty. Li Si (李斯) created the small seal script, Cheng Miao (程邈) created the clerical script, and Wang Cizhong (王 次仲) created the *bafen* script, which incorporates "eighty percent of the small seal script and twenty percent of the clerical script" (八分小篆，二分隸法). *Bafen* script is the standard script of the inscription of the "Linked Arcs and Concentric Circles Mirror" of the Han dynasty. Typical inscriptions of the "Sunlight Linked Arcs and Concentric Circles Mirror" include:

May you see the light of the sun

The universe is made bright

or:

May you see the light of the sun

And forge me not

The former inscription is the most common. The standard inscription of the "Illumination Mirror" (昭明鏡) is:

Its inner pure element illuminates

Brightness that resembles sun and moon

My heart is in high spirit and I wish to pledge my loyalty

Yet it is plugged and will not express freely.

The character *xi* (兮) is a common expletive that can often be found in the Songs of Chu. When making

Han TLV mirror with spiritual animals 神獸規矩鏡

Han magic mirror 見日連弧透光鏡

Han grass leaves by the light of sun linked arcs and concentric circles mirror 見日之光草葉連弧紋鏡

and inscribing mirrors, most craftsmen paid close attention to the aesthetic arrangement of the characters, in order to achieve a balanced look on the inscription band. One way to accomplish this is adding particles and expletives to fill extra space. An extreme example is a variation of the standard inscription of the "Illumination Mirror", where a particle *er* (而) is inserted between every two characters of a sentence like "Its inner pure element illuminates" (內清質以昭明), transforming the whole sentence into a barely illegible "Inner er pure er element er illuminates er brightness er that er resembles er sun er and er moon" (內而青而以而昭而明而光而夫日而月而).

If we take the expletive *xi* from the standard inscription of the "Illumination Linked Arcs with a band of inscription Mirror" (昭明連弧紋鏡) quoted above, the remaining 24 characters resemble both the clerical and seal script, and when "held up to the sun, the designs and characters on the back appeared distinctly in the reflection", precisely fitting Wang Du's description of the ancient mirror in "*gujing ji*".

Besides Wang Du's "*gujingji*", records and discussions of the light penetration mirror can be found in many sources across the dynasties, such as *Records of Clouds and Mist Passing Before One's Eyes*" (*yunyan guoyan lu* 雲煙過眼錄) by Zhou Mi 周密, *Brush Talks from the Dream Brook* (*mengxi bitan* 夢溪筆談) by Shen Kuo 沈括 in the Song dynasty, *Manuscript in Seven Categories* (*qixiu leigao* 七修類稿) by Lang Ying 郎瑛, *Minor Knowledge about Things and Their Principles* (wuli xiaoshi 物理小識) by Fang Yizhi 方以智 in the Ming dynasty, and *Fascination with Lenses and Mirrors* (*jingjing lingchi* 鏡鏡詅痴) by Zheng Fuguang 鄭復光 in the Qing dynasty.

Shen Kuo offers the following explanation in the 19th volume of his work *Brush Talks from the Dream Brook*:

There exists certain "light penetration mirror", which have about twenty characters inscribed on them in an ancient style which cannot be interpreted. If such a mirror is exposed to the sunshine, although the characters are all on the back, they "pass through" and are reflected on the wall of a house, where they can be read most distinctly.

Those who discuss the reason for this say that at the time the mirror was cast, the thinner part became cold first, while the (raised part of the) design on the back being thicker, became cold later, so that the bronze formed (minute) wrinkles. Thus although the characters are on the back, the face has faint lines (too faint to be seen with the naked eye).

From this experiment with light, we can see that the principle of vision may be really like this. I have three of these inscribed "light penetration mirrors" in my own family, and I have seen others treasured in other families, which are closely similar and very ancient; all of them "let the light through". But I do not understand why other mirrors, though extremely thin, do not "let light through". The ancients must indeed have had some special art. (Joseph Needham's translation. *Science and Civilisation in China: Volume 4, Physics and Physical Technology; Part 1, Physics*. Cambridge University Press, 1962, 95.)

In fact, research shows that the so-called "light penetration" is actually an optic effect of reflection from uneven surfaces. When the mirror is cast in the rapid cooling process, because the raised part of the design on the back is thicker and thus cools more slowly than the rest of the mirror, the surface of the mirror acquires a slight unevenness that corresponds to the patterns on the back of the mirror. The surface is carefully polished afterwards to conceal the unevenness so that it becomes invisible to the eye. Therefore, when held up to the sun, the reflection from the uneven surface shows the characters and designs on the back of the mirror.

3. Tang "King Qin Detecting Gall Mirror" （秦王照膽鏡）

According to Shen Kuo's description, when a semi-transparent mirror is exposed to the sunshine, "although the characters are all on the back, they 'pass through' and are reflected on the wall of a house." There is a similar account in *"gujing ji"*. On New

Han its inner pure element illuminates mirror 內清昭明連弧鏡

Tang mirror of King Qin detecting gall 秦王照膽鏡

Year's Day of the ninth year of Daye, a Buddhist monk from the Western Regions came to Wang Du's house to beg. Impressed by his unusual appearance and manners, Wang Du's brother invited him to the house and prepared food for him. Upon his request, Wang Du's brother showed him the mirror. The monk took the mirror in his hands and danced with joy, revealing that this mirror had several magical appearances, one of which being the semi-transparent mirror: if painted with a gold ointment and sprayed with pearl dust, the light reflected from the mirror will penetrate the wall.

Another magical appearance of the ancient mirror is a "Detecting Gall Mirror"（照膽鏡）. The monk said with a sigh, "if you smoke it with incense of gold and wash it with liquid jade before you apply the ointment and pearl dust, it will enable you to see the inner organs of man. The only pity is that it provides no cure for the ailments that it enables you to diagnose." The monk was actually referring to a "King Qin Detecting Gall Mirror"（秦王照膽鏡）that can reflect the internal organs of the palace ladies. It is said that there are two different "King Qin Detecting Gall Mirrors". One of them is the "*qin wang zhao dan inscriptions Mirror*"（瑞獸銘帶賞得秦王鏡）of the Tang dynasty with auspicious animals and a band of inscriptions with a five-character quatrain:

I was given a King Qin mirror

I wouldn't trade it for a thousand pieces of gold；

There is nothing to do with detecting the gall,

It is mainly a reflection of my tranquil mind.

The other one is the legendary "King Qin Detecting Gall Mirror" that was in the Qin palace during the Warring States period. According to an entry in *Miscellaneous Records of the Western Capital* (*Xijing zaji* 西京雜記）, after the fall of the Qin dynasty, when Liu Bang, Emperor Gaozu of the Han dynasty, first entered the Xianyang palace, he found all kinds of rare treasures that the First Emperor of the Qin had collected, including a five-branched lamp of blue jade, a thirteen-string lute adorned with seven precious stones, and a jade flute with twenty-six holes. Among them is a square mirror:

"It is four feet wide, five feet and nine inches high, and its outside and inside are both bright. When one walks up to look into the mirror, his/her reflection will appear upside down. If one comes with one hand on heart, his/her intestines and five internal organs will distinctly show up in the mirror, without any obstruction. When someone with internal ailment looks into the mirror with one hand on heart, the mirror will localize the cause of the ailment. Moreover, if a woman harbors any licentious thoughts, the mirror will expose her expanded gall and quivering heart. The First Emperor used to examine his palace ladies with this mirror, and anyone with an expanded gall and quivering heart would be executed."

The outside and inside of the mirror both being bright may indicates that it is transparent from front to back. Its ability to illuminate one's inner viscera, or expanded gall and quivering heart caused by licentious thoughts, may well be the magical quality of this legendary mirror. Even as a legend, it still inspired the romantic imagination of the Tang people. If a mirror can reflect one's gall, surely it is also able to illuminate one's heart and reveal one's nature. With this notion they composed verses like "It has nothing to do with detecting the gall, but mainly as a reflection of my tranquil mind". And in the famous verses composed by the *Chan*（Zen）Buddhist master Shenxiu（神秀）and Huineng（慧能）in the famous competition of stating their understanding of the Buddhist mind（heart），"the heart is like a bright mirror's stand"，and "the bright mirror also has no mirror's stand"，the mirror is also used by both as a metaphor of the heart or mind.

Tang mirror of coiling dragons 盤龍鏡

4. Tang "Mirror of the Coiling Dragon"（盤龍鏡）

In "*gujing ji*"，not only can this ancient mirror drive away the evil, it can also cure disease：

There was then a famine in the land and the people suffered greatly from hunger and disease, particularly in the regions of Pu and Shan. Among my officers there was a man by the name of Chang Lung-chu, a native of Hopei, whose entire household, numbering more than a score, was stricken with sickness. Taking pity upon them, I went to his house with my mirror and left it with Lung-chu with the instruction that he should uncover it at night. When this was done the sick all rose from their beds with their fevers completely gone. They said that Lung-chu had come into the room with a moonlike object in his hand and that its light had chilled them like ice and driven away their fevers. Since it did not occur to me that this service would cause the mirror any harm, while it might save a multitude of people, I instructed Lung-chu to take the mirror and turn its magic emanations on the other people in the district who were afflicted, but that night the mirror made a strange, chilly, and penetrating noise and did not stop for a long while. In the morning, Lung-chu came to me and said, "I dreamed last night that I was visited by a man with the head of a dragon and the body of a snake, wearing a red hat and a purple robe. He told me that his name was Purple Gem and that he was the spirit of the mirror."

By naming the minor officer Longju (dragon steed 龍駒), Wang Du is actually making an allusion to the "Lobed Mirror with the Coiling Dragon"（葵花盤龍鏡）that was once prevalent during the Tang dynasty. The way Longju cures disease with the moonlike round mirror, and his dream about the spirit of the mirror "with the head of a dragon and the body of a snake, wearing a red hat and purple robe", can also be easily associated to the "Lobed Mirror with the Coiling Dragon". The coiling-dragon mirrors of the Tang dynasty can have single or double coiling dragons. On the back of most mirrors with a single coiling dragon, there is a flying dragon with scales, manes, claws and horns, soaring in high spirits among the flowing cloud design. Its rotund knob looks like the dragon's pearl, and the brocade belt or bright colored cord that is passed through the knob to hang the mirror is especially eye-catching.（Yao He's 姚合 poem "On Mirror"（詠鏡）has the following two lines: "Both ends of an embroidered cord seek to emerge from the dragon mouth's knob, foiled flowers blossom vibrantly in the box"（繡帶共尋龍口出，菱花爭向匣中開）. The dragon's pearl is often placed between the coiling dragon's head and tail. Sometimes the design becomes even more vivid where the dragon turns its head toward the pearl, as if taking it in and out of its mouth.

There are a number of Tang poems on the coiling-dragon mirror. For example, the first poem of Li Bo's（李白）"Written for a Beauty's Mirror on Grievances, Two Poems"（代美人愁鏡二首）has the following lines:

A beauty gives me a precious coiling dragon mirror

Candles shine on my gold-threaded robe

She frequently uses her red sleeve to brush on the bright moon

Just to save brightness to illumine both of us.

Meng Haoran's（孟浩然）five-character regulated verse "Grieving a Clear Mirror with Zhang Mingfu"（同張明府清鏡嘆）reads:

I am a lady with a coiling dragon mirror

It emits clear light often in daytime

Since dust has gathered, it looks like a moon in the mist ;

When in grief, I use it to look at myself

And signed vainly over my growing white hair

I have a message to tell the frontier man

"How could you stand for such long separation ? "

And Bai Juyi's（白居易）"A Thought on a Mirror"（感鏡）reads:

My lady bids me farewell

And leaves her mirror in a box

Since her flowery face is gone

There is no hibiscus in the autumn water.

For years, the box is closed,

There are red dusts covering the bronze

Today I wipe it clean

And look at my pined countenance

There are heavy sorrows after looking into the mirror

On its back, there are two coiling dragons.

Mid-Yangzi river multiple refined mirror 唐代江心百鍊鏡

5. "Mid-Yangzi River Multiple Refined Mirror"（江心百鍊鏡）

The fifth mirror is an extension of the coiling-dragon mirror. In *"gujing ji"* , Wang Du gave the mirror to his brother Wang Ji upon his long journey to the mountains and rivers, to expose demons and fend off evil spirits. When Wang Ji was crossing the Yangzi River at Guangling in the Jiangnan area, suddenly a violent wind started to rage, and his boat was about to be overturned by the big waves. As soon as Wang Ji took out the mirror and shone it over the river, the wave quieted down. The description of Wang Ji holding a mirror in the middle of the Yangzi River calls forth the image of the "Mid-Yangzi River Multiple Refined Mirror" of the Tang dynasty. In *Supplement to the History of the Tang Dynasty*（Tang *guoshi bu* 唐國史補） by Li Zhao 李肇 , there is an entry in the chapter "Imperial Mirrors from Yangzhou" that offers an interesting account of the "Mid-Yangzi River Multiple Refined Mirror": "Yangzhou once produced a mid-Yangzi mirror（江心鏡）and sent it to the imperial court as a tribute. It was made at the Yangzi River on the fifth day of the fifth month. Some said that the mirror was only smelted for sixty to seventy times, not a hundred times as claimed. Mirrors of this type are very difficult to make, yet easy to break. Many of them can make sound." Bai Juyi also wrote a poem "Multiple Refined Mirror"（百鍊鏡）:

What a multiple refine mirror! Its model is out of ordinary

Day and hour to cast are divine and unique

Amidst the river, above the waves, inside the boat

On the fifth day of the fifth month at noon.

Once polished with pearl dusts and gold ointment to shine

It turned into a pool of autumnal water

And was about to be sent to the moon palace.

The Yangzhou governor himself placed a sealing tape

This mirror is not made for women of the human world

At its back, there is an imperial flying dragon

People therefore called it Emperor's mirror.

I have heard from Emperor Taizong of Tang

Who often used mirror as metaphor for people:

Mirror illuminates past and present

Not merely for the reflection of faces.

The security of four seas is in his palm

Pacifying a hundred lords is always in his mind

Then I know this is a different Emperor's mirror

It is not the Yangzhou multiple refined bronze.

From this poem we know that this "multiple refined mirror" that "at its back, there is an imperial flying dragon"（背有九五飛天龍）is a "coiling-dragon mirror". *Extensive Records of the Reign of Great Tranquility (Taiping guangji* 太平廣記）includes an entry "Li Shoutai"（"李守泰"）from *Records of Extraordinary Events (Yiwen lu* 異聞錄 ）: "In the third year of the Tianbao Reign, on the fifteenth day of the fifth month, Yangzhou sent a "amidst the river mirror"（水心鏡）to the imperial court, which is nine inches in both width and height, clear and bright in the sunlight. On its back there is a coiling dragon, three feet four and a half inches in length, in a lifelike posture. The Emperor Xuanzong was amazed when he saw this mirror." Then Li Shoutai, the military officer of Yangzhou who escorted the mirror to the capital, explained that the mirror was made on the fifth day of the fifth month on the Yangzi River, by a craftsman named Lü Hui（呂暉 Sunray Lu）, with the assistance of an old man named Longhu（龍護 Dragon Protected）and a boy named Xuanming（玄冥 Dark Spirit）, who disappeared before the mirror was completed（presumably became one with the mirror）. Afterwards Emperor Xuanzong always had great success when he prayed for the rain using this mirror.

The fifth day of the eighth month is Emperor Xuanzong's birthday. During the Tang dynasty this day was made a national holiday and named "Thousand-Autumn Festival". On this day horses were trained to dance to the beat of the music and hold wine cups in their mouths to present to the emperor. Besides, the court officials also presented the emperor with bronze mirrors and the "dew-collecting sacks" that had an auspicious meaning, as birthday gifts. The emperor in return awarded the officials bronze mirrors to express his will and intention. Emperor Xuanzong composed two "Distributing Mirrors to My Nobles in Thousand-Autumn Festival"（千秋節賜群臣鏡）poems:

Once the Thousand-Autumn mirror was casted

Light emits from its multiple refined bronze

I distribute the mirrors among nobles,

Wishing them to see phenomena with a clear mind

On the pavilion, they look penetrating cold

By the window, the moon shadow arrives.

There are birds holding long embroidered ribbons in their beaks

To show deep feelings towards our ties.

And

Auspicious dews and flowery ribbons

The precious wheel is icy cold

Comparing it to the pavilion moon

We all celebrate these happy hours.

The image of bird holding a ribbon (*shoudai* 綬帶)appears in both poems. The character *shou* 綬 (ribbon) is homonymous with *shou* 壽 (longevity). The image of a magpie holding a flower ribbon in its mouth is a traditional auspicious design on the bronze mirrors of the Tang dynasty. Add a moon to this design and it will become a "Lobed Moon Palace Coiling Dragon with Ribbon Mirror" (葵花月宮盤龍銜綬鏡).

Du Fu wrote lines "Precious mirror are given to the nobles, troops are returning from foreign lands" (寶鏡群臣得，金吾萬國回) in his poem "On Thousand-Autumn Festival, Two Poems" (千秋節有感二首), yet a coiling dragon mirror of the Tang dynasty found in Xi'an has the characters "qianqiu " (thousand-autumn 千秋) in its inscription on the back. The "thousand-autumn mirror" (千秋鏡) in the poem may be the coiling dragon mirrors that were awarded to the officials in the thousand-autumn festival. Or "thousand-autumn mirror" could be a general terms for all types of mirrors that the emperor gave the officials, including coiling dragon mirrors.

The basic functions of the mirror include reflecting light, revealing one's heart and nature, and illuminating the supernatural world, like the heavenly mirror. However, it is the following inscription on a Tang mirror that captures the quintessential quality of any mirror: "Clear as still water, bright as the autumn moon, pure luminance contained within, water chestnut flower blooming without." With its emphasis on the ancient mirror's clearness and brilliance, *"gujing ji"* is actually an optical text that has magical qualities. During the solar or lunar eclipse, the ancient mirror grew dim and lost its brilliance due to the lack of light, and "when the sun had recovered completely its luminosity, the mirror too shone with its former brilliance". On the fifteenth day of the lunar month, if placed in a dark room, "it will radiate rays of light to the distance of several rods". At a night with the full moon, when Wang Du and his friend put the ancient mirror and a bronze sword side by side in a dark room with all the light shut out to test their brightness, "presently the mirror shone forth with a light that brightened up the room like day, but the sword along side of it gave no light at all".

Upon seeing the light-penetration mirror, the Buddhist monk from Western Regions left instructions to polish the mirror: "If you smoke it with incense of gold and wash it with liquid jade before you wipe it with the gold ointment and pearl dust, even if buried in earth, the mirror will not grow dim." Wang Du and his brother followed the monk's instructions and everything turned out as he said. The method of polishing bronze mirrors is also recorded in the chapter "Necessity of Training"（xiuwu 修務）in *Huainanzi* 淮南子: "When a mirror is just taken out of its mould, it is so dim that one cannot see his own face. Only after being rubbed with black tin and polished with white felt, can it reflect one's hair, brow, and other fine details." The gold ointment and pearl dust described in *"gujing ji"* may be the "black tin" in *Huainanzi*, a mixture of lead powder and mercury, or a polishing material made from cassiterite.

Because of its brightness, the mirror is believed to be able to illuminate the supernatural world that is otherwise invisible to the human eye. One obvious function of the mirror is to expose the original form of demons that have transformed into humans. In *"gujing ji"*, besides records about the mirror exposing and vanquishing all kinds of ugly animal spirits like the snake, ape, turtle, shark, rooster, weasel, mouse, and gecko, the most touching episode is about a thousand-year old fox that transformed into an attractive maid named Parrot. She was unfortunately exposed by the mirror and could not escape. She asked Wang Du to cover the mirror for a while so she could drink and have one last moment of joy. Intoxicated, she rose and danced and sang the following song:

"O magic mirror, magic mirror !

Alas, my life, alas, my life !

Since I cast off my own form,

How many dynasties have risen and fallen ?

Though life is indeed sweet,

It is vain to mourn death.

So why cherish only this world ?

Why cling only to this life ? "

The mirror represents the final destiny of both foxes and humans, from which there is no escape.

In *"gujing ji"*, the accounts of all kinds of different extraordinary events and spirits are derived from the ancient mirror's multiple magical properties. This can only be achieved through the intricate framework made up of the five mirrors discussed above. One single mirror is unable to sustain the narrative development and variation of twelve marvels. Making use of his vast knowledge about bronze mirrors, along with the imaginative power in his accounts of marvelous events, the author has created an unprecedented romance about mirrors.

第三章

一面銅鏡還是五面銅鏡？

唐傳奇〈古鏡記〉視覺文本的探求

前言：

唐人傳奇有〈古鏡記〉一篇，隋唐山西人王度所撰，誌怪述異，辭章藻麗，涵義深幽，迂迴曲折，是傳奇文體的壓卷之作。內述王度得侯生贈古鏡一面，持之不但可辟邪怪，更會在日月薄蝕，鏡面便昏昧無光，日月光復，隨即光彩如昔。此鏡亦可在日下，鏡背圖型能被日光穿透，投影牆壁。

文內又據胡僧云，如依法以劑藥把鏡拭洗乾淨，能照見人之六腑五臟。王度曾以此古鏡贈弟王勣，以壯遠遊。勣攜鏡出入長江流域名山大川、叢林草莽，皆能降魔辟邪，驅獸伏波。後來聽從高士「天下神物，必不久居人間」的勸告，將鏡攜回歸還其兄。數月後，度聞匣中悲鳴，其聲轉宏如龍虎咆吼，開匣視之，已失鏡之所在。

作者在文首曾以這種惘然若失與處身喪亂的感慨，作為追憶陳述古鏡十二種異跡的緣由。他說，「今度遭世擾攘，居常鬱怏，王室如燬，生涯何地，寶鏡復去，哀哉！今具其異跡，列之於後，數千載之下，儻有得者，知其所由耳」。

由此可知，這篇以古銅鏡異跡為主體的文本追述，在不同事件中顯露出鏡子不同的特異功能。表面看似是一面銅鏡傳奇，由於情境各異，鏡隨景變，卻發展成多面銅鏡特徵的各自表述，極為引人入勝。青銅鏡背，形相特殊，歷朝銅鏡圖型設計，均各蘊含豐富文化、神話、宗教、文學與美學內涵。〈古鏡記〉作者除自文字中詳細描繪鏡子的各類特徵，更藉豐沃的文字意象，召喚出實物的視覺形象，進而在文本中互相重疊（overlap）、互換（interchange）、互感（interplay）及互補（reciprocate），形成一種奇特的視覺文本（visual text）。本文即是對「視覺文本」定義的探討與體驗，以及對出現在故事中各類銅鏡的歷史文化內涵追溯探源。

第一面：「四神十二生肖鏡」

〈古鏡記〉內，侯生當初把一面古鏡贈予王度，告知如持此鏡，則百邪不侵。鏡子的描述是這樣的：

鏡橫徑八寸，鼻作麒麟蹲伏之象，遶鼻列四方，龜龍鳳虎，依方陳佈。四方外又設八卦，八卦外置十二辰位，而具畜焉。辰畜以外，又置二十四字，周遶輪廓，文體似隸，點畫無缺，而非字書所有也。侯生云：「二十四氣之象形」。

觀上所述，應是一面漢魏六朝的「四神十二生肖鏡」。此類鏡種發展至隋唐初為之大盛，但隨即轉型入「狻猊瑞獸銘帶鏡」。其實漢鏡與隋唐鏡最大差別除圖案設計外，主要仍在於銘文字體的差異。漢鏡多用篆隸小字銘文，字跡古雅拙樸。隋唐鏡多用大字楷書銘文，字跡典雅秀麗。

但上面引文有載：「又置二十四字，周遶輪廓，文體似隸，點畫無缺」，即是指風格較近於漢代四靈博局鏡的篆體小字銘文。如以隋唐的「四神十二生肖鏡」、「狻猊瑞獸銘帶鏡」或「瑞獸團花鏡」而言，多屬三十二字。例如「狻猊瑞獸銘帶鏡」的：

　　靈山孕寶，神使觀爐
　　形圓曉月，光清夜珠
　　玉臺希世，紅妝應圖
　　千嬌集影，百福來扶

或「瑞獸團花鏡」的：

　　煉形神冶，瑩質良工
　　如珠出匣，似月停空
　　當眉寫翠，對臉傳紅
　　依窗繡晃，俱含影中

二十四字的鏡銘則有三種，因字數較少，銘帶空間較寬闊，多為大型楷書銘字。二十四字銘文一種是從唐武德到高宗年間極為普遍的「光流素月」鏡，以「狻猊瑞獸銘帶鏡」居多，其銘文為：

　　光流素月，質稟玄精
　　澄空鑒水，照迴凝清
　　終古永固，瑩此心靈

其他兩種為隋朝的「窺莊鏡」及「團圓鏡」，前者銘文為：

　　窺莊益態，韻舞鴛鴦
　　萬齡永保，千代長存
　　能明能鑒，宜子宜孫

後者銘文為：

　　團圓寶鏡，皎皎升臺
　　鸞窺自舞，照日花開
　　臨池滿月，睹貌嬌來

觀諸王度為隋末唐初人，所以很可能是取後二種隋代二十四字楷書銘文的「窺莊鏡」或「團圓鏡」。故事中假托為隸書銘文，則是想以象形文字，襯托出後面侯生的「二十四氣之象形」這句話。

所謂四靈或四神，是依循漢朝博局鏡（TLV）布局於東南西北的四方神獸，分別為青龍、白虎、朱雀、玄武，亦即上引文所謂的龜龍鳳虎（玄武為龜蛇交纏）。

漢代博局四神鏡標準銘文中除開首一句「尚方作鏡真大好」外，經常會提到辟邪的四神如「左龍右虎辟不祥，朱雀玄武順陰陽」。

十二生肖按十二時辰的子、丑、寅、卯、辰、巳、午、未、申、酉、戌、亥，分別配搭以十二動物的鼠、牛、虎、兔、龍、蛇、馬、羊、猴、雞、狗、豬。這種以動物作為吉祥保護物，是隋唐民間流傳的信念。日後十二生肖也成為道教的神祇，如元朝山西永樂宮道教壁畫上就繪有十二生肖神君，與八卦神君、二十八星宿、三十二天帝君等神祇並列。唐代陶俑中有所謂「四神十二時」，即是指墓室排列的一組保護者陣容，包括禽畜人身的十二生肖，一對文臣武將或一對天王俑。

所謂鼻，實即鏡背上用作繫繩或布條的鏡鈕（knob）。本來此類魏晉南北朝鏡種的「四神十二生肖鏡」，多為渾圓鈕（rotund knob），有別於戰國鏡的弦紋鈕（fluted knob），或西東漢神獸規矩鏡的圓型鈕。至於「麒麟蹲伏之象」，則類似戰國鏡的大型鏤空鈕（chased knob），但代以一座蹲伏麒麟的伏獸圓鈕，也是吉祥物。「遶鼻列四方」，是指麒麟圓鈕外方，亦即銅鏡所謂的「內區」，為一方型鈕座，座外分布青龍、白虎、朱雀、玄武四神。四角外方，列以卦象。卦象外為鏡子「外區」，再分成十二格，每格各置一生肖，分別排列出十二時辰的十二生肖圖象。

第二面：「透光鏡」

〈古鏡記〉在描述完「四神十二生肖鏡」後，緊接又有以下數句：

承日照之，則背上文畫，墨入影內，纖毫無失。舉而扣之，清音徐引，竟日方絕。

屆此這面古鏡已自「四神十二生肖鏡」搖身一變，而成為西方人稱之為「魔鏡」（magic mirror）的漢代「透光鏡」。透光鏡不是一種鏡種，而是因為它照向日光如「草葉紋鏡」）居多。日光與昭明，均指鏡上標準銘文，似篆似隸，非篆非隸。其實自秦代始，書寫文字發生了重要的改革演變，李斯作小篆、程邈作隸書、王次仲作八分。這種「八分小篆，二分隸法」的字體叫做「八分」，正是漢代連弧鏡銘文的標準字體。日光鏡銘文有：

見日之光，天下大明

或：

見日之光，長毋相忘

等類字句，尤以「天下大明」的連弧鏡最多。昭明鏡標準銘文為：

內清質以昭明，光輝象夫兮日月

心忽揚而願忠，然雍塞而不泄

其中「兮」字為虛字，有如《楚辭》。工匠製鏡立銘，多注意字型的美感分配以及均衡，以便銘刻在鏡子的一圈銘帶上。所以常需用一些虛字，以填塞空間。最嚴重的例子是昭明鏡的另一種銘文，全鏡銘文只斷續零碎用了一些「內清質以昭明」的句子，其他則布滿「而」的虛字，成為似是而非的「內而青而以而昭而明而光而夫而日而月而」的銘文。

因此上面「昭明連弧紋鏡」的鏡上銘文，如果去掉「兮」字，似篆似隸，剛好二十四字，堪可符合王度文中的字數，更且「承日照之」，鏡背圖案顯現，「纖毫無失」。

透光鏡除隋唐王度提及，歷代均有，宋朝周密《雲煙過眼錄》、沈括《夢溪筆談》、明朝郎瑛《七修類稿》、方以智的《物理小識》、清朝鄭復光《鏡鏡詅痴》皆有記載或研討。沈括《夢溪筆談》卷十九〈器用〉內有下面一段解釋：

世有透光鑑，鑑背有銘文，凡二十字，字極古，莫能讀。以鑑承日光，則背文及二十字，皆透在屋壁上，了了分明。人有原其理，以為鑄時，薄處先冷，唯背文上差厚後冷，而銅縮多。文雖在背，而鑑面隱然有跡，所以於光中現。予觀之，理誠如是。然予家有三鑑，又見他家所藏，皆是一樣，文畫銘字無纖異者，形制甚古，唯此一樣光透，其他鑑雖至薄者，皆莫能透，意古人別自有術。

其實據研究指出，所謂透光，是一種光學反射作用。主要是在鑄造過程中急速冷凝，使鏡背圖案在厚薄程度上產生較大凹凸度，再在平面加工磨礪，掩飾其表面較明顯凹凸不平地方，把鏡子對著日光，便會反射出明暗不同效果，這就是所謂「透光鏡」。

第三面：「秦王照膽鏡」

上面的透光鏡，按沈括所謂，若「鑑承日光，則背文及二十字，皆透在屋壁上」，在〈古鏡記〉內亦有同樣記述，大業九年正月朔旦，有胡僧行乞到王度家，王度兄弟見其神采談吐不俗，遂招入府具食，並出鏡示僧。僧睹鏡跪捧欣躍，並謂此鏡有數種靈相，其一靈相即透光鏡，若「以金膏塗之，珠粉拭之，舉以照日，必影徹牆壁」。

另一靈相卻是一面照膽鏡。文中僧人歎息說，「更作法試，應照見腑臟。所恨卒無藥耳」。胡僧所指，是一張能照宮人腑臟的秦王照膽鏡。此鏡應有兩種，一是唐朝鑄造的瑞獸銘帶「賞得秦王鏡」，內有五言絕句：「賞得秦王鏡，判不惜千金；非關欲照膽，特是自明心」。

另一則是戰國時代傳說在秦宮的「秦王照膽鏡」。《西京雜記》內載，秦亡後，漢高祖劉邦初入咸陽宮，見到始皇所藏各種珍寶異物，如青玉五枝燈、飾有七寶的十三弦琴、六孔玉管等。其中有方鏡一面，廣四尺，高五尺九寸，表裡有明，人直來照之，影則倒見。以手捫心而來，則見腸胃五臟，歷然無礙。人有疾病在內，則掩心而照之，則知病之所在。又女子有邪心，則膽張心動。秦始皇常以照宮人，膽張心動者則殺之。

表裡有明，就是裡外均透明之意。至於能見腸胃五臟或是心邪而膽張心動，皆為傳說中這面銅鏡的特異功能吧了。即使如此，也就啟發了唐人的浪漫想像，鏡既可照膽，當然亦可明心見性，因而遂有「非關欲照膽，特是自明心」之句。當然禪宗神秀、慧能的「心如明鏡台」，「明鏡亦非台」，直指本性，清水見底，明鏡照心，亦使鏡子產生很大的隱喻作用。

第四面：「盤龍鏡」

這面古鏡不但辟邪，更可治病，文本內有這麼一段：

時天下大飢，百姓疾病；蒲陝之間，癘疫尤甚。有河北人張龍駒，為度下小吏，其家良賤數十口，一時遇疾。度憫之，齎此入其家，使龍駒持鏡夜照。諸病者見鏡，皆驚起，云：『見龍駒持一月來相照，光陰所及，如冰著體，冷徹腑臟。』即時熱定，至晚並愈。以為無害於鏡，而所濟於眾，令密持此鏡，遍巡百姓。其夜，鏡於匣中，冷然自鳴，聲甚徹遠，良久乃且。度心獨怪。明早，龍駒來謂度曰：『龍駒昨忽夢一人，龍頭蛇身，朱冠紫服，謂龍駒，我即鏡精也，名曰紫珍。』

小吏姓名為張龍駒是一種文學的附會手法，使龍駒持有如滿月的圓鏡治病，以及龍駒夢見鏡精「龍頭蛇身，朱冠紫服」，正是隋唐流行一時「葵花盤龍鏡」的聯想。唐朝盤龍鏡種，有單盤龍或雙盤龍。但大部分的單盤龍鏡背上，是一尾吐舌舞爪、鱗鬣爪角悉具，昂揚飛騰於流雲紋間的飛龍。渾圓鏡鈕有如龍吐之珠，尤其自鏡鈕穿出以懸掛的錦帶或彩色繩索，十分亮麗（姚合〈詠鏡〉詩內更有「繡帶共尋龍口出，菱花爭向匣中開」）。銅鏡龍珠多位於盤龍首尾之間，有時龍首回咬吞吐，極為生動。唐人歌詠盤龍鏡不少，李白〈代美人愁鏡二首〉其一，即有「美人贈此盤龍之寶鏡，燭我金縷之羅衣。時將紅袖拂明月，為惜普照之餘暉」之句。孟浩然的五言律詩〈同張明府清鏡嘆〉亦有「妾有盤龍鏡，清光常晝發，自從生塵埃，有惹霧中月。愁來試取照，坐嘆生白髮，寄語邊塞人，如何久別離」。白居易〈感鏡〉亦云：「美人與我別，留鏡在匣中，自從花顏去，秋水無芙蓉。經年不開匣，紅埃覆青銅，今朝一拂拭，自照憔悴容，照罷重悵惘，背有雙盤龍」。

第五面：「江心百煉鏡」

　　第五面鏡其實是第四面「盤龍鏡」的延伸。故事中作者以鏡贈其弟王勣遠遊，出入名山巨川，照妖辟邪，及至遊江南，將渡廣陵揚子江，忽地風起波湧，頃將覆舟，勣攜鏡照江中數步，波濤盡息。於揚子江心攜鏡，不禁讓人想起唐朝的「江心百煉鏡」，唐朝李肇《唐國史補》下卷〈揚州貢鏡〉一條內云：「揚州舊貢江心鏡，五月五日揚子江所鑄也。或言無百煉者，六七十煉則止。易破難成，往往有鳴者」。白居易更有〈百煉鏡〉一詩：

> 百煉鏡，熔範非常規
>
> 日辰處所靈且奇，江心波上舟中鑄，
>
> 五月五日日午時，瓊粉金膏磨瑩已，
>
> 化為一片秋潭水，鏡成將獻蓬萊宮，
>
> 揚州長吏手自封，人間臣妾不合照，
>
> 背有九五飛天龍，人人呼為天子鏡。
>
> 我有一言聞太宗，
>
> 太宗常以人為鏡，鑑古鑑今不鑑容，
>
> 四海安危居掌內，百王治亂懸心中，
>
> 乃知天子別有鏡，不是揚州百煉銅。

　　由此可知，「背有九五飛天龍」的百煉鏡，亦即是「盤龍鏡」。《太平廣記》231引內載《異聞錄》〈李守泰〉一則，「天寶三載五月十五日，揚州進水心鏡一面，縱橫九寸，青瑩耀日，背有盤龍，長三尺四寸五分，勢如生動。玄宗覽而異之。」於是進鏡官揚州參軍李守泰解釋說，在鑄鏡時有一老人名龍護，攜一小童名玄冥，助鏡匠呂暉於五月五日午時揚子江中，鑄成盤龍鏡一面，鏡成之前，失龍護玄冥所在（暗示兩人化入鏡中）。後來唐玄宗以此鏡祈雨，風虎雲龍，無不靈驗。

　　唐代每年八月初五，為玄宗生辰，被稱為千秋節。除了會舞蹈的馬匹，隨著音樂起舞，「奮首鼓尾，縱橫應節」，口啣酒杯向皇上獻上壽酒外，臣子也會向皇帝獻上鏡子和代表吉祥的承露囊。皇帝亦有回賜臣子銅鏡以明其心志的習俗，唐玄宗曾寫有〈千秋節賜群臣鏡〉兩首詩：

葵花月宮盤龍啣綬鏡

鑄得千秋鏡，光生百煉金。分將賜群後，遇象見清心。

台上冰華澈，窗中月影臨。更銜長綬帶，留意感人深。

另一首為：

瑞露垂花綬，寒冰澈寶輪。對茲台上月，聊以慶佳辰。

兩首詩都有提到銜綬帶，壽綬同音，那是指喜鵲口銜花綬帶的一種唐代鏡子吉祥圖案，如果加上明月影照，那就是一面「葵花月宮盤龍銜綬鏡」了。

杜甫〈千秋節有感二首〉內，亦有「寶鏡群臣得，金吾萬國回」之句。但在陝西西安出土的一面唐朝「盤龍鏡」，鏡背方銘竟鑄有「千秋」兩字，「背有九五飛天龍，人人呼為天子鏡」，可能詩中的千秋鏡即是「盤龍鏡」，用來在千秋節賞賜給群臣，也是可能。或看，千秋鏡是一個總括詞，包括天子賞賜給群臣的不同鏡種，內裡亦有「盤龍鏡」。

其他

　　鏡子的基本功能在於折光反射，明心見性，洞悉幽玄，有若天鏡。而鏡之為鏡，唐鏡銘文有所謂「湛若止水，皎如秋月。清輝內容，菱華外發」。所以〈古鏡記〉其實是一種具備靈相的「光的文本」（optical text），它特別強調古鏡的光澤清朗。日月蝕時，因為缺光，鏡面昏昧，無復光色，「俄而光彩出，日亦漸明。比及日復，鏡亦精朗如故」。每月到了十五，「則出鏡於暗室，光嘗照數丈」。甚至有一次王度與友人把古鏡與一柄青銅劍相鬥比試光澤，於月望時，共置鏡劍在一間密閉無隙的暗室，「俄而鏡上吐光，明照一室，相視如畫。劍橫其側，無復光彩」。

　　及至胡僧得識絕世寶鏡的透光鏡，留下磨鏡之法，「但以金煙薰之，玉水洗之，復以金膏珠粉如法拭之，藏之泥中，亦不晦矣。遂留金煙玉水等法，行之，無不獲驗」。這些都是打磨銅鏡的方法，西漢劉安《淮南子》〈修務〉內指出：「明鏡之始下型，矇然未見形容，及其粉以玄錫，摩以白旃，鬢眉微毫可得而察。」金膏珠粉就是玄錫之類鉛粉與水銀合成的「鉛汞劑」或是「錫石」（酸化錫）的研磨劑。摩以白旃，就是用白毛氈反覆磨擦鏡面，使之光滑明亮。

　　由於鏡子的明亮能夠洞悉幽玄，它顯然能把幻變為人身的妖怪，影照還原為本來的禽獸本尊。除了一些醜陋蛇妖猿龜、蛟魚雄雞、鼠狼、老鼠、壁虎被神鏡殲滅現出原形外，最令人感動的一幕莫如一隻老狐，變形成為一名大宅婢女，名叫鸚鵡，端莊秀麗。不幸遇上神鏡，無所遁形，遂求一醉以死，酒後奮衣起舞而歌：「寶鏡寶鏡，哀哉予命。自我離形，於今幾姓？生雖可樂，死必不傷。何為眷戀，守此一方！」狐狸如人，鏡似大限，大限一臨，人狐皆難倖免。

　　因此我們可以這樣說，〈古鏡記〉藉鏡子種種特異功能，牽引出各類不同的幻怪精靈。如果沒有上述五面鏡子的多元構架，單憑一面鏡子的單一定義敘述，實難支撐十二種靈異怪聞的敘述發展與變調。作者利用豐富的銅鏡知識，配合獨特的想像與怪談，寫出了一篇獨步千古的鏡子傳奇。

參考資料 書籍・王度，〈古鏡記〉，取自《唐人傳奇小說》，世界書局，台北，1972四版，3-9.
　・辛冠潔，《陳介祺藏鏡》，文物出版社，北京，2001.
　・守屋孝藏（蒐集），《方格規矩四神鏡圖錄》，京都國立博物館，日本京都，1969.
　・《中國青銅器全集》no.16《銅鏡》，文物出版社，北京，1998.
　・Donald H. Graham Jr. Collection, *Bronze Mirrors: From Ancient China*, 1994.
　・《故宮銅鏡選萃》，國立故宮博物院，台北，1971.
　・《歷代銅鏡》，國立歷史博物館，台北，1996.
　・《息齋藏鏡》，國立歷史博物館，台北，2001.
　・孔祥星・劉一曼，《中國古銅鏡》，藝術圖書公司，台北，1994.
　・沈括，《夢溪筆談》，胡道靜校注，中華書局，香港，1987.
　・《西京雜記》，曹海東注譯，三民書局，台北，1995.
　・劉安，《淮南子》，熊禮匯注譯，三民書局，台北，1997.

29. Mirror with auspicious animals and "*qin wang zhao dan*" inscriptions 秦王照膽鏡

Sui-Tang Dynasty（581-907 AD）   Diameter: 9.3cm

Initially, the early Sui-Tang mirrors strayed little from their Han predecessors, workshops may have even used the same molds from the earlier dynasty. However, this is a transition piece, an excellent example that marks the Sui-Tang craftsmanship beginning to deviate from recycled Han forms. Like the Han mirrors, this object also has three main components: the rim, inscription, and central registers. However, a plain framing border no longer exists, instead, the rim immediately inclines into the inner well, with a pair of saw-toothed borders decorating its beveled surface. The inscriptions have also changed both stylistically and topically. The pair of hachured ribbons

buffering both sides of the written register (see examples in the Han illumination mirrors) has disappeared, and now, the inscribed band buttresses inclined edge. The characters on this inscription also look larger, the script is clearly belonged to the "standard" style (*Kai shu* 楷書) which looks similar to modern Chinese. The text reads:

I was given a King Qin mirror
I wouldn't want to trade it for a thousand pieces of gold ;
There is nothing to do with detecting the gall,
It is mainly a reflection of my tranquil mind.

賞得秦王鏡、判不惜千金、非關欲照瞻、特是自明心

This inscription hearkens back to a myth regarding the Qin emperor, who possessed a mirror that reflected back one's inner body instead of his or her outward superficialities.[1] In the past, Han inscriptions often sought to allude to cosmological allusions and wards against inauspicious events. Now, these inscriptions seem to draw from historical fable rather than philosophical thought.

The details on the central register reveal further changes between the two dynasties and allude to specific characteristic typologies that will come become more concrete as the Sui and Tang Dynasty continues. The central decoration is now sunk into another well, with a saw-toothed pattern running along a raised, concentric boundary. In the past as seen in the 東漢三羊四乳四神 mirror, the four Divine beasts would walk around the register. Now, there

are four mythical beasts similar to dogs or foxes, prancing in the central band, replacing the mythical creatures. The large, hemispheric knob, adopted in the Han mirrors remains at the center of the mirror. Now however, a thin beaded pattern decorates the base of this handle, replacing a circular base or square base. Despite the mirror's extremely worn surface, it is still a representative object that visually summarizes the stylistic changes from one dynasty to another.

1 | Chou. Ju-His. *Circles of Reflection, The Carter Collection of Chinese Bronze Mirrors*（Ohio: Cleveland Museum of Art, 2000）, 62-3.

30. Mirror with 4 auspicious animals 隋四瑞獸鏡

Sui-Tang Dynasty（581-907 AD）   Diameter: 11.5cm

Adaptations to the Han typology continue, and now, there are certain embellishments that characteristic of the Sui-Tang Dynasties. As seen in the previous example, four auspicious animals running clockwise around the central register, their feet barely touching the outer, raised, double-scalloped ring. This mirror is extremely well preserved, and we now see that these beasts are dog-like creatures. The ground pattern behind the animals is dense with foliage ; exotic fauna with curly leaves, and long, serpentine vines weave an intricate backdrop. All of these

decorations rotate around a central hemispheric knob set on a circular base. The outer register is also incredibly ornate. Another set of auspicious animals sprint clockwise around a tangle of curling vines full with bunches of grapes. All of the decorations on the mirror are cast plastically in a high relief, giving great depth to the piece. The rim inclines inward with a beveled edge and has two saw-toothed rings at its outermost, raised edge. These so called "auspicious animals" are most likely a misnomer for "lions" in medieval China which were pronounced as "*suanni*"（archaic Chinese 狻猊）that came from India to China before the Christian era. However, according to Liang Shang-chun（梁上椿）, an early modern mirror specialist, these running animals in the mirrors do not appear like lions, but a hybrid of lions, tigers, foxes, wolves and dogs.[1]

As for grapes, it is obvious Persian and central Asian influences when new wine making grapes was introduced to Tang China together with the knowledge of making grape wines. For further details, see Berthold Laufer, *Sino-Iranica* (volume 15, no.3) *Chinese Contributions to the History of Civilization in Ancient Iran*, General Books, Chicago, 1919, and Edward Schafer, *The Golden Peaches of Samarkand*, UC Press, 1963, chapters on "Wild Animals" and "Foods."

31. Mirror with 4 auspicious animals and "*zhao ri lin chi*" inscriptions 唐四獸照日臨池鏡

Sui-Tang Dynasty（581-907 AD）　　Diameter: 10.5cm

We still have the same inner register seen in the previous piece, with four auspicious animals running through lush foliage, radiating from a plain hemispheric knob. However, this mirror substitutes the outer register with decorative grape vines for an inscriptive band. The text reads:

Facing the mirror to the sun, foliated flowers emerge

Taking it to the pond, it is a full moon；

My husband looks at it to put on his cap and gown

I use it to complete my make-up.

照日菱花出，臨池滿月生

官看巾帽整，妾映點妝成

The first couplet of the above inscription originates from a first rhyme-prose "Essay on the Mirror"（鏡賦）in Chinese literature written on the bronze mirror by Yu Xin（庾信）in 6th century AD in which the mirror is compared to the sun and the moon, and the shape of the mirror is like a foliated flower. The reflection of such a mirror also suggests strongly a "light penetration mirror"（透光鏡）：

When the mirror is faced to a pond, a moon emerges

When facing the sun, a foliated flower appears on the wall.

臨水則池中月出，照日則壁上菱生

Despite an almost identical design, there are slight differences between this mirror and the previous one, highlighting the lost-wax casting technique used during the Sui and Tang Dynasties. While the previous mirror's ground pattern has sharp, clear shapes, the leaf decorations in this piece are of a lesser quality due to its lack of clear lines and gradations. This indicates the constant reuse of likely a single wax mold, where one typology and variations of it could be cast multiple times to mass produce one piece. This mirror might have been cast later on, after manufacturers already used the same mold many times. The variation between the outer registers also indicates the use of lost-wax casting. Inscriptive rings or the grape-vine register could easily be exchanged with one another as other decorative wax pieces could be affixed to the original casting.[1]

---

1 | D.H. Graham , Suzanne Cahill, Tseng Yuh Ecke, Toru Nakano ed. *Bronze Mirrors from Ancient China: Donald H. Graham Jr. Collection*（Hong Kong, 1994）, 16-17.

32. Large mirror with grapes and auspicious sea-lions 唐海獸葡萄鏡（大）

Sui-Tang Dynasty（581-907 AD）　　Diameter: 10.8cm

More and more, the Sui-Tang mirrors increase their ornamentation and complexity. The rim has forty-nine, tiny "cloud-floral" motifs which decorate its edge.[1] Inside the mirror has two spaces, the outer register and inner register separated by a raised ring ; however, the two spaces meld into one another with a grape-vine pattern. In the

outer register, eight magpies fly in all different directions, surrounded by dense flora and vines. This foliage and grape decoration bleeds into the inner register and surrounds four mythical sea mammals. Their bodies curve into an arc, and their faces turn upward towards the viewer though there is no particular direction in which they move. The vine decorations evolve, and four ornate acanthus leaves with curled edges sit at four axes around the raised border. At the center of the mirror is a large knob in the form of an animal. Replacing the usual hemispheric knob, the animal's body swells and curves to form the round shape of the small handle.

1 ｜ Chou, p.66

33. Large Bronze-Mercury mirror with grapes and auspicious sea-lions 唐水銀海獸葡萄鏡（大）

Sui-Tang Dynasty（581-907 AD）   Diameter: 17cm

    This mirror has a light brown color rendered by its mixture of bronze and mercury. Its decorations emulate the previous mirrors, following typical elements of the typology. The rim slants inward with small cloud-floral designs on its edge. Small birds fly throughout the outer register, and now, dragonflies and bees also appear the space. The usual grape vine pattern completes the ground pattern, decorating the inner and outer register. A raised ring restricts the center of the mirror, where four marine animals and a pair of birds with ornate plumage rotate around a zoomorphic central knob.

34. Medium mirror with *Lingzhi* and auspicious sea-lions #1 唐海獸靈芝葡萄鏡（中）之一

Sui-Tang Dynasty（581-907 AD）　　Diameter: 9.5cm

This medium mirror is a variation to its larger counterpart. puffed clouds pattern the outer rim, and the mirror then dips inward to create an inner well, where there is a middle register with the grape-vine pattern. The vine leaves are reminiscent of curling acanthus leaves often seen on Grecian friezes. Among this pattern, six birds fly around, interspersed throughout this space. A raised ring isolates the mirror's central register, which frames a large zoomorphic knob. The animal curls its body with its front legs outstretched as if ready to pounce. Four sea-lions swim around this central creature, alternating between facing inward and outward. Each animal has a small round head and pair of ears, and its body curves and tapers into a single flipper. The same acanthus pattern in the middle register, now without grapes, decorates the ground pattern behind these animals. Compared to the previous pieces, the grapes and sea-lion decoration in this mirror is simplified and pared down, allowing for more space between each embellishment. The viewer is able to clearly identify the distinct flora and fauna and the weaving vines pattern. This piece could have been one of the first cast in its mold, thus explaining its high quality of craftsmanship.

35. Medium mirror with grapes and auspicious sea-lions #2 唐海獸葡萄鏡（中）之二

Sui-Tang Dynasty（581-907 AD）   Diameter: 9.5cm

We have yet another variation of the grape and sea-lion ornamentation in these medium sized mirrors. The outermost rim with cloud decorations has disappeared, leaving only two main registers in the mirror. The main register now has a greater variation of flora and a lack of animals. The space overflows of grapes, and small arched tendrils hold this bountiful crop of fruit. Intertwined among this are two larger branches or flowers, laying horizontally on opposite axes from one another. Sporadically interspersed among the grapes and branches are smaller round fruit that protrude from the surface of the mirror. The boundary between the central and the outer, main register has deteriorated. Instead, a ring of grapes and vines surround the center of the mirror and separate the two spaces. As usual, the central register features an animal transformed into the mirrors knob. While often ostentatiously decorated, this space has a plain, undecorated ground pattern, leaving ample space for four sea lions swim around the knob.

36. Medium mirror with grapes and auspicious sea-lions #3 唐海獸葡萄鏡（中）之三

Sui-Tang Dynasty（581-907 AD）　Diameter: 10.8cm

This mirror has two parts, a central register, and outer concentric ring. Like the previous two mirrors, this piece's decoration continues vary the grapevine motif. Small birds and dragonflies alternate between small bunches of grapes, and framing this is a frieze of flat leaves and small protruding blossoms. This lines the edge of the register like a rim and adds more fauna to the typical curling vine embellishments. The central space has a zoomorphic, animal knob, and four sea lions alternate swimming centripetally and centrifugally around it. Patterning the edge of this register are small bunches of grapes and leaves.

37. Small mirror with grapes and auspicious sea-lions #1 唐海獸葡萄鏡（小）

Sui-Tang Dynasty（581-907 AD）   Diameter: 10.1cm

Now, with a small mirror, the grapes and sea lion motif has simplified significantly, yet still retains its most identifying qualities. The outer register consists only of thin curling vines with small blossoming protuberances that form a border along the mirror's rim. The mirror is extremely worn, but it is still possible to identify the four curling shapes within the central space as sea lions. These animals have small tails along with their hind flippers, a small variation from the usual depiction of these creatures. The central knob is a simpler, hemispheric knob, and bunches of grapes typical to the motif appear along the raised ring that bounds the space.

38. Small mirror with grapes and auspicious sea-lions #2 唐海獸葡萄鏡 (小)

Sui-Tang Dynasty（581-907 AD）　Diameter: 10.1cm

This mirror is incredibly worn, its embellishments are difficult to discern. However, it is still possible to see thick vines and grapes decorating the outer register. A raised ring bounds the center register that has an eroded, small hemispherical knob. Some remnants of leaves and grapes decorate the edge of the register, and four large, raised protuberances could be the sea lions that commonly rotate around the knob.

39. Mirror with paired phoenixes and brocade ribbons 唐雙鸞唧綬鏡

Sui-Tang Dynasty（581-907 AD）　　Diameter: 16cm

  Save for a crack running across the diameter, this piece is incredibly well preserved with its decorations clear and identifiable. The border of this mirror is thin and plain, leaving room more room for surface embellishments. A small, round knob sits on a eight-petal flower base. Facing it on either side is a pair of phoenixes. Their tail feathers are incredibly ornate, curling into one another. The mythical birds raise their wings, ostentatiously displaying overlapping layers of feathers. On the perpendicular axes, a pair of animals prances across the mirror parallel to one another, as if about to leap off of the surface. The animal above has a single horn and hooves, and the creature below looks like a dog with a dragon's head. These are possibly the qilin or pixie, two guardian animals from the Han Dynasty, now interpreted on a Tang mirror.[1] The background is completely undecorated, highlighting the four mythical beasts as the piece's only, and intricate embellishment.

40. Lobed mirror with paired magpies and brocade ribbons 唐葵花雙鵲啣綬鏡

Sui-Tang Dynasty（581-907 AD）   Diameter: 16cm

This piece is similar to the previous work, especially its motifs. The mirror has eight lobes ; its edges take on the shape of petals, and its central knob sits on a worn base that looks like a flower as well. The surface is incredibly eroded, thus we must rely on common stylistic forms to help identify the embellishments on this piece. Like the previous mirror, there are four animals on the flat surface, each in a pair. One set is the deer and pixie, prancing parallel from each other. Facing one another, wedging the central knob, is a pair of magpies. They style is similar to that of the phoenixes. These birds also have their tail feathers are ostentatiously displayed made of detailed casting work. Now, the two creatures each bite a tassel in their beaks. This is a common motif seen in various Tang mirrors.[2] Between the pixie are two small swirling clouds, perhaps indicating how the viewer should orient the mirror.

1 | Chou. Circles of Reflection, 72-73
2 | Chou. Circles of Reflection, 69.

41. Mirror with 6 "*baoxianghua*" Rosette flowers 唐寶相六花鏡

Sui-Tang Dynasty（581-907 AD）   Diameter: 16.8cm

This mirror has a rounded, raised border, which frames an expansive, flat surface. At the center sits a small hemispherical knob sitting on a 12-petal base. Around this is a small raised ring. Rotating around this main "flower" are six flowers. Three of these look like rosettes or peonies, with voluminous petals blossoming from their centers. In the other set, each bloom has six petals and a central pod encasing seven seeds 1These six flowers cluster tightly towards the central flower are the only decorations on the mirror's otherwise smooth, plain surface.

"*Baoxianghua*"（寶相花）, literally translated as "Holy Image flower" is but a generally term for a grouping of blossoms, either of lotus or peonies under apparent Buddhist decorative influences.

42. Plain mirror with concentric circles 唐弦圈素鏡

Sui-Tang Dynasty（581-907 AD）　Diameter: 9.8cm

Erased of any embellishment, this plain mirror has a smooth undecorated surface interrupted only by a few concentric rings. A large hemispheric knob sits at the center of the mirror, and thin raised ring surrounds and creates a shallow well around it. This is the only ornamentation on the piece except for a raised concentric ring that adjoins the plain beveled rim.

Module Systems and Style of the Song Plain Bronze Mirrors

Song, Liao, Jin

Looking into the trajectory of the dynamic development of the artistic style, it is indubitable that Chinese bronze mirrors reached a great apex in the Warring States and the Han-Wei period, and transitioned into yet another climax in the Sui and the Tang. The Song dynasty, however, is often regarded by the scholars as "the age of deterioration" due to the plainness of its mirrors. Song mirrors emphasized practical values, not decorative patterns on the backside, which "degraded" the aestheticism of the exquisite, sumptuous Tang mirrors to a mere subordinate to the practicality of social life. Kong Xiangxing and Liu Yiman determine the Sui-Tang to be the period of "high development of Chinese bronze mirrors" in history, while considering the Song to be the period of "gradual deterioration of Chinese bronze mirrors". They believe that Song mirrors "are mainly chronological and in lack of a representational model due to the insufficiency of the records of archaeological excavations, which is why scholars have failed to summarize or identify the characteristics and typology of the bronze mirrors of this period"; they further point out that following the late Tang and the Five Dynasties, during the coexistence of and confrontation between the Song and its foreign neighbors—the Liao, the Xixia, and the Jin—the fluctuation of successive regimes might have well been the historical and political reasons for the gradual decline of Song mirrors.[1] In the section titles to the plates of *Lianxing shenye, yingzhi lianggong* (Refined shape, divine forging, lustrous quality, and fine workmanship), a 2005 publication of select bronze mirrors in the collection of the Shanghai Museum, Sui-Tang mirrors are regarded as "glamorous and kaleidoscopic", while Song mirrors are, though not disparagingly, included in the "secular and miscellaneous bronze mirrors of the Song, the Liao, the Jin, the Xixia, the Yuan, the Ming, and the Qing". With the simply put "secular and miscellaneous", Song mirrors are, like commoners in crude clothes, put amid the secular ranks of the Han people and various groups of foreigners.[2]

Shen Congwen（沈從文）mentions the deterioration of Song mirrors from two angles:

Speaking of the art and craftsmanship of the mirrors, the development into the specialized officially-

---

[1] Kong Xiangxing and Liu Yiman, *Zhongguo gutongjing* (Chinese ancient bronze mirrors) (Taipei: Yishu tushu gongsi, 1994), 138. However, the two authors put forward an opposite view about Song mirrors in another work of theirs; the *Tongjing jiancang* (Connoisseurship of bronze mirrors) (Changchun: Jilin kexue jishu chubanshe, 2004), which mentions specifically the renowned, graceful and delicate "mirror of entwining branches and flowers and herbs", claiming that this type of low-relief flower-and-herb mirrors "even from the view of art and crafts... occupies an important place in the history of the development of Chinese bronze mirrors and should not be overlooked." See page 56.

[2] Shanghai Museum, *Lianxing shenye, yingzhi lianggong* (Refined shape, divine forging, lustrous quality, and fine workmanship: a publication of the select bronze mirrors in the collection of the Shanghai Museum) (Shanghai: Shanghai shuhua chubanshe, 2005), 6.

manufactured mirrors in the Song can be compared to the coda to a piece of elegant music. The boundless wisdom, rich skills, and infinite creativity of the working class changed with the development of the society and shifted its focal point to other aspects of art creation—kilning porcelains, sculpting lacquers, weaving gilt brocades, marking lines, etc. Though bronze-work also made progresses of varying degrees in several subfields... for instance... saddles refined by works of gold and silver... miscellaneous pieces of iron weaponry, often with gold or silver inlaid... antiquarian bronze vessel imitations made in the Song Xuanhe period... and the square burners with refined brocade ground pattern cast by Lady Jiang in the Shaoxing period of the Southern Song, which was peculiar in style among bronze artifacts.

Shen goes on to say,

In fact, the art of mirror making was apparently in decline coming to the Southern Song, which no longer remained the emphasis of art production especially in the south. At the time, the handicraft industry in metropolitan cities such as Yangzhou was disrupted by war, where old mirrors were melt down and recast into copper coins or other supplies. Household mirrors for general usage focused on practicality and not patterns. In cities of Huzhou, Raozhou, and Lin'an, the bronze mirrors manufactured by nationally renowned workshops and retailers—the Zhangs, the Mas, and Second Uncle Nian of the Shi Family, were often plain and unadorned with only a trademark of the retailer shop on the backside.[3]

Actually, the remark of Southern Song mirrors being "focused on practicality and not patterns" refers to the evolved patterns of the way mirrors were used, which had little to do with aesthetics. The function of the fluted knobs of Warring States mirrors or the perfectly round knobs of Han-Wei and Sui-Tang mirrors was to be strung by a ribbon or a colorful cord (commensurate with the size of the mirror) through the hole of the knob, so that the mirror can be held or hung. Large mirrors with ties of ribbons through the knob have been unearthed in the Han tombs of Mawangdui, Hunan, and the tomb of King Nanyue of the Western Han, Canton: the *panchi* (coiling dragon) mirror from the Mawangdui tomb no. 1 measures 19.4cm in diameter, while the mirror stand composite with gold and silver inlaid from the tomb of King Nanyue reaches a 29.8cm diameter﹔both are large enough to have a mirror mount included, which were not found in the excavation, and so it seems that these mirrors were still hung by the strings or held by the servants.[4] While using, such a mirror was either held in the hand or strung by a ribbon and hung and placed upon a low mirror

3 | Shen Congwen, "Gudai jingzi yishu (The art of ancient mirrors)", in Huahua duoduo tantan guanguan (Many flowers, many urns) (Nanjing: Jiangsu meishu chubanshe, 2002), 48.
4 | Chen Jianming ed., Mawangdui hanmu chenlie (The exhibition of the Mawangdui Han tombs) (Changsha: Hunan Museum, 2004), 9﹔Guangzhou xihan nanyuewang mu bowuguan ed., Xihan nanyuewang mu bowuguan zhenpin bacui (Select precious items from the Museum of the tomb of King Nanyue of the Western Han), 57. The most persuasive evidence for the stringing of mirror by a ribbon comes from the mural paintings of the tomb of Zhao Daweng at Baisha in the Yu County of Henan, dated the third year of the Yuanfu period of the Northern Song (1100) (facsimiles of the illustration in the collection of the Chinese Museum of History), which show the family members of the clan-leader and landlord Zhao Daweng dressing up in front of the mirrors in their daily life. See Shen Congwen, "116—Dressing up and Banqueting in Song murals, Fig. 178", in Zhongguo gudai fushi yanjiu (Research on Chinese ancient clothing) (Shanghai: Shanghai shudian chubanshe, 2002), 456.

Han coling dragon mirror with colorful cords excavated from Mawangdui 馬王堆鈕座穿繫綏帶蟠螭鏡（湖南博物館）

King Nanyue of Han mirror with knob bands 南越王墓綏帶穿繫帶托銅鏡（廣州西漢南越王墓博物館）

holder（ancient Chinese had used to sit on the floor mats prior to the Tang-Song）, just as seen in a scenario of the painting on silk, *Admonitions of the Court Instructress*（女史箴圖）attributed to Gu Kaizhi（顧愷之）, which shows a woman holding and looking into a bronze mirror on the right, and on the left, another woman sitting in front of a mirror holder letting a maidservant combing her hair while she watches the reflection in the mirror.

Whether or not the painting was done by Gu Kaizhi of the Eastern Jin is still questionable. Shen Congwen argues pointedly that the Admonitions was originally painted by Zhang Hua（張華）to admonish Empress Jia, and that the combing woman in the painting has the twin-coiled coiffure typical of the Western Han. Therefore, the painting was "in fact painted as a record of the hairstyles of court instructress, just as it was done by the brush-holding woman in the beginning of the scroll"；but this point is irrelevant to the discussion here and will not be further investigated.[5] For this reason, the hand-held mirror naturally

Gu Kaizhi——Admonitions of the court instructress 顧愷之「女史箴圖」（大英博物館）

attends to the decorative patterns at the back and strives for an eye-attracting, heart-pleasing look with an addition of expressive omens and auspicious symbols ; the four-spiritual-beasts TLV mirrors of the Han and the sea lions-and-grapevine mirrors of the Tang are such examples.

The Chinese in the early days sat on the floor mats and beside low tables, when the mirror holders were made simple, convenient, and small in size, such as the gilt-bronze mirror holder of the Eastern Han which has a crescent-shape groove for the mirror to fit in. This type of mirror holders was made of heavy metal, unsophisticated in shape, and with rather short stem supports, which means that presumably they were placed on higher tables or held by maidservants when one looked into the mirror to dress up. Similar features can be found in the later "rhinoceros-gazing-at-the-moon" bronze mirror rest, which is likely a derivative of the same type of mirror holders.

The extant mirror holders, either excavated or collected, are all made of bronze, for which reason they have been kept intact. The other wooden holders have but all rotten and disappeared over the vicissitudes of thousands of years, leaving only groups of holders and mounts made of rosewood or red sandalwood (*pterocarpus indicus*) in the Ming and the Qing. The composition and carving of these holders, however, betray the features of a modern style, while the air of antiquity is never recaptured.[6]

From the Song and the Ming on, chairs have become an essential part of domestic furniture and influenced the making of other objects at home, including the mirror. One table with two chairs has become a standard set in the house ; chairs are higher, and the both decorative and functional mirror holder put on the table immediately stands out. As one sits in the chair, the mirror holder is placed on the table to clamp and support the mirror ; sometimes a long slender rod is used to insert through the hole of the knob at one end, while the other end is inserted into the mirror holder (such holders were placed on the floor mats in the Han-Wei and the Six Dynasties ; see the *Admonitions* scroll), which has since gradually replaced the hand-held mirrors tied by thick cords or cloth ribbons. Notably, once the rather wide tying ribbon was abandoned, the knob of the bronze mirror has become increasingly smaller, as epitomized by the tiny, round, and sometimes ingot-shaped knobs in the Song and the Ming.

When one sits in front of the mirror holder facing the mirror, the backside of the mirror is rarely seen and the aesthetic requirement for the patterns is lowered ; therefore it makes sense that the backside appears plain and unadorned. To make it easier to be placed in the holder, a Song mirror has the general quality of being even, firm, and thin throughout the body, measuring about 0.3cm in thickness, which quite differs

5 | Shen Congwen, Tongjing shihua (Talking about the history of bronze mirrors) (Shenyang: Wanjuan chuban gongsi, 2005), 196. This book is an expanded and edited edition based on the Tangsong tongjing (Tang and Song mirrors), an earlier work by Shen in 1956.
6 | Wang Du, Xizhai Cangjing (Mirror collection of the Xi Studio) (Taipei: Museum of History, 2001). The book records a private collection of various types of Qing wooden mirror-holder sets. See 233-236.
7 | With regard to the practical functions of bronze mirrors, aside from archival evidence and extant objects, the author of this paper also referred to chapter "Ancient Bronze Mirrors", in Zhongguo wenming shihua (Talking about the history of Chinese culture) (author unknown) (Taipei: Muduo chubanshe, 1983), 357-363. For the advancement and evolution of mirror holders, refer to Zhou Ya, "Tongjing shiyong fangshi de kaogu ziliao fenxi" (Analysis of the archaeological documents on the way of using bronze mirrors), note 2, 54-66.

from the thick and heavy body of a Tang mirror.[7] But an overview of the scale of the bronze mirrors over the dynasties suggests that, whether to be put in the holder or held in hand, the size of the mirror determines the way of placement. A mirror less than 8 cm in diameter should be held by the hand, not put on the holder.

Even though unadorned, the mirror is in no less splendid. Song plain mirrors（素鏡）were variegated in form and shape: in addition to the square, the oblong, and the ones with handles, there were also six- and eight-sided floral mirrors derived from the lobed or

Tang sea lions and grapes mirror 唐海獸葡萄鏡（台北故宮博物院）

foiled mirrors of the Tang. There was the heart-shaped mirror, alternatively regarded as the peach- or shield-shaped, whose small scale made it likely a hand-held mirror or a mirror in the palm. Moreover, there were mirrors in the full charge of Daoist spirits, which took the shape of a hanging bell, a tripod, or a cloud-chime, displaying the typical artistic atmosphere of the time. Since the round and the square are the basic shapes

Han TLV with four spritual beasts mirror
漢博局規矩四靈獸鏡（台北故宮博物院）

Wei-Jin mirror stand with rhinocero gazing at the moon
魏晉鏡犀牛望月青銅鏡座

Song plain square mirror 全素方鏡

Song Rao Zhou Ye family rectangular mirror with inscriptions
饒州葉家久煉銅照子記長方鏡

Song Shi family
mirror with a handle
承租石六十郎柄鏡

of all mirrors, the irregular shapes—the burner, the bell, the tripod, and the cloud-chime mentioned above—were short-lived and disappeared quickly, which have nevertheless left a point of departure for posterity to easily identify and verify Song mirrors by formal features.

There is indeed the historical evaluation that the Song underwent continuous warfare, suffered the shortage of mineral deposits, while its handicraft industries were hindered by unstable social factors, but this statement is not entirely true in all respects. Instead, the urban economy of Song cities was developing vigorously; the rise of the middle-class stimulated commerce and trade, and as catalysts and lubricants, people of the middle-class enabled general application of the aristocratic culture and helped enhance the culture of the citizenry. The population of the Northern Song capital Bianjing（汴京 nowadays Kaifeng 開封）reached one million, and the city was flourishing as floral brocade. The Southern Song focused on maritime transportation, which pushed commerce and trade to a greater scale; its capital Lin'an（臨安 nowadays Hangzhou）had a 1.2 million population, where wine shops, teahouses, theaters, and plazas were all over the place. From dawn to dusk, the streets and alleys were bustling with people. The prosperity of Bianjing can be read from the *Dongjing menghualu* (Records of the Eastern Capital, a dreamt utopia 東京夢華錄), a jotting-fiction by Meng Yuanlao（孟元老）; while the magnificent views of the southern capital Lin'an can be found in the *Ducheng jisheng* (Magnificence of the capital city 都城紀勝) by Naideweng of the Guanpu garden（灌圃耐得翁）, the *Fanshenglu* (Records of prosperity and magnificence 繁勝錄) by the

Song Jian kang prefecture made by 8th uncle Mao foiled mirror with inscription on the right side
建康府茆八叔煉銅照子葵花鏡（右銘文）

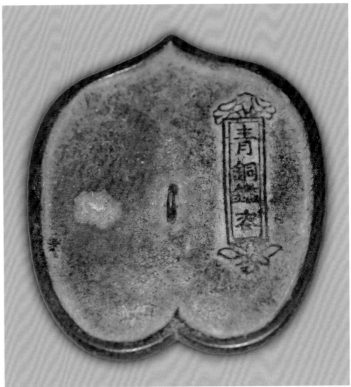

Song peach mirror with inscriptions 青銅鑑容鏡（右銘文）

Song Rao Zhou Ye the 3rd foiled mirror
饒州棚下葉三家煉青銅照子葵花鏡（右銘文）

Song lobed plain mirror 菱花素鏡

Song Hu Zhou peach mirror made the Shih family with inscriptions on the left
湖州石念四郎真煉白銅照子（左銘文）

Old Man of the West Lake（西湖老人）, the *Mengliulu* (Records of a yellow-millet dream 夢粱錄) by Wu Zimu（吳自牧）, and the *Wulin jiushi* (Old stories about Wulin 武林舊事) by Zhou Mi（周密）. They depict food, holidays and public festivities, including various performing folk arts in the street ; the chapter of "plazas and performers" in the *Ducheng jisheng* includes a record about the art of "*shuohua*"（説話 talks, or colloquial tales）, a form of the literary genre *xiaoshuo*（小説 fiction）, which serves as an invaluable primary source for studying the script-based fictions (prompt tales, *huaben xiaoshuo* 話本小説) of the Song and the Yuan:

> The colloquial tales are performed in four schools: the first is the *xiaoshuo* (minor talks), which is called "*yinzièr*" (silver-lettered flute), and its contents include love affairs, spirits and monsters, and marvels and strange occurrences. The lawsuit tales include stories of sword fighting, chasing with the cudgel, and sudden obtaining of fame and fortune. The iron-cavalry tales are about things in the battlefield—soldiers, horses, and bells and drums. The sutra tales interpret Buddhist writings. The Buddhist solicitation tales tell the stories of how believers comprehend the essence of Buddhist teachings. The historical tales narrate the documents, histories, literature, and biographies of previous dynasties, including stories of rise and fall and of contesting and conquering. The story-tellers are awesome, because they, by telling the stories of a past era or of a past generation, are capable of making an immediate disillusionment...[8]

The widespread of fictions nurtured the interest and taste of the consumers and made the myths and tales familiar and congenial to the population, which spurred the depiction of folklore, tales of the divine and celestial beings, and Buddhist and Daoist stories as decorative patterns on Song mirrors. Such mirrors include the "mirror of Xu You and Chao Fu"（許由巢父鏡）, the "mirror of Zhong Kui catching the ghosts"（鍾馗捉鬼鏡）, the "mirror of the moon Rabbit pestling under the laurel tree"（月桂玉兔搗杵鏡）, the "mirror of a Wu water-buffalo panting at the sight of the moon"（吳牛喘月鏡）, the "mirror of Wang Zhi watching the chess game till the haft of his axe goes rotten"（王質觀棋爛柯鏡）, the "mirror of a celestial being with the tortoise and the crane"（仙人龜鶴鏡）, and the "mirror of a celestial being slaying the dragon"（仙人斬龍鏡）, etc.

Another artistic achievement of Song mirrors lies in the mirror of entwining branches, flowers, and leaves, which belongs to a low-relief decorative pattern in full display of the delicate virtuosity of the highly refined brushwork (*gongbi* 工筆) on flowers and herbs. Its ingenious design and the smooth, flowing lines are in direct contrast in artistic treatment to the aforementioned mirrors of folklore and legends.

Looking back again into the history following the late Tang and the Five Dynasties to the great unification of the empire under the Northern Song, in merely 16 years（963-979）, Emperor Taizu of the Song, after his accession to the throne through the Chenqiao Mutiny, succeeded in conquering the regional regimes of the Southern Tang, the Later Shu, and the Wuyue by the remainder of his military prowess. Except for the Sixteen Prefectures of Yan and Yun ceded to the Khitans in the Later Tang, the majority of China was unified, and the political confrontations among the separate, ambitious local authorities taken shape in the

Tang were quickly dispelled. As the Later Shu of Sichuan, the Southern Tang of Jiangnan, and the Wuyue of Zhejiang were spared from war and pillaging, folk art and crafts enjoyed continued development in several places. The woven brocade and lacquer ware of the Later Shu were gorgeous and graceful ; the local kilns of Cizhou in the north and Jizhou in the south were remarkable for the ingenuity of the mind and the creativity in art expression ; while during the Wuyue of Qian, the celadon ware of the mystic-color kiln（祕色窯）was unique and unsurpassable of its time.

We can further say that, even when the Song entered the stage of confrontation against the Liao, the Xixia, and the Jin, its still advancing handicraft industry with specialized craftsmanship, especially bronze mirror casting, was not at all in its twilight, except that "the boundless wisdom, rich skills, and infinite creativity of the working class changed with the development of the society and shifted its focal point to other aspects of art creation—kilning porcelains, sculpting lacquers, weaving gilt brocades, marking lines, etc." as Shen Congwen claims.

But the quantity, the techniques, and the requirement of bronze production in the Song all far surpassed previous dynasties. Because of the rapidly expanding commerce and trade system and the increasing flow of currency, the demand for bronze became greater day by day ; and when the supply failed to meet the demand, rigid sumptuary laws on bronze were promulgated with frequent bans on bronzes. In the manufacturing of objects of daily life, brass was mainly used for making mirrors, bells, and gongs. The mirror industry was still very advanced in the Southern Song ; however, whenever a mirror was to be used or sold by a commoner, usually the official procedure of "paying taxes for mining"（投稅獲鑿）had to be observed.[9]

Notably, the mirrors of the Song, the Jin, the Yuan, the Ming, and the Qing used a new type of alloy containing an extremely high percentage of copper, which reached to 73.7%. In contrast, the percentage of tin was lowered to 7.1%, that of lead to 13.1%, while zinc was raised to a 10% and above. But the scarcity of copper was not the major cause ; the reduction of tin was to reduce the brittleness of bronze so it became more durable. He Tangkun（何堂坤）in his analytic study of the chemical makeup of bronze mirrors points out: "the change in social customs and people's heightened knowledge of the properties of materials were in fact the main causes of the change in the makeup of mirrors after the Song. The lack of copper might have indeed made a few impacts, but such impacts were not direct but at most indirect and secondary factors".[10]

The inclusion of a low proportion of tin has indirectly influenced the appreciation and appraisal of Song mirrors by posterity. Because of the low tin contained, it is rare to see a Song mirror with "black-lacquer antique" (heiqigu 黑漆古) excavated after a thousand years, while ancient Han and Tang mirrors contained a considerable amount of tin and appeared dark, lustrous, reflective, and delightful. The author's point

8 | Guanpu Naideweng, Ducheng jisheng（Magnificence of the Capital City）, in Meng Yuanlao and others, Dongjing menghualu ; wai sizhong（Records of the Eastern Capital, a dreamt utopia ; and four other works）（Beijing: Wenhua yishu chubanshe, 1998）, 86.

9 | Tian Zibing, Zhongguo gongyi meishushi（History of Chinese Art and Crafts）（Taipei: Danqing tushu youxian gongsi, publishing date missing）, 305-307.

10 | He Tangkun, Zhongguo gudai tongjing de jishu yanjiu（A technological study on Chinese ancient bronze mirrors）（Beijing: Zijincheng chubanshe, 1999）, 62.

on this matter coincides with the paper "Qingtongqi 'heiqigu' ceng xingcheng jili tantao" (Exploration on the formation of the layer of "black-lacquer antique" on bronze vessels〈青銅器「黑漆古」層形成肌理探討〉) submitted by Hua Chuanping (花傳平) and other five co-authors to the 1985 Conference of Chinese History of Metallurgy in Shaoxing, though He Tangkun does not agree with the point that the emergence of the black-lacquer antique is induced by the chemical inverse segregation effect (反偏析作用) of tin.[11]

The plainness and simplicity of Song mirrors in fact also came from an artistic subversion. Such a subversive action resembles, just as in Hegel's dialectic theory, the progression of a "thesis" based on a set of original, coherent concepts, to its "antithesis" which goes against former concepts, and finally to a "synthesis" in which the antagonism is given up to allow a development toward unification and integration. In other words, it is universally applicable to the development of all things that whenever a certain thing reaches a certain stage, it must transform into something opposite, and that the cause of this transformation does not come from the external world but exists in the own body of this very developing thing.

In the dialectic, three-stage development from the thesis to the antithesis and then to the synthesis, Song mirrors did not stand out in history as the epitome of the synthetic movement, but the interaction with Tang mirrors could be viewed as an antithetical response in style. Just as in the field of porcelain, the simple elegance and transcending spirit of Ru and Ding wares of the Song (in resemblance of humble, unadorned, and graceful lacquer wares) were in the sharp contrast to the exuberant and flamboyant tricolor-glazed porcelain (sancai 三彩) of the Tang. From the emergence of the Five Kilns onward, the rusticity of Cizhou ware (磁州窯), the variegated Jizhou ware (吉州窯), and the peculiar greenish yellow of Yaozhou ware (耀州窯) can all be seen as a result of the transformative and self-subverting process in the development of art.

The delicate beauty and sheer purity of Song mirrors is exactly a transformative subversion to the exuberant, sumptuous art style of the Tang. However, it is still undeniable that the delicate and artful mirrors manufactured from the Northern Song to the beginning of the Southern Song gradually became rough and crude in the late Southern Song, which should be attributed more to political and economic reasons than to aesthetic frustrations.

The so-called inscribed plain mirror refers to a mirror with a plain, unadorned back, which contains only an inscription of the address of the workshop or the name of the manufacturer within a square frame. The earliest instance of this type of mirrors appeared in the Zhenghe period of the Northern Song, and the same type lasted in the Southern Song in Lin'an. The inscription of "qingtong zhaozi" (bronze mirror, 青銅照子) or "jianzi" (mirror 鑑子) was made to avoid mentioning Zhao Jing (趙敬), ancestor of Emperor Zhao Kuangyin, since the "jing" (敬) in his given name and the "jing" (鏡) meaning mirror are homophones.[12] Also in the inscription is the proclamation "wubi" (unmatched), "zhenlian" (authentically cast) or "zhenzheng" (authentic), all pointing to genuine mercantile goods of supreme qualities. These plain mirrors were made in the six major regions of mirror production in China, and the most representative ones were the Shis（石家）of Huzhou, the Ye's（葉家）of Raozhou, the Maos（茆家）of Jiankang, the Gongs（龔家）of Chengdu, the Mius（繆家）and the Zhaos（趙家）of Suzhou, and the Wangs（王家）of Hangzhou（Lin'an）. On the other hand, inscribed plain mirrors were often valued by weight: the price was sixty to a hundred *wen*（文, a unit of currency）per *liang*（兩, a unit of weight）. The lobed inscribed mirror（may not be bronze, but from highly carbonated raw iron）made by Daoist Shi of Huzhou contains a two-line, ten-character inscription in a frame on the right of the mirror reading "Daoist Shi of Huzhou/ Has cast and produced this raw iron alloy mirror"（湖州石道人法煉生鐵鏡）, while in the frame on the left is another line of five characters reading "A full one hundred〔*wen*〕per *liang*"（每兩一百足）. Indeed with authentic goods comes solid price.

In the six regions of mirror manufacturing, the most famous were the Huzhou（now Wuxing）workshops which sold mirrors nationwide. Of the Shi family, the most renowned was the second brother of the father's generation, Shi Nian（石念）, whose plain mirrors in the inscription of "Bronze mirrors by the Second Uncle Nian of the Shi Family in Huzhou" were the most plentiful. Other members of the family included Second Son, Shi San（Third of the Shis）, Third Uncle, Fourth Son, Tenth Son, Fifteenth Son, and so on. The original shop of Shi Nian was located to the west of the street facing the South Temple in Huzhou, and his mirrors bore the inscription of "shop of the authentic bronze mirror by Second Uncle Nian of the Shi Family, in the west of the street facing the South Temple in Huzhou"（湖州南廟前街西石家念二叔真青銅照子記）. Other retailer shops of the Shi family were probably located around the Yifeng Bridge in Huzhou, because the plain mirrors of the Shis were usually inscribed with "Authentic and pure bronze mirror by the Shis of the Yifeng Bridge in Huzhou"（湖州儀鳳橋石家真正一色青銅鏡）. According to the *Wuxing zhi*（Gazetteer of Wuxing）of the Jiatai period, the Yifeng Bridge was located within the lively urban center of Huzhou in the Southern Song. The same gazetteer also records that the bridge was originally built in the Tang and then destroyed by fire in the third year of the Shaoxi period of the Southern Song；in the following year it was rebuilt and renamed Shaoxi Bridge. Therefore, all mirrors of the Shis bearing the inscription of the Yifeng Bridge must have been manufactured before the third year of the Shaoxi period（1192）.[13]

With regard to pictorial composition, the inscribed plain mirrors features a framed inscription, which turns into a unique textual pattern within the pure and unadorned art space. It is at once texts and an image. Taking Shi Nian's work, the "authentic bronze mirror by Second Uncle Nian of the Shi Family, in the west of the street facing the South Temple in Huzhou" as an example, this 11 by 11 cm square mirror has a small

---

11 | Ibid., 194, 243, 253.

12 | Zhou Zuoren mentions his possession of two pieces of Song mirrors in his "Gudong xiaoji"（"A short record of the antiques"）. One is a square mirror of Xue Jinhou bearing the sixteen-character inscription of "Hollowing the center", and the other is a lobed mirror with the inscription of "Mirror cast by Fifteenth Son of the Shi Family in Huzhou". Zhou then cites Qing scholar Wang Rizhen's Huya（lit. lake-elegance）, volume nine, pointing out that the terms zhaozi, jianzi（鑑子）, and jianzi（監子）were used to avoid the character "jing". He further mentions the account of once obtaining a "Moon-Palace mirror" of the Tang: "Thief Agui brought forth a mirror with an image of the Moon Palace at the back, which I purchased for a dollar. This mirror is also recorded in the Tenghua tingpu（List of mirrors of the Vine-flower Pavilion）and is certainly a Tang mirror, which unfortunately has been lost now." See Zhou Zuoren, Kucha suibi（Essays of bitter tea）, in Zhou Zuoren quanji（The complete works of Zhou Zouren）, vol. 3（Taipei: Landeng wenhua）, 9-11.

13 | Here the information is from "258: Inscribed mirrors of the Shi family in Huzhou", Tongjing pian（Bronze mirrors）, vol. 2（Taipei: Taipei Palace Museum, 1993）, 338.

Song Hu Zhou square plain mirror with inscriptions on the right
湖州南廟前街西石家念二叔真青銅照子記（右銘文）

round knob at the center of the back, and on the right is a three-line, eighteen-character inscription set within a frame. That is to say, the external frame of the square mirror contains in itself an oblong frame of inscription, just as a square wall having the opening of an oblong window. Each of the three lines in the frame of inscription consists of exactly six characters in an orderly manner, which like a borrowed scene through a window fills the entire space of the oblong frame. But the beholder of the mirror looks into not a landscape of mountains, water, and trees, but a textual scenery composed of rectangular blocks of characters!

The aesthetic design of this mirror is to center around the focal point of the square mirror—the small round knob—and create a contrasting composition of the round and the square. Additionally, the left of the knob is left blank while the right contains the eighteen-character inscription and its frame, creating a tension between the void and the solid. Such a design concept of using inscribed texts as pictorial modules resonates with German scholar Lothar Ledderose's monograph, *Ten Thousand Things—Module and Mass Production in Chinese Art*. Ledderose believes that the Chinese written language bespeaks a visualized thinking；no matter which type of writing is concerned—from the Lessor Seal Script to the more evolved Clerical and Regular Scripts, even including the transition from traditional to simplified Chinese—the structure of a character remains to be a combination of "modules". For instance, comparing the two groups of "*jun, chuan, xuan*", and "*ji, xun, tao*", which write as "鈞，釧，鉉，and 記，訓，討" in traditional Chinese and "钧，钏，铉" and "记，训，讨" in simplified Chinese, the fundamental change happens but in the basic modular radicals "*jin*"（金）and "*yan*"（言）, thus suggesting the importance of discerning the "modules". The "modules" seen by Ledderose are undetected by common Chinese from the use of their own native language. The way of dealing with the individuality and totality in art using the concept of "modules" or the "modular system" can be termed as the "Constructuralism" of art. The "modular system" conceptualized by Ledderose considers the totality of an artwork as an integral pattern put together by the parts（as in the case of the exceedingly hard jigsaw puzzle that he solved by farsightedly following a line of horizon in his childhood）, and it proves widely applicable. On the terra-cotta armies of the Qin, he traces the interrelationship between the manufacturing of individual modules and the overarching modular system, pointing out that, to ensure the timely completion of the mass production of tens of thousands of terra-cotta soldiers, "Only the use of modules made possible the most extraordinary feat of the terra-cotta army: the enormous quantity of diverse figures. Only by devising a module system could their makers rationalize production to such a degree that, with the material and time available to them, they were able to meet the expectations of the emperor—the creation of a magic army that would protect his tomb for eternity". Even the Nanking Cargo of the early Qing export blue-and-white porcelain salvaged from the pelagic sea outside Indonesia can be identified as having a modular system, since the integral pattern painted on a teacup or a saucer is formed by putting together individual modules of flowers and herbs.[14]

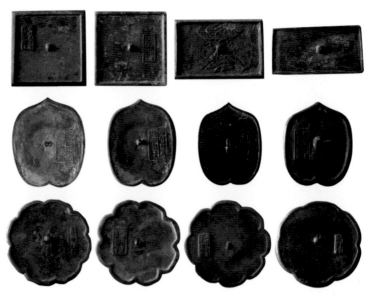

Modular system with inscription frames in Song plain mirrors 宋素鏡模件系統

The inscribed plain mirrors of the Song in fact also belonged to a large-scale "modular system"；the square frame of inscription in the above example of the "authentic bronze mirror by Second Uncle Nian of the Shi Family, in the west of the street facing the South Temple in Huzhou" was but one of the fundamental "modules". Apart from square ones, there were also inscription frames of other shapes made by many different workshops and retailers, which appeared in oblong, lobed, and heart-shaped (or pear-shaped) mirrors and constitute a series of modules or a modular system. We can derive a "modular system" of the overall shape of the mirror by taking the square, the oblong, the lobed, or the heart shape as different modules；moreover, for each of these shapes, we can further derive a second level of modular system concerning the various "inscription frames". In this way, the seemingly simple inscribed plain mirrors of the Song possess a unique artistic appeal via the glamour of its modular system.

In association of the Song plain mirrors, the splendor of the unadorned（素以為絢兮）, just as Confucius says, lies in the practical function. Colors and adornments are better applied only after the purity of the original（繪事後素）. Sitting beside and gazing into a Song inscribed plain mirror, one should see in the reflection a clearer and more dazzling image of the "entrancing, dimpling smile" and the "beautiful glancing eyes"（巧笑倩兮、美目盼兮）of an ancient beauty in the Books of Songs（*Shijing*）.

---

14 | Lothar Ledderos, *Ten Thousand Things—Module and Mass Production in Chinese Art*（Princeton: Princeton University Press, 2000）. For written Chinese, refer to the first chapter of the book, "The System of Script", 9-23. For the terra-cotta army, see chapter three, "A Magic Army for the Emperor", 51-73. The Nanking Cargo and export porcelains can be found in chapter four, "Factory Art", 75-97. The caption to the figure on page 93 contains a small error: Fig. 4.14 should be twelve sets of "bowls and plates" instead of the smaller "teacups and saucers". The "Nanking Cargo" salvaged from the Geldermalsen includes three types of glaze with regard to the teacups and saucers--blue and white, Batavian brown, and the Japanese-style Imari. A small blue-and-white teacup measures 6-7 cm in diameter, and a saucer between 10-11 cm. Small teacups and saucers of Batavian brown have blue-and-white illustrations in the inside while the outside uses the color of brown, a glaze sometimes also regarded as "caf au lait"；they have the same diameters as their blue-and-white counterparts and were cherished by Islamic peoples. The "Imari" porcelains are resplendent and colorful and are very easy to identify. In Fig. 4.14, those in the diameter of 11.5 or 17.5 cm should be medium-sized bowls and plates, but not small teacups and saucers. The one in Fig. 4.20 is 11.5 cm in diameter and has an illustration of a huge spray of peony with bamboo and rocks, which belongs to a small saucer of "Batavian brown".

第四章

素以為絢兮

宋代銘文素鏡風貌

《故宮文物》月刊，
台北，2007，10月，
295期，68-77頁。

若以青銅鏡風格發展起伏的脈絡看來，毫無疑問，自戰國到漢魏為一大巔峰，到了隋唐又轉折入另一高潮。然而到了宋代，論者多歸咎其素面相見，在銅鏡史的位置屬「退化期」。宋鏡重實用價值，鏡背不尚紋飾，使唐鏡華麗豐腴的唯美主義，一落而為社會現實生活的附屬樣品。孔祥星、劉一曼把隋唐鏡釐定為發展史的「中國銅鏡的高度發展」期，把宋鏡發軔為「中國銅鏡的日趨衰落」期。他們認為宋鏡「考古出土的資料不充分，除紀年鏡外，缺乏標準鏡，因此，學者對這個時期銅鏡的特徵和類型並沒有好好加以總結和鑒定」，但繼指出殘唐五代十國後，宋與遼、西夏、金等外族的鼎立與對峙，政權前後交替的歷史政治因素，似乎就是宋鏡日趨衰落的原因[1]。2005年上海博物館出版館藏銅鏡精品的《練形神冶，瑩質良工》一書圖版章回內，雖未謫貶，然亦把隋唐鏡呼為「絢麗多姿的隋唐銅鏡」，宋鏡則歸納入「世俗繁雜的宋遼金西夏元明清銅鏡」，一句「世俗繁雜」，宋鏡便如布衣庶人，躋身漢人及異族諸色人種的世俗行列。[2]

沈從文曾自兩種角度提到宋鏡的衰退。他指出：

如以鏡子工藝美術而言，發展到宋代特種官工鏡，已可說近於曲終雅奏。勞動人民的豐富智慧和技巧以及無窮無盡的創造力，隨同社會發展變化，重點開始轉移到新的燒瓷、雕漆、織金錦、刻線等等其他工藝方面去了。青銅工藝雖然在若干部門還有不同程度的進展……例如……金銀加工的馬鞍裝具…鐵兵器雜件也常錯縷金銀……宋宣和的仿古銅器……南宋紹興時姜娘子鑄細錦地紋方爐，在青銅工藝品中還別具一格。

沈先生並繼續指出：

不過製鏡工藝事實上到南宋已顯明在衰落中，特別是在南方，已再不是工藝生產的重點。這時揚州等大都市的手工業多被戰爭破壞，原有舊鏡多熔化改鑄銅錢或供其他需要。一般家常鏡子，重實用而不尚花紋。在湖州、饒州、臨安聞名全國的「張家」、「馬家」、「石家念二叔」等等店鋪所做青銅照子，通常多素背無花，只在鏡背部分留下個出售店鋪圖記。[3]

其實所謂南宋鏡子「重實用而不尚花紋」，主要是使用方式的演進，與美學無關。戰國鏡的弦型鈕座（knob）、漢魏、隋唐鏡的渾圓鏡鈕功用，均是用綬帶或綵繩（視乎鏡之大小）套出其中，以持或縛掛。湖南馬王堆漢墓出土銅鏡及西漢南越王墓均曾出土鈕座繫有綬帶的大型銅鏡，馬王堆一號墓的蟠螭鏡直徑 19.4 公分；南越王墓的錯金銀複合帶托銅鏡直徑更長達 29.8 公分，都是大鏡，應有鏡座，然未見出土，可見仍為繫掛或侍僕手持。[4] 用鏡時，拿在手裡，或用綬帶縛架掛放在較低的鏡台上（唐宋以前，古人多席地而坐），就如同顧愷之「女史箴圖」絹本內的一段，右邊有人手執銅鏡自照，左邊有人對著鏡台由侍女臨鏡梳妝照影。

此畫是否東晉顧愷之所作，存疑。沈從文更直言所謂《女史箴》本張華諷賈后而作，畫中梳髮婦女為西漢雙環髻髮型。因而此畫「其實卷首執筆婦女係畫古代宮廷女史髮髻而作」，因不屬本文討論，不深究。[5] 因此，如是手執鏡，自然注意及鏡背紋飾，以力求美觀賞心悅目及表現主題的祥瑞，像是漢博局規矩四靈獸鏡，或唐海獸葡萄鏡等。

早期几桌席地而坐，鏡架簡便形小，譬如東漢鎏金銅鏡架，把鏡套入如一彎新月的鏡架槽內便可。這類鏡架金屬沉重，型簡、座柄矮短，當是放在較高几桌，或由侍女持之以讓妝者觀照。後來的青銅犀牛望月鏡托，大同小異，應是此類鏡架的演變。

目前出土或收藏的鏡架座均為銅製，方能保存全貌。所有其他木製架座千年滄桑歲月，均已朽蕩無存，僅賸明清花梨木或紫檀木等的木質鏡座架組，但架疊雕鏤，已是近代風貌，無復漢唐古韻。[6]

宋明以後，椅座已為生活家具，影響其他器形制，鏡子就是其一。房內一桌二椅的標準陳設，坐具較高，放在桌上較具美感及實用的鏡座隨即脫穎而出。人坐椅上，鏡座置放在桌用來架持鏡子，或用一條幼長桿條套咬入銅鏡鈕孔，接插入鏡座（此種鏡座在漢魏六朝時就置放在席地上，可參看「女史箴圖」），從此逐漸取代穿手入寬繩或布帶的手持鏡。尤其用以縛掛的綬帶寬闊，一旦捨棄，銅鏡鈕座遂變狹小，宋明兩朝的細圓及元寶型鈕座就是典型。

鏡台前梳妝面對鏡面，極少看到鏡背，圖案美觀需求度減低，鏡背素面無紋，亦是道理。為了便於上架，宋鏡一般質身均較堅薄，約0.3公分，與厚重唐鏡鏡身並不相同。[7] 但瀏覽歷代銅鏡體積，上架或手持，均視乎鏡之大小。小於8公分的鏡子僅宜掌中，不宜上架。

即使素面，風韻無減。宋素鏡造型多姿多采，除方型、長方型、有柄型的鏡子外，又有繼承自唐代葵花、菱花而成的六稜或八稜花鏡；還有一種雞心鏡，又稱桃型或盾型鏡，體積較小，應仍為手持鏡或掌中鏡。另外，又有道教氣息濃厚的掛鐘型、鼎型、雲板型，極具時代風貌。但因圓、方鏡種仍為所有鏡子基本型式，上面不規則的爐、鐘、鼎、雲板鏡型僅曇花一現，留給後人鑑證宋鏡一個容易的特徵切入點。

宋代戰禍連綿、礦藏匱缺、手工藝受制於不穩定社會民生等因素，固是一種歷史評價，但並非放諸四海皆準。其實宋代城市經濟發展仍非常蓬勃，中產階級興起帶動商貿，他們的媒觸潤滑作用，使貴族文化普及，也使市民文化提昇。北宋汴京（開封）人口達一百萬，繁華如花錦。南宋重視海路交通，商業貿易

1　孔祥星、劉一曼《中國古銅鏡》，台北：藝術圖書公司，1994。p.138。但二氏在另一專著《銅鏡鑑藏》內對宋鏡又提出另一種相反的肯定看法，特別提到宋代秀色纖纖著名的「纏枝花草紋鏡」，認為這類用淺浮雕處理的寫生花草紋鏡子，「即使從工藝美術而言，……在我國銅鏡發展史上也佔有重要位置，也是不應忽視的。」見氏著，長春：吉林科學技術出版社，2004，p.56。

2　上海博物館，《練形神冶，瑩質良工──上海博物館出版其館藏銅鏡精品》，上海：上海書畫出版社，2005，p.6

3　沈從文，〈古代鏡子藝術〉，見《花花朵朵壇壇罐罐》，南京：江蘇美術出版社，2002，p.48。

4　《馬王堆漢墓陳列》，湖南博物館，p.9。《西漢南越王墓博物館珍品拔粹》，廣州西漢南越王墓博物館編，p.57。有關綬帶縛掛鏡子梳妝最具說服說服力的證據為「河南禹縣白沙北宋元符三年趙大翁墓壁畫」（中國歷史博物館藏摹本繪）內有宗室地主趙大翁家眷在日常生活對鏡梳妝描繪。見沈從文，〈116──宋墓壁畫梳妝和宴飲，圖178〉，《中國古代服飾研究》，上海：上海書店出版社，2002，p.456。

5　沈從文，《銅鏡史話》，瀋陽：萬卷出版公司，2005，p.196。此書原據沈早年著作《唐宋銅鏡》（1956）加編而成。

6　王度《息齋藏鏡》，台北：歷史博物館，2001，該書記錄私人收藏有清代木質鏡架組多種，見 pp.233-236.

7　有關銅鏡的實用功能，本文作者除利用文獻及實物引證外，尚參考了《中國文明史話》一書內〈古代的銅鏡〉一章，作者不詳，台北：木鐸出版社，1983，pp.357-363。鏡架鏡台的進化演變，參閱周亞，〈銅鏡使用方式的考古資料分析〉一文，見註2, pp.54-66.

規模更大，臨安（杭州）人口亦達一百二十萬人，酒肆茶坊，勾欄瓦舍遍處皆是。從早到晚，大街小巷，人群攢動。讀筆記小說孟元老《東京夢華錄》可知汴京盛況，讀灌園耐得翁《都城紀勝》、西湖老人《繁勝錄》、吳自牧《夢梁錄》、周密《武林舊事》可悉南渡臨安的繁觀勝景。除飲食及節日民俗喜慶，還有民間的百戲伎藝，《都城紀勝》〈瓦舍眾伎〉條內有小說文類「說話」記載，為宋元話本小說珍貴的原始資料：

> 說話有四家：一者小說，謂之銀字兒，如煙粉靈怪、傳奇。說公案，皆是博刀趕棒，及發跡變泰之事。說鐵騎兒，謂士馬金鼓之事。說經，謂演說佛書。說參請，謂賓主禪悟道等事。講史書，講說前代書史文傳，興廢爭戰之事。最畏小說人，蓋小說者能以一朝一代故事，頃刻間提破……。[8]

小說的普及，薰陶消費者的興趣傾向，民眾對神話傳說熟悉而具好感，帶動宋鏡紋飾以大量的民俗傳說及神仙佛道故事，其中包括「許由巢父鏡」、「鍾馗捉鬼鏡」、「月桂玉兔搗杵鏡」、「吳牛喘月鏡」、「王質觀棋爛柯鏡」、「仙人龜鶴鏡」、「仙人斬龍鏡」等。

宋鏡另一藝術造詣為纏枝花葉紋鏡，那是一種淺浮雕紋飾，呈現細緻的工筆花卉畫風，匠心獨運，線條流暢。與前面的民俗神話人物鏡粗糙的藝術處理手法，恰成正比。

再觀殘唐五代十國到北宋大一統的帝國局面，短短十六年（963～979），宋太祖挾陳橋兵變、黃袍加身的餘威，次第用兵平滅南唐、後蜀、吳越等國。除在後唐割讓給契丹的燕雲十六州，中國大致已統一。從此唐代藩鎮割據，獨霸一方的分峙煙消雲散。更因四川後蜀、江南南唐、浙江吳越等地均未受兵燹，民間工藝發展在個別地區持續不輟。後蜀織錦與髹漆，瑰麗典雅；北方磁州窯及南方吉州窯等民窯創思活潑、屢見巧意；吳越錢氏青瓷祕色窯，獨步一時。

我們甚至可以說，即使宋朝進入與遼、西夏、金朝對峙局面，手工業與工藝的發展，除了像沈從文先生在前面所謂的「勞動人民的豐富智慧和技巧以及無窮無盡的創造力，隨同社會發展變化，重點開始轉移到新的燒瓷、雕漆、織金錦、刻線等等其他工藝方面去了」外，銅鏡的鑄作並非日落崦嵫。

但是銅的產量、技術、需求在宋代都超越前代，更由於貿易急速發展，貨幣流通，需銅日亟，管制亦嚴，供不應求，屢有銅禁之事。黃銅在日常生活器具中，主要用來製造銅鏡、鐘或鑼等，銅鏡業在南宋依然非常發達。但民間使用或出賣銅鏡，很多時也要經過官府一道「投稅獲鑿」的手續。[9]

需注意的是，宋金元明清鏡使用一種新合金，含銅量極高，達 73.7%，錫含量相反低至 7.1%，鉛 13.1%，含鋅量亦提高至 10% 以上。但缺銅並非主因，減錫，是減少青銅的硬脆度而更耐用。何堂坤曾在銅鏡化學成份分析研究指出「社會習俗的變化，以及人們對材料性能認識水平的提高，才是宋後銅鏡成份改變的主要原因，缺銅事可能也發生過一些影響，但不是直接的；至多是間接的、次要的因素。」[10]

宋鏡這種低錫現象，間接影響了後人對宋鏡的喜愛及評價。因為低錫，千年後出土宋鏡呈黑漆古不多，不若漢唐古鏡因具相當錫量而呈黑漆古，幽光鑑人，十分討好。筆者此觀點與 1985 年紹興「中國金屬史學術討論會」花傳平等六人提出的論文〈青銅器「黑漆古」層形成肌理探討〉的看法不謀而合。儘管何堂坤先生並不同意黑漆古的呈現，乃錫的「反偏析作用」所致。[11]

其實宋鏡素樸，亦是來自一種藝術反動。這種反動行為有似黑格爾（Hegel）辯證理論中，從一個概念同一性發展下來的「正論」（thesis）、到概念自我對立的「反論」（antithesis）、再到概念放棄對立而趨向統一整合的「綜論」（synthesis）。換句話說，宇宙萬物發展的公式，凡是某一事物到達某一程度，必會轉化成與自身相反的東西，而且轉化原因並非來自外界，而實存在於發展事物的本身。

宋鏡在正、反、合三段的歷史辯證裡，雖未能臻達集大成綜合，然與唐鏡的正反互動，理應視為風格上正反的辯證。就如在陶瓷上，宋代汝、定的淡雅高逸（猶如樸實無華的典雅漆器），與唐代華麗鋪張的三彩恰成正比。五大名窯以降，磁州的野趣，吉州的千般變幻，耀州的翠黃異色，均可視為一種藝術發展下自身的轉化反動過程。

宋鏡纖秀素淨，正是對唐代華麗豐腴風格一種藝術反動轉化。但是無可否認，北宋到南宋初期製作精緻巧麗，入南宋後期質素便日呈粗簡，卻是事實，此乃政治經濟原因多於美學挫敗。

所謂銘文素鏡，是指鏡背素面無紋，僅以方框銘刻店號地址或製鏡人名字。此鏡種最早出現在北宋政和年間，一直延續入南宋臨安。銘文內稱鏡子為「青銅照子」或「鑑子」主因是避諱趙匡胤之祖趙敬，「敬」、「鏡」兩字同音。[12] 此外又稱「無比」、「真煉」或「真正」，均指正宗的商號精品。這些素鏡以全國六大產區為主，最具代表性分別有「湖州」石家，「饒州」葉家、「建康」茆家、「成都」龔家、「蘇州」繆、趙家、「杭州」（臨安）王家。此外，銘文素鏡經常以重量計值，每重一兩，售六十文到一百文，湖州石道人葵花銘文鏡，鏡右框書銘文二行十字「湖州石道人法煉生鐵鏡」，左側另框一行五字，上鑄「每兩一百足」，可謂貨真價實。

六大鑄鏡地區，以湖州作坊最為有名，銷售全國。石家以父執輩排行第二的石念鑄鏡名氣響亮，銘文素鏡「湖州石家念二叔青銅照子」最多，其他家族成員有二郎、石三、三叔、四郎、十郎、十五郎等人。石念老店在湖州南廟前街西，鏡銘標有「湖州南廟前街西石家念二叔真青銅照子記」。其他石家店舖應就在湖州儀鳳橋一帶，因石家素鏡多銘有「湖州儀鳳橋石家真正一色青銅鏡」。據嘉泰《吳興誌》載，儀鳳橋位於南宋湖州的熱鬧市區。又，該橋原建於唐代，南宋紹熙三年毀於火。翌年重建改稱紹熙橋，因此凡鑄有儀鳳橋銘文之石家鏡應是製於紹熙三年（1192）之前。[13]

自美術構圖而言，銘文素鏡以方框文字在素淨空間形成一種獨特文本圖案。它既是文字，也是圖象。就以石念「湖州南廟前街西石家念二叔真青銅照子記」為例，這面長闊各 11 公分的方鏡鏡背中心有一細小圓型鈕座，右邊以方框置三行十八字銘文。也就是說，方鏡型的方框內又含長方框銘文，有如四方牆壁再開一面長形窗子。框內三行銘文，每行整齊六字，似窗戶借景，填滿整個長框空間。持鏡人看過去不是山水樹木，而是方形文字組合而成的文本景觀！

這面方鏡的美學設計，是以四方鏡子中間細圓鈕座作為中心焦點，做成一圓一方的對比構圖。另又

8　　灌園耐得翁《都城紀勝》，見孟元老《東京夢華錄》（外四種），北京：文化藝術出版社，1998，p.86.

9　　田自秉《中國工藝美術史》，台北：丹青圖書有限公司，出版日期缺，pp.305-307。

10　　何堂坤《中國古代銅鏡的技術研究》，北京：紫禁城出版社，1999，p.62。

11　　見上著，何堂坤，p.194, 243, 253。

12　　周作人在〈骨董小記〉一文內提及收有宋鏡兩面，一為薛晉侯「既虛其中」十六字銘文方鏡。另一為「湖州石十五郎鍊銅照子」葵花鏡。周氏並引清人汪日楨《湖雅》卷 9，指出照子、鑑子、監子均因避「敬」字嫌。另又提到曾得唐「月宮鏡」一面：「小偷阿桂攜來一鏡，背作月宮圖，以一元買得，此鏡《藤花亭譜》亦著錄，定為唐製，但今已失去。」見周作人《苦茶隨筆》，《周作人全集三》，台北：藍燈文化，pp.9-11。

13　　此處資料取自「285：湖州石家銘文鏡」《銅鏡篇下冊》，台北故宮博物院，1993，p.338.

在圓鈕左邊留白，右邊以十八字銘文框格，一虛一實。這種以銘文作為圖型基本模件（modules）的設計觀念，就像德國學者雷德侯（Lothar Ledderose）在其專著《萬物：中國藝術的模件與量產》（*Ten Thousand Things—Module and Mass Production in Chinese Art*）內，認為中國書寫文字是一種視覺思維，無論自小篆進化入隸書、楷書，甚至自繁體字進化入簡體字，它們的結構仍然是「模件」的組合。譬如兩組繁體字的「鈞、釧、鉉」、「記、訓、討」進化入簡體字的「钧、钏、铉」、「记、训、讨」，其基本變化亦僅自基本模件的「金」與「言」，由此可見辨別出「模件」的重要。雷德侯看到中文書寫的「模件」，是一般中國人自本國文字警覺不到的。由「模件」或「模件系統」去處理藝術的個別性與整體性，可稱為藝術的「結構主義」。雷德侯這種「模件系統」（modular systems）觀念，拼湊合成整體圖案（patterns）去處理藝術的整體觀念（就像他小時憑著宏觀追隨一條地平線破解了一個很難玩的拼圖遊戲 jigsaw puzzle），可謂無往而不利。他不但追蹤處理秦兵馬俑個別模件的製作與模件系統的關係，千萬秦俑遂能如期量產完成（mass production）——「惟模件應用才能顯出秦俑隊伍製造技藝的超卓本色：包括各色各樣的千軍萬馬。惟靠模件系統設計才能讓工匠們儘量利用手上材料與時間去量材而用，造出皇帝要求臻達的一隊神兵，保護陵寢千秋萬世。」，就連印尼外海沉船撈起的清初青花貿易瓷「南京貨運」（Nanking Cargo），也可在杯碟上描繪的個別花卉模件，拼湊出整體構圖的模件系統。[14]

宋代銘文素鏡其實也是一個大型「模件系統」，上面舉隅「湖州南廟前街西石家念二叔真青銅照子記」內的銘文方框，只是其中一個基本「模件」。除方鏡外，還有許多不同店號作坊的銘文圖型出現在其他長方鏡、葵花鏡、雞心鏡內，形成一系列的模件或模件系統。我們可以以不同的鏡型模件如方、長方、葵花、或雞心排列成一個以銘文方框作主題的整體「模件系統」，也可以單獨以方型或長方型鏡種、葵花鏡種、雞心鏡種排列出不同模件的「銘文方框」模件系統。如此一來，看似簡單的宋代銘文素鏡，自有其藝術獨特的模件系統風姿。

素以為絢兮，夫子說得不錯，以實用功能而言，繪事後素，臨照宋代銘文素鏡，更能自倒影中看到更多更絢麗的巧笑倩兮、美目盼兮。

14｜Lothar Ledderose，Ten Thousand Things—Module and Mass Production in Chinese Art, Princeton: Princeton University Press, 2000。處理書寫文字可參閱該書第一章〈書寫系統〉，pp.9-23；秦俑，第三章〈造給始皇帝的神兵〉，pp.51-73。「南京貨運」（Nanking Cargo）貿易瓷可參閱該書第四章「工廠藝術」，pp.75-97。惟 93 頁內圖片說明稍有錯誤，圖 4.14 應為十二套碗碟（bowls and plates），而非體積較小的茶杯碟（teacups and saucers）。「南京貨運」沉船「蓋德麻森號」（Geldermalsen）打撈出來的茶杯碟釉色可分三種：青花（blue and white）、「巴達維亞赭」（Batavian brown）及東瀛式「伊萬里」（Imari）。青花小茶杯 teacup 直徑 6cm 至 7cm 間，碟 10cm 至 11cm 間。「也達維亞赭」小茶杯碟內繪青花，外壁用赭色釉，有時亦稱「奶咖啡色」（cafe au lait），直徑與青花杯碟相同，為伊斯蘭國家所喜愛。「伊萬里」金碧輝煌似五彩，極易辨認。書中圖 4.14 稱直徑有 11.5cm 及 17.5cm 者，應為青花中型碗碟，而非小茶杯碟。圖 4.20 即為 11.5cm 內繪大朵牡丹竹石的「巴達維亞赭」小碟。

43. *Hu Zhou* Shi family's 2nd uncle *Nien* square mirror 宋湖州石家念二叔素方鏡

Song-Liao Dynasty（907-1279 AD）　　Diameter : 11.3×11.3cm

New shapes, such as this square mirror, also begin to appear during the Song Dynasty as a result of increased mass production. This piece has a plain, surface with single, thin border framing its edges. Its only embellishment is the inscription on the right side of the square, which states:

湖州南廟前街
西石家念二叔
真青銅照子記

The inscriptions state in great detail of the Shi family's 2nd uncle whose shop is located in the west side of the front street before the South temple. It also states that it is an authentic bronze mirror made by the 2nd uncle Nien.

44. *Hu Zhou* Shi family's plain mirror #1 宋湖州石家素鏡

Song-Liao Dynasty（907-1279 AD）　Diameter : 11.3×11.3cm

This mirror has a slightly curved, raised rim but possesses the same square shape as the previous piece. These two mirrors also have an almost identical inscription. The writing is now on the upper left hand side of the surface and says:

湖州真石家
念二叔照子

The first line authenticates this piece as a work cast in, the 石家 , or Shi family workshop of Huzhou in Eastern China. The second line indicates the mirror's owner, a second uncle. These two lines are also seen in the previous work, indicating that these inscriptions were commonly duplicated and transposed onto various pieces. At the center of this piece is a small hemispheric knob, much like the other one work.

45. *Hu Zhou* Shi family's plain mirror #2 宋湖州石家素鏡

Song-Liao Dynasty（907-1279 AD）　　Diameter：12.5×12.5cm

　　We now see an exact replication of the above mirror, with yet again, the same inscription at a different location on the surface. The mirror has thin raised border that frames the mirror's plain surface. This piece's inscription is less clearly engraved；perhaps it is a later reproduction from the same mold as our previous pieces. All three mirrors are made in Huzhou from the Shi family workshop as indicated by the inscription.

46. *Hu Zhou* Shi family's 2ⁿᵈ uncle *Nien* plain lobed mirror 宋湖州石家念二叔葵花素鏡

Song-Liao Dynasty（907-1279 AD） Diameter : 13.5cm

We saw lobed mirrors beginning to be produced in the Tang dynasty, and in the Song Dynasty, this becomes a popular ornamentation to the otherwise plain object. This mirror has eight lobes, each of them linked together to create the shape of a flower. The same inscription from mirrors 44 and 45 is also cast on the left side of this piece. The small, central knob on this mirror is broken, but it looks likely to have been a plain round one.

47. *Hu Zhou* Authentic Shi family's plain lobed mirror 宋湖州正石家葵花鏡

Song-Liao Dynasty（907-1279 AD）　　Diameter：15.5cm

Yet again, the shape of the mirror changes but the surface of the object continues to be plain and undecorated except for an embossed inscription indicating its workshop and owner. This mirror now has six wide lobes that link together to form the shape of a flower. The inscription is on the right side, but it has eroded significantly and is difficult to read. A small looped knob sits at the center of the piece.

48. *Hu Zhou* 石承祖六十 plain mirror with handle 宋湖州承祖石六十帶柄素鏡

Song-Liao Dynasty（907-1279 AD）　　Total Length：17.2cm　　Diameter of face：9.9cm　　Width of handle：2.1cm

　　This mirror exhibits a new invention in the Song Dynasty: a mirror handle. The piece is much like the other lobed mirrors, with five lobes that create a floral shape. However, the sixth "lobe" at the bottom of the piece transforms into a long, undecorated handle that is rounded at the end. The central knob, seen in all of the previous mirrors, now disappears. A flat, raised border frames the entire piece including this new, extra element. The inscription also slightly differs. It reads:

承祖石六十

　　This simply states that there have been 60 (or 16) generations of the Shi workshop though it is an ambivalent, nebulous term often used by younger generations. Despite this, the seal once again indicates the mirror's manufacturing location.

49. Square mirror with coin designs 宋金錢紋方鏡

Song-Liao Dynasty（907-1279 AD）　　Diameter：13.5cm

　　In the Han Dynasty, we have seen TLV patterns with a central square embellishing a round mirror. Now, a square mirror frames a central circular pattern surrounding a small central knob. Within the circle is a repeating, interlocking pattern of floral copper coins, each with four flat leaves. The circular shape gives a sense of a coin at the center, and small lines decorate the remaining space in each corner of the mirror.

50. *Rao Zhou* Ye family rectangular mirror 宋饒州葉家長方鏡

Song-Liao Dynasty（907-1279 AD）　　Length：7.5cm　　Width：12.6cm

The Song dynasty had two main, manufacturing centers for mirrors, one in Huzhou（now in Zhejiang province）and the other in 饒州, or Raozhou（now in Jiangxi province）. This particular piece's inscription indicates that it is from the latter location. The first line states:

饒州葉家

久煉銅照子記

Which means "a long casted bronze mirror made from the Ye family in Raozhou".

The first line identifies the piece as a work of Raozhou, specifically from the Ye family workshop. The second line states that this is a copper smelted mirror. This object also has a new rectangular shape, which is also easy to duplicate and mass-produce. A thin, plain raised border frames the shape, and its inscription is on the right side of the mirror's surface. Completing the piece is a small round knob at its center.

51. *Rao Zhou* rectangular mirror 宋饒州長方鏡

Song-Liao Dynasty（907-1279 AD） Length：7.5cm Width：12.6cm

    This is could easily be a reproduction of the previous mirror, cast from the same mold. It has the same small, central knob, as well as raised border. However, there is no inscription on this piece, and only the shape gives us indication of its workshop and place of production. Perhaps these inscriptions used on various pieces were a detachable piece that could be attached to different mirror molds.

52. *Jian kang* prefecture Mao family's 8th uncle lobed plain mirror 宋建康府茆八叔葵花素鏡

Song-Liao Dynasty（907-1279 AD）　Diameter : 13.5cm

This mirror is similar to the other pieces, and has six lobes that create a floral shape. Specifically, this piece is a 葵花 *kui hua* mirror because of its large petals that lends to its floral shape. The surface is plain except for an inscription that reads:

This mirror is from the Jian Kang prefecture（present Nanking）, the Mao family's eighth uncle, a bronze mirror.

建康府茆八叔

煉銅照子

53. *Hu Zhou* Shi family's Peach mirror 宋湖州石家桃心鏡

Song-Liao Dynasty（907-1279 AD）   Length：12.9cm   Width：10.5cm

We have returned to Huzhou, and we see that a new peach shaped mirror is also produced by the same Shi family workshop. Like the square and rectangular mirrors, a raised, plain border frames this shape, and yet again, the inscription remains similar to the others, stating the mirror's production place and workshop, type of mirror （copper）. A small round knob sits at the center ; only the shape of the mirror has altered from the previous pieces（see #45-47 produced presumably in the same place and workshop）.

54. *Hu Zhou* Shi family 念四郎 Peach mirror 宋湖州石念四郎桃心鏡

Song-Liao Dynasty（907-1279 AD）   Length：12cm   Width：10.6cm

A similar peach shaped mirror with a broken central knob now has a slightly different inscription on the left side of its plain surface. The inscription reads:

湖州石念四郎

真煉銅照子

It is a bronze mirror made by the 4th son of Shi Nien. This is a simple variation that personalizes the typical inscriptions on the Song mirrors. Like the piece before, there are various permutations of shapes and embossed seals that add ornamentation to the otherwise undecorated mirrors. It too as a small hemispheric knob though it is broken.

55. *Rao Zhou* Zhou family the 2nd Son's Peach mirror 宋饒州周二家桃心鏡

Song-Liao Dynasty（907-1279 AD）　Length : 12cm　Width : 10.7cm

This mirror is now produced in Rao Zhou, but still uses the peach design. This one is slightly more square-shaped than the previous example. A small knob sits at the center, and an inscription, mostly illegible, is on its left.

It reads "bronze mirror made by the 2nd son of the Chou family from Raozhou".

饒州
周二家鍊銅照

56. *Rao Zhou* Ye Family casted Peach mirror #2 宋饒州葉家久鍊桃心鏡之二

Song-Liao Dynasty（907-1279 AD） Length : 12cm Width : 10.7cm

Compare this mirror with another Ye family workshop piece, mirror #50. The pieces are cast in two different shapes, and the peach mirror likely had a larger knob. Despite these differences, both have identical inscriptions on their surfaces:

饒州葉家父

鍊銅照子記

Once again, we see a reuse of the same seals and shapes, most likely to allow for mass-production pieces from these workshops.

57. Peach mirror with *"qing tong jian rong"* inscriptions 宋「青銅鑑容」桃心鏡

Song-Liao Dynasty（907-1279 AD）　　Length : 9cm　　Width : 7.4cm

　　This peach mirror has a unique inscription. Instead of indicating a locale and production workshop, it reads: *"qing tong jian rong"* , or translated roughly as, this is a bronze mirror which reflects back one's appearance.

　　We have not seen inscriptions describing the aesthetics and utilitarian use of these bronze mirrors since the Han Dynasty. Furthermore, the object's seal is highly individualized. Floral embellishments decorate the ends of rectangular frame around the inscription. The knob is delicate and consists of narrow strip of metal, differing from the usual thicker, round knobs. Its well-preserved condition and detailed inscriptive decoration might suggest that this mirror was not mass-produced or that it was one of the first cast from its mold. Surely though, it differs slightly from the other pieces we have seen.

58. Double phoenix rectangular mirror 宋雙鳳長方型鏡

Song-Liao Dynasty（907-1279 AD）　Diameter : 11cm

　　This rectangular mirror has a green patina on it, and its embellishments are faded ; however, it is still possible to see two phoenixes, their wings both outstretched on the surface. The birds' beaks turn towards a small hemispheric knob with a flattened top at the center of the mirror. The two creatures are raised decorations cast on the surface of the mirror, and there is no inscription indicating its workshop or place of production.

59. *Hu Zhou* Shi Family lobed mirror with waves designs 宋湖州石家波濤紋葵花鏡

Song-Liao Dynasty（907-1279 AD）　　Diameter：14.5cm

　　This is yet another variation of the undecorated Song mirrors where the workshop has added further intricate embellishments to the work's surface. This is an eight-lobed mirror in the shape of a flower, with a small hemispheric knob at the center. Most of the Song bronze pieces are left undecorated except for its inscription, but this mirror has a linear, billowing wave pattern that covers its entire surface. This is reminiscent of the Warring States mirrors（see mirror 3）, where a ground pattern decorates the mirror. There is still an inscription on the left on the knob, which reads:

湖州石家

清銅照子

Like most inscriptions, it simply indicates that the mirror was made by the Shi workshop in Huzhou.

60. Double phoenix long handle round mirror 宋雙鳳帶柄圓鏡

Song-Liao Dynasty（907-1279 AD）   Total Length：16.4cm   Width of mirror face：8.6cm   Width of handle：2cm

We have an even more ornate example of the double-phoenix design, now on a circular mirror with a long handle. The two birds circle one another and their heads facing with their mouths open and snapping at each other. The workshop has included extremely ornate details from the phoenixes' curling, ornate tails to the feathers on their wings. A plain raised border frames the back of the mirror, and a plain handle protrudes from the bottom of the piece. At the base of the handle, there is a small inscription, which reads: 關家照子, which means "a mirror casted by the Guan family".

61. Mirror with 5 dragons chasing pearls 宋五龍戲珠鏡

Song-Liao Dynasty（907-1279 AD）   Diameter : 18cm

    Many Song workshops copied the ornamentation seen in the Tang and previous dynasties and cast them as later pieces. In this circular mirror, we have a plain border that frames two intricate but heavily eroded, decorative registers. Dragons fly around the outer register, chasing pearls that are incased in a ring of flower petals. An incised ring frames the inner register with a slightly flattened, round knob at its center. The outer register's motif repeats itself again with possibly another dragon turning in a circle, curling around the knob. A green patina and severe corrosion has significantly damaged the mirror, making the design difficult to determine. However, the organization of this mirror is reminiscent of the serpentine mirrors in the Warring States period（see mirror #1）, where intertwining dragons were a common decorative motif.

62. Lobed mirror with woods and floral designs 宋林徑花樹葵鏡

Song-Liao Dynasty (907-1279 AD)　　Diameter : 16cm

　　An entire forest scene decorates the surface of this eight-lobed mirror with a beveled border. On the edge of the outer register, eight foiled brackets echo the floral shape of the piece. Five blooming flowers face outward and further decorate this space. At the center of the mirror is a wooded area with various fauna adjoined by a small path. The viewer feels as if he or she is viewing a part of a larger forest scene through this space. Only the round knob at the center disrupts this view.

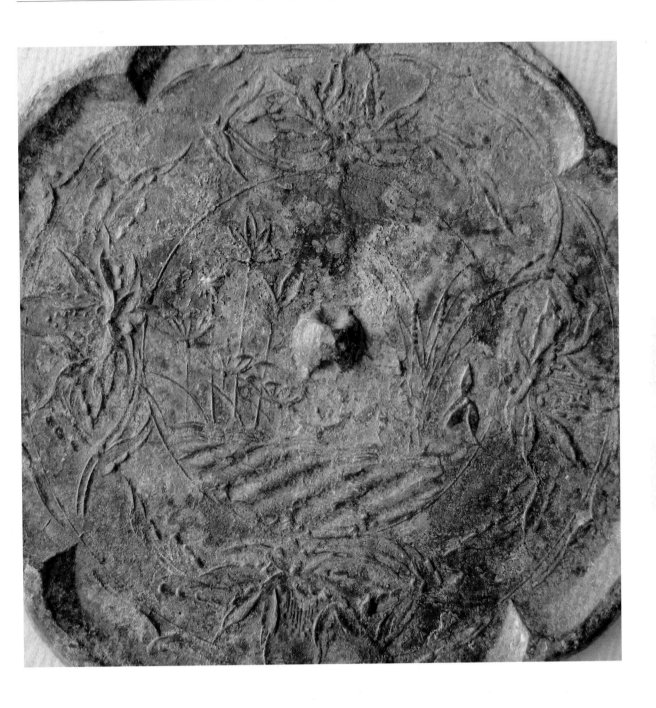

63. Mirror with the legend of Liu Yi as messenger for the dragon princess 宋柳毅傳書鏡

Song-Liao Dynasty（907-1279 AD）　　Diameter : 17.8cm

At the center of this mirror is a round knob with a flattened top. Surrounding this handle is an image from the Chinese fable of Liu Yi and the dragon princess. On the left of the knob are faded, thin striations, suggesting the rolling waves of a river. Standing on this water are two figures, one of them presumably the dragon princess, who in this myth is unhappy with her marriage. She asks Liu Yi, who walks past the river on his way to take his civil examination, to bring a letter to her father that asks for help. There are three other figures on the mirror, likely her attendants, two below the knob, and one on the right of it, but is unclear who is Liu Yi in the piece. It is also apparent that the creator of this piece chose to add further detail to the mythological scene. On the edge of the mirror, connected to plain circular border, there seems to be two posts of a fence. On the top half of the piece, a beautifully ornate tree shades the scene with its bushels of leaves.

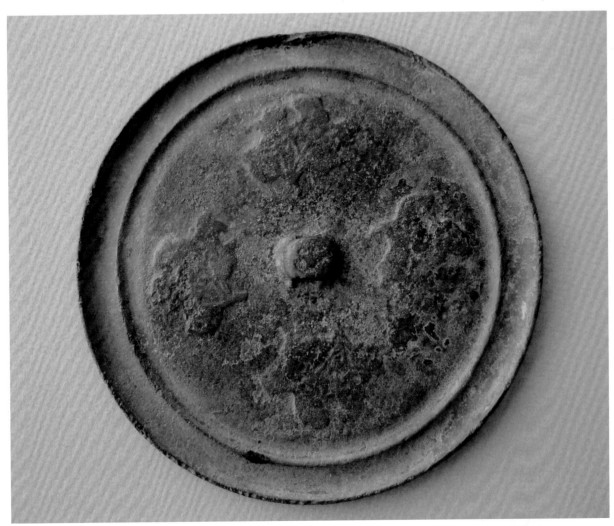

64. Large Song 4 flower mirror 宋四團花弦圓鏡

Song-Liao Dynasty（907-1279 AD）　　Diameter : 12.5cm

　　This round mirror has four flowers decorating its plain surface. The edge of the central decoration bevels inward towards a raised ring. This separates the floral motif from a concave, outer border. A round knob, its top flattened, sits at the center of the mirror. This decoration is reminiscent of a Tang style mirror,（see mirror 41）with six flowers surrounding its central knob. The Song version of this is much more simplified, with no decorations framing the knob, and only four blooms present, leaving an ample amount of empty space.

65. Eight trigrams mirror in the shape of "Ya" character
宋八卦亞字鏡

Song-Liao Dynasty（907-1279 AD）   Diameter : 12.3cm

This mirror has four wide lobes, leaving a large, square-like space for decoration. On its surface, a circle frames the 8 trigrams of the *I-Ching*（*The Book of Changes*）, a text on cosmology and divination. These radiate from the center where a small, flattened central knob sits on a blooming, six-petal flower. The ring of trigrams is large and takes up most of the decorative back of the mirror. However the workshop still includes small curling lines that embellish the space between the central decoration and the four lobes.

66. Lobed mirror with people 宋人物葵花鏡

Song-Liao Dynasty（907-1279 AD）　Diameter : 12cm

We have seen embellishments with mythological figures as well as scenic flora, and now, this mirror incorporates a secular scene of a single figure standing next to a tall tree. On the left of a thin, narrow knob, is the outline of a tree trunk with small gnarls on its surface. One branch has broken off and now lies at the base of the trunk. The tree droops over the scene framed in a circle, and large blossoms hang over the figure in the piece. This woman wears a long costume with various folds and layers delineated on his sleeves and dress. A train extends from her clothing, trailing behind her. Our figure holds a thin staff in his/her hands as they stand under the large, overarching tree.

67. Peach shaped mirror with door ring and *"an ming gui bao"* inscription 宋安明貴寶劍鏡──環扣

Song-Liao Dynasty（907-1279 AD）　　Diameter：17cm　height

This is an incredibly ornate peach shaped mirror, with various embellishments decorating its surface and knob. On the surface of the mirror are archaic inscriptions, which say:

安明貴寶

弗劍而鏡

Translated, it says that it is the treasure（貴寶）swords from the An Ming Temple（安明）in Nanking . This is possibly a Taoist mirror referring to the exorcist swords stored in the An Ming Temple 安明寺 in the Southern Chi 南齊 of the Six Dynasties. Taoists are fond of using mirrors and swords for exorcism. Superimposed upon this is a large, square knob that protrudes from the top of the "peach." Affixed to this is a large door ring with various grooves carved into its circular shape. This is piece is quite different from the various small knobs and handles we have seen in Song, Liao, and Jin mirrors.

68. Liao-Jin double-carp mirror with Mirror Bureau inscriptions 遼金鏡子局官雙魚鏡

Song-Liao Dynasty（907-1279 AD）   Diameter : 11.4cm

The double-carp imagery is an auspicious congratulatory sign seen in mirrors during the Jin and Liao dynasties[1]. Two large carp fish, a symbol of fertility or fecundity in China, swim in opposite directions in a faint, incised ground pattern of billowing waves. Details show the numerous fish scales on their bodies as well as the webbing on their fins and tails. A plain, raised circular frame bounds this image, and a small round knob sits at the center of the mirror among the waves. A small inscription states that this is a mirror casted by the Liao Dynasty government mirror bureau.

69. Liao mirror with auspicious beast and chrysanthemum petals 遼瑞獸鈕菊瓣圓鏡

Song-Liao Dynasty（907-1279 AD）　Diameter : 11.5cm

We have a Liao mirror whose decorations rise from the surface and are cast plastically, giving the piece a unique sculptural quality. In place of a knob, a frog sits at the center of a blooming chrysanthemum. Small, adjoining rings line the interior edge of this space, and a miniscule saw-tooth pattern trims the outside edge. The chrysanthemum has three layers of petals. Twelve small, round leaves bloom from the flower's center, each spaced slightly apart. Underneath, this is a set of large petals, each delineated with their central vein delineated, and plastically engraved to curl up. Peeking out from behind these layers are the corners of twelve petals, the last layer of the flower. The ground pattern on which the chrysanthemum sits is equally ornate. They look to be semicircular leaves, with one edge tapered and pointing away from the center. This embellishment is a continuous frieze that frames the outside of the flower. A plain, raised border frames these decorations, bounding them within a circular shape.

70. Liao-Jin Double fish mirror 遼金雙魚鏡

Song-Liao Dynasty（907-1279 AD）　Diameter : 12.2cm

We have seen this motif before（see mirror #68）, where two fish swimming in opposite directions on the surface of a round mirror. Now, the decoration is more simplified ; instead of a ground pattern, two small rolling waves on either side of a round, flattened knob, isolating each animal in two separate halves of the mirror. Further embellishments show the scaled texture on the fishes' skin, and faint hachures decorate their fins. A raised ring bounded by an indented rim frames the decoration and edge of the piece.

71. Song "*ding hai zan ting*" inscription mirror 宋「丁亥贊廷」銘文鏡

Song-Liao Dynasty（907-1279 AD）　Diameter : 8.9cm

Four characters surround found sides of a large, flattened round knob on a round mirror. Framing the piece is a thick, plain raised border. When read from the top, then bottom, then right to left, the inscription "丁亥" was year 1107 A.D. during the Northern Song Emperor Zhao Zi（徽宗趙佶）of the Huizong era under the reign title of "Daguan"（大觀）, however, "zan ting" is appears to be the name of the casting manufacturer.

This is a Song Dynasty "chronology mirror" in which the reign era was inscribed in indicate the time it was casted.

72. Song "*bing shen ben li*" mirror 宋「丙申本立」鏡

Song-Liao Dynasty（907-1279 AD）　　Diameter : 9cm

　　Now, we have a piece fashioned from the same mold as the previous mirror, with a raised, plain border and a short inscription that surrounds the piece's round, flattened knob. The year "*bing shen*" was 1056 AD during the Southern Song emperor Zhao Shu of the Yingzong（英宗趙曙）era under the 3rd year of the reign Zhihe（至和三年）.

73. Song plain round mirror 宋全素圓鏡

Song-Liao Dynasty（907-1279 AD） Diameter : 9.6cm

The back of this mirror is completely undecorated save for its round, flattened knob. It seems to have a slightly concave shape, which curves and dips slightly inward towards the center. Perhaps there may have been a thin flat border since some parts of the mirror seem to flatten into a rim, but overall, there seems to be no embellishments at all.

74. Song floral lobed mirror 宋團花葵鏡

Song-Liao Dynasty（907-1279 AD）　Diameter : 13cm

　　Various, delicately cast floral motifs decorate this bronze mirror. At the center of mirror sits a small round, flattened knob surrounded by a blossoming flower with 18 round petals. A granulated ring frames this central design. In an outer register surrounding this, seven alternate between facing and turning away from the center. Thin stems surround each blossom and connect each of them together. Around this is another fine, granulated ring. The shape of the mirror echoes its decorative element. The raised border of this mirror is separated into six lobes, creating the shape of a large flower.

75. Song 8 figures mirror with handle 宋八人物帶柄鏡

Song-Liao Dynasty（907-1279 AD）　　Total Length : 17.8cm　　Diameter of mirror face : 9.6cm　　Width of handle : 1.8cm

　　Long handles appear on the Song Dynasty mirrors, replacing the round knobs commonly seen. Much like the double phoenix mirror（雙鳳帶柄圓鏡）, a raised border frames the edge of the entire piece. Eight figures in various postures decorated the back of the mirror. Due to erosion and encrustation, they are blurry.

76. Song floral mirror 宋團花鏡

Song-Liao Dynasty（907-1279 AD）　　Diameter : 12.8cm

　　This piece has a small, round knob, which sits on a flattened, blossom. Four flowers of the same species surround it and rotate around the center. A plain border frames all this. Another Song mirror exhibits a similar floral pattern（see mirror 74）, where blossoms surround a single central knob. Furthermore, this is also reminiscent of a Tang piece（see mirror 41）with six flowering buds and a similar plain border.

77. Song multi-nipple TLV foiled mirror 宋多乳釘博局菱花鏡

Song-Liao Dynasty（907-1279 AD） Diameter : 11.8cm

The TLV design was common in the Han Dynasty, and now in the Song Dynasty, workshops transposed this motif onto mirrors of different shapes. Compare this piece with one of the earlier TLV Han pieces, mirror #26, "TLV mirror in New Han Dynasty by Wang Mang, The Second Year of the Xinfeng Reign, Xin Dynasty（15AD）王莽新漢 TLV鏡 . Its Song counterpart continues to have a square frame with twelve nipples. These surround a central knob just like the original piece. It is possible that further embellishments surrounded the central knob, but the mirror's heavily eroded surface makes it difficult to discern. Remnant outlines of four T's are still present, protruding from the central, square boundary, and two nipples decorate either side of these letters. Two stylistic features help us identify this as a Song Dynasty mirror rather than a Han Dynasty piece: the knob and shape of the mirror. While the Han Wang Mang TLV mirror has a large hemispheric knob, this object has the typical Song Dynasty knob, which is round but flattened at the top. Furthermore, this piece has six elaborate lobes that create a floral shape. Its form is common to the Song Dynasty whereas most Han TLV mirrors were circular in shape.

78. Song Nian the Second plain foiled mirror 宋念二菱花素鏡

Song-Liao Dynasty（907-1279 AD）　Diameter : 15.5cm

　　This is an eight-lobed mirror, crimped so they emulate the shape of a blooming flower. The knob is small and flattened at the top. Though the inscription on the left of the piece has eroded, the last two characters, "念二", has been seen in various other inscriptions stamped on other Song mirrors.

79. Song hanging plain mirror 宋掛式素鏡

Song-Liao Dynasty（907-1279 AD）   Diameter : 7.1cm   Width of hanging knob : 1.2cm

The surface of this mirror is undecorated save for a slightly raised border and central round, flattened knob. This piece is also unique as it has an extra knob. Protruding from the top of the mirror is a flat looped knob. This would allow the mirror to be held by hand using the central knob or hung on a wall with the other.

80. Song "*Jing-shan zi zao*" mirror with inscriptions on knob 宋敬山自造銘鈕鏡

Song-Liao Dynasty（907-1279 AD）   Diameter : 7.5cm

This is a new type of mirror that we have not seen before. The piece is smooth and undecorated except for its knob. Instead of a round, flattened shape, this mirror's knob is button-like and protrudes from the center like a short, circular column. Its face is flat and wide leaving room for the object's only embellishment, a small inscription. It reads "*Jing-shan zi zao*" translated as self-made by Jing-Shan the caster. Much like the earlier mirrors with phrases such as, 湖州真石家 and 真青銅照子記 , this is decoration is simply an identifying placard for the mirror's production locale and authenticity.

81. Song "*ying yang*" mirror 宋榮陽鏡

Song-Liao Dynasty（907-1279 AD）　　Diameter : 7cm

Like earlier mirrors with four characters, this piece only has inscriptive decorations. A raised border bevels and dips into the inner well of this circular mirror. At the center is a large hemispheric knob, different than the usual flattened, round knobs prevalent in the Song dynasty. In spindly font, the letters say "*ying yang*" 榮陽 , which is a county（xian 縣）in Henan Province in Northern Song.

82. Song mirror in remnant condition 宋殘素鏡

Song-Liao Dynasty（907-1279 AD）　　Diameter : 6cm

　　This is a Song mirror whose surface either has been eroded and/or damaged by age, or the mirror production itself lent the piece to be defective. The round shape and round, flattened knob on the piece is still clear ; however, all other decorative elements are mostly illegible. On the left of the knob, judging by the raised, rectangular shape of the damaged ornamentation, there may have been an inscription describing the place of production. There is also a slightly raised line on the right of the knob, perhaps indicating another inscription, also unfortunately illegible.

83. Song Huzhou Li Family lobed mirror 宋湖州李家葵花鏡

Song-Liao Dynasty（907-1279 AD） Diameter : 11.7cm

This is a plain six lobed mirror in the shape of a flower with only an inscriptive seal on its face. The characters are damaged but are able to indicate that the 李家 , or Li family workshop of Huzhou produced this mirror. Because of the similarity in seals and the characters in these pieces, it is easy to surmise what the inscription would likely have said despite damage that may erode the writing.

84. Song Huzhou Shi ju-ye's authentic lobed mirror 宋湖州祖業真石家葵花鏡

Song-Liao Dynasty（907-1279 AD） Diameter : 14.4cm

　　This is an eight-lobed miror, now with a smaller, narrower knob, and a clearer, and more intricate inscription on the face. It says 湖州祖業真石家煉銅鏡. This identifies the piece as an object cast in Huzhou a genuine bronze mirror from the workshop pasted down from the Shi family's ancestors. Like various other pieces, it serves as an identification that tells us where these bronze pieces were commonly produced.

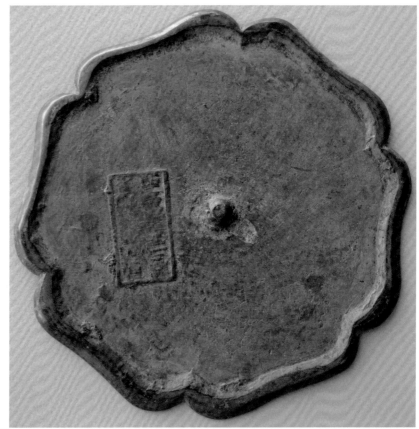

85. Song Huzhou lobed mirror with inscription in blurry condition 宋湖州葵鏡（字不辨）

Song-Liao Dynasty（907-1279 AD）　　Diameter : 8.3cm

　　This mirror has six lobes, creating a flower shape to the piece that is common to the Song mirrors. Like other lobed mirrors, it has a small round, flattened knob at its center, and a small rectangle on its surface indicating an inscription. The words have been eroded or were badly cast, causing the characters to be illegible. Nevertheless, by identifying these other specific stylistic typologies, the mirror is easily identified as a Song piece.

86. Song blurry square mirror 宋漫漶方鏡

Song-Liao Dynasty（907-1279 AD）　　Length：10.2cm　　Width：10.2cm

　　We have yet another mirror where its inscription is blurred beyond recognition. Its square shape, small, flattened round knob, and remnants of an inscriptive seal's border all suggest that it is a Song Dynasty mirror. However, the inscription itself, which usually indicates the place of production, is illegible. This superficial damage could be ancient, caused by a lack of attention while casting the piece, or the mirror's surface could have been eroded from age.

87. Song mirror with inscribed "*qi bin yu*" on knob 宋祁賓宇銘鈕素鏡

Song-Liao Dynasty（907-1279 AD）　　Diameter : 14.3cm

　　This mirror follows the same decorative motif as mirror #80. The surface is smooth and undecorated, but its central knob is larger with a flat surface. Surrounded by a round border, a small inscription now decorates the surface of this new type of knob. Read vertically, three characters read: *qi bin yu*, which is the name of the craftsman. On either side of this phrase are two characters, "*bao huan*" 包換 , which means return（exchange）guaranteed.

88. Song bundle floral round mirror 宋簇花圓鏡

Song-Liao Dynasty (907-1279 AD)   Diameter : 18cm

There are a variety of Song floral motifs (see mirrors 74, 76), but this piece has a unique type of ornamentation. Covering the entire surface of the circular mirror are various blooming flowers, overlapping and unfolding over one another. Unlike other pieces where there are only a few flowers that rotate around the central knob, all of the decorative elements in this piece meld together without a pattern or sequence. A plain border bounded by a repetitive frieze made of petals frames the ornately embellished surface. The design is made in low relief making it difficult to clearly discern the pattern.

89. Song plain round mirror 宋素圓鏡

Song-Liao Dynasty（907-1279 AD） Diameter : 7.3cm

This is a completely plain, undecorated piece. The mirror is circular and slightly concave. At its center is a large, round knob.

90. Song plain square mirror 宋素方鏡

Song-Liao Dynasty（907-1279 AD）　Length : 10cm　Width : 10cm

This is another undecorated mirror, now in the shape of a square. A thin raised band frames the plain surface, and a small hemispheric knob sits at the center.

91. Song plain mirror with refined circles 宋細弦紋素鏡

Song-Liao Dynasty（907-1279 AD）　　Diameter : 8.4cm

This piece has a thick border that bevels inward at the edge. A thin raised ring isolates this from the large, plain surface on the mirror. Another ring cast in low relief closely adjoins this. At the center is a small, flattened hemispheric knob. Though simplistic, these small details evoke the concentric circle embellishments popular in the Warring States period. Perhaps the Song Dynasty workshops sought to adapt these designs to decorate otherwise plain mirrors.

92. Song plain mirror single refined circle 宋細弦素鏡

Song-Liao Dynasty（907-1279 AD）　　Diameter : 8.4cm

A raised ring isolates this mirror into two parts, its center and beveled border. It has a large flattened hemispheric knob, and the concentric ring is cast in high-relief, creating more depth and dimension to the mirror's plain, undecorated surface.

93. Song plain lobed mirror（inscription illegible）
宋菱花素鏡（字不辨）

Song-Liao Dynasty（907-1279 AD）　　Diameter : 15.5cm

This is an eight-lobed mirror with a small-flattened round knob, and an illegible inscription positioned on the left side of the piece. Each lobe tapers slightly at the center, creating the effect of pointed petals.

94. Song Xue Huai Quan self-made mirror with inscriptions on knob 宋薛懷泉自造銘鈕鏡

Song-Liao Dynasty（907-1279 AD）　Diameter : 9.8cm

On this piece, the decorative inscription is found on the face of its knob, an adaptation from the rectangular seal often found on Song mirrors. Like other mirrors cast in this style, this inscription also indicates the piece's place of production. Reading down from the center then the right and left, the inscription indicates Xue Huai Quan （薛懷泉）, the renowned craftsman and workshop in the city of Huzhou with an affirmation of authenticity. Framing the entire piece is a plain, wide border.

95. Song Xue Huai Quan mirror with inscriptions on knob
宋薛懷泉銘鈕鏡

Song-Liao Dynasty（907-1279 AD）　　Diameter : 10.1cm

　　This is another plain, slightly concave mirror, with a flat, inscribed knob. However, the inscription has faded significantly making it illegible.

96. Song Xue Huai Quan mirror with inscriptions on knob
宋薛懷泉銘鈕鏡

Song-Liao Dynasty（907-1279 AD）　　Diameter : 9cm

　　We have yet another mirror produced in the same place as indicated by its inscription, "*Xue Huai Quan zao*" 薛懷泉造 on its flattened, central knob. This is a shortened version of the previous mirror's ornamentation but still indicates the workshop and authenticity. The surface of the piece continues to be undecorated.

97. Song Xue mirror with inscription on knob 宋薛銘鈕鏡

Song-Liao Dynasty（907-1279 AD）　Diameter：7.1cm

This mirror is cast in the same manner as the previous works. Its surface is undecorated, and only a large, flat, columnar knob decorates the center of the piece with an inscription. The characters are damaged but presumably indicate the place of production.

98. Song "Jin-quan" mirror with inscriptions on knob
宋近泉銘鈕鏡

Song-Liao Dynasty（907-1279 AD） Diameter : 9.1cm

We have the same type of mirror with an undecorated surface and flat knob, but a new inscription. The last characters are eroded, but the first two say *Jin-quan*（近泉）or, the name of the mirror maker. Despite coming from two different workshops, the mold used for these Song mirrors was widely used in various bronze workshops.

99. Song round mirror with "*qian qiu jin jian, xun ye pin kan*" inscriptions
宋「千秋金鑑，勳業頻看」銘文鏡

Song-Liao Dynasty（907-1279 AD）　Diameter : 15.5cm

The inscriptions of this mirror came from two literary allusions in the Tang dynasty. "*qian qiu jin jian*"（千秋金鑑 Golden Reflections of Thousand Autumns）refers to the ten chapters of political advisements and criticisms written by the Tang poet-courtier Zhang Jiu-ling（張九齡）who submitted them to Emperor Xuanzong（玄宗）on his birthday during the reign of the 24th year of Kaiyuan. Among the many treasures and rarities given to the Emperor by his noblemen, the royal highness preferred these ten chapters under the title "Collections of the Golden Reflections of Thousand Autumns" in which the poet wrote: "With the mirror, you reflect your own appearance. With the people, you reflect your own good and evil."（以鏡自照見形容，以人自照見吉凶）.

The other line of inscription "*xun ye pin kan*"（勳業頻看 Look frequently at meritorious achievements）refers to a couplet of Du Fu's（杜甫）poem "On the River"（江上）in which the poet says, "With meritorious achievements in high office, I frequently examine myself in the mirror；Dismissed from the office, I lean alone in a pavilion"（勳業頻看鏡，行藏獨倚樓）.

100. Song double dragon lobed mirror with handle 宋雙龍帶柄葵花鏡

Song-Liao Dynasty (907-1279 AD)　　Total Length : 15.8cm　　Diameter of mirror face : 9.5cm　　Width of handle : 2cm

　　This mirror is highly ornate with a dragon motif decorating its back. The creature breathes fire from its mouth, sending swirling flames from its mouth to its tail. The animal mimics the shape of the object and turns in circles. Adding further embellishment, a handle attaches itself to the bottom of the piece, and the mirror is cast in a six-lobed, floral shape.

Yuan, Ming and Qing Dynasties

Yuan, Ming and Qing Dynasties

101. Ming Hongwu 22nd year reign cloud-dragon mirror 明洪武廿二年雲龍鏡

Ming Dynasty（1368-1644 AD） Diameter：11.4cm

This Ming dynasty mirror has a round, circular shape framed by a plain wide rim. At its center, an intricate design motif portrays a dragon soaring through a cloud pattern created by faint, hachured lines. Cast in high-relief, further details show the mythical beast's hind leg tangled with its long tail, and infinitesimal scales coating the dragon's long, snake-like body. The creature turns to the left, facing an ornate inscription, which says:

Made on the 1st day of the 1st month in Hongwu 22nd year reign

洪武二十二年正月日造

To add further embellishment, wave-like swirling clouds isolate the inscription to the left from the dragon covering most of the mirror's surface. At the center is an extremely small, circular knob, flattened on top. The dragon motif is popular after the Yuan Dynasty and into the Ming, where it symbolizes the emperor.[1] This mirror was made during the 22nd year of the Hongwu Emperor's reign (1389AD), during the early Ming Dynasty.

1 | Graham, 286.

102. Ming cloud-dragon mirror 明雲龍鏡

Ming Dynasty（1368-1644 AD） Diameter：11cm

We have yet another piece with a dragon motif, but cast in a different manner. The ornamentation of this mirror is reminiscent of the Warring States, where we see pieces such as the Warring States mirror with coiled dragons（戰國蟠螭紋鏡，see mirror 1）, where flat, intersecting serpents decorate the face of a round, plain framed, mirror. Now, we have a flat rim again, with a smaller concentric ring, which isolates the main pattern. At the center, sitting on a circle framed by another concentric ring is a small, flat-faced, round knob. On the main register, we see the face of

a single dragon, its mouth open and its face turned to the side. One of its three-clawed arms extends forward; we possibly see a small wing extending from its snake-like body. Unlike the Warring States piece, where the repetitive pattern evenly distributes itself across the face of the mirror, this Ming mirror's decoration seems off-balanced. As the dragon's body knots and intersects with itself, the ornamentation remains concentrated mostly in the upper part of the mirror. The lower third of the mirror is relatively undecorated and uninterrupted by the dragon's curling body. Furthermore, the top third of the mirror clearly delineates the body of the mythical creature with its head, legs, and body all cast in low-relief. The pattern becomes more abstracted and more difficult to differentiate the animal from other decorative embellishments.

103. Ming 3 cloud dragon Han imitation mirror 明三雲龍仿漢鏡

Ming Dynasty（1368-1644 AD）　　Diameter：10.5cm

Like the Song, Liao, and Jin Dynasties, the Ming Dynasty also borrowed motifs from their predecessors. Here, we see the popular saw-toothed pattern prevalent in Han Dynasty mirrors. Furthermore, the Ming workshop sought to emulate the concentric ring design also popular in the early bronze mirrors. The rim has a plain, thick rim, and a thinner concentric ring, which adjoins the saw-toothed embellishment. At the center, bounded by another raised ring are the faint forms of three dragons. Much like the *kui* dragons,（see mirror 5）, they rotate around the large, hemispheric knob, which sits at the center of the mirror. There are still remnants of scales decorating the spine of each creature, as well as their hind legs and tails. Thick swirling lines, possibly suggest a ground pattern of clouds. The mirror is in poor condition : either it was crudely cast or was badly preserved. Despite this, we can still identify older motifs reused in a modern piece readapted to serve a new meaning.

104. Ming hand mirror with "*lian jin san yuan*" inscriptions #1 明「連進三元」掌中鏡之一

Ming Dynasty（1368-1644 AD）　Diameter：5.6cm

　　This piece has a specific phrase, 連進三元, which wishes the bearer success in passing three levels of examination which are 1/ the civil examination at the provincial capital（鄉試）, 2/ civil examination at the national capital（會試）, and 3/ civil examination in the imperial palace（殿試）. Read from top to bottom, right to left, the four characters decorate most of the mirror and surround a protrusion with a flattened top, presumably the worn remnants of a knob. Bounding the inscription is a granulated border and thin raised ring, which isolate this middle register from the edge. The piece bevels outward and has a thin, decorated raised rim.

105. Ming hand mirror with "*lian jin san yuan*" inscriptions #2 明連進三元掌中鏡之二

Ming Dynasty（1368-1644 AD）　　Diameter：5.6cm

We have another Ming mirror with a similar description but a different decorative motif. This time, the circular mirror has a thin raised border and a single raised ring which bounds the central register. In faded, large script, it says, "連中三元" which means passing the three levels of civil examinations.

At the center of the mirror sits a thin, fluted knob. Comparing this and the previous piece, we see now that these mirrors with similar inscriptions could easily be mass-produced with only slight stylistic variations.

106. Ming mirror with (*qing xian*) inscriptions 明清閑鏡

Ming Dynasty（1368-1644 AD） Diameter：7.2cm

We now have a mirror with a beveled rim that creates a deep well on the face of the piece. In this central space, two pairs of figures frame the words "*qing xian*"（清閑, or leisure）, which is cast above and below the mirror's flattened, round knob. It is possible that there is a 5th figure near the right edge of the mirror, but the details of this piece have worn away. There is another decorative element on the left edge as well.

107. Ming mirror with "*wei shan zui le*"（The Joy of Charity）inscriptions 明為善最樂鏡

Ming Dynasty（1368-1644 AD）　　Diameter：6cm

    This inscriptive mirror says, "*wei shan zui le*"（為善最樂）, or the act of kindness or charity brings the greatness happiness. The characters are large and decorate either side of a large lobed knob whose top has been flattened. The script looks contemporary, and the words are the only embellishment on the surface of the piece. A single concentric ring isolated the central decoration from the plain rim with a raised edge.

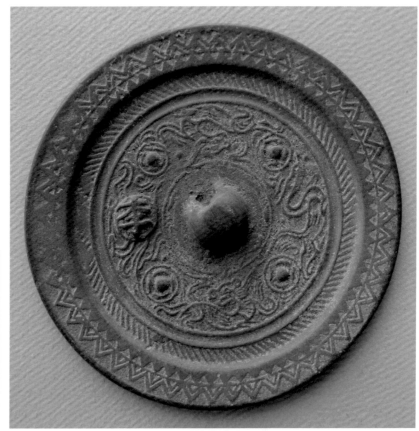

108. Ming Li's imitation of a Han 4 nipple 4 divine beast mirror 明李氏仿漢四乳四靈鏡

Ming Dynasty（1368-1644 AD）　　Diameter：9.5cm

　　Ming Dynasty bronze workshops often produced works inspired by or copied from Han Dynasty pieces；thus, how can we discern between the two eras？This Ming Dynasty mirror uses a four nipple, four divine beast decorative motif that we have seen before（see mirror 14 and 17）. Now, however, its central, round, flattened knob is a stylistic element characteristic of the later dynasties rather than the Han. The wide border has two registers, an outer one with a double saw-toothed pattern, and an adjoining band with a single-saw-toothed design. None of the mirrors in this collection have these two saw-toothed friezes placed next to one another for such an ornate frame. A hachured and indented band frame the main register with four divine beasts, the Blue dragon of the East, the Vermilion Bird of the South, the White Tiger of the West, and the Black Turtle of the North. Four nipples each set in circles isolate the mythic creatures into four distinct spaces. What seems most telling of this mirror's later production is the button-like insignia, 李, superimposed whether the Black Turtle is cast. This indicates the workshop or imitator's creator, and only from the Song dynasty onward do we have inscriptions that suggest bronze mirrors' production context. Here we have a cleverly cast piece which reuses an old, popular motif for a new, more secular era.

109. Ming Lu-made imitation of a Han 4 nipple 4 divine beast thick border mirror
明呂造仿漢四乳四靈寬緣鏡

Ming Dynasty (1368-1644 AD)　　Diameter：11.5cm

　　This is another Ming mirror inspired by its Han predecessors. On the main register, the four divine beasts are now further abstracted, with possibly a celestial companion included in the motif. Superimposed at oppose sides are two characters, "Lu Zao" (呂造), which likely indicates this piece was cast or made by the craftsman with a surname Lu. Buttressing either side of this band are two hachured rings. One of these bands isolates the central motif, a thick raised ring surrounding a flattened, round knob at the center of the mirror. On the outer edge, a thick plain border rims the entire piece.

110. Imitation Tang lobed erotic mirror 明風月仿唐瑞獸葵花鏡

Ming Dynasty（1368-1644 AD） Diameter：11.5cm

There are remnants of four figures rotating around the central, flat-topped hemispheric knob. These easily could have been the dog-like creatures seen in various Tang mirrors, and small cloud-like motifs decorate the outer border. Due to the corroded condition of the mirror, it can only be suggested that there might be erotic images behind these four figures. It is clear however, that this is not a Tang Dynasty original and rather a more contemporary replica. The large flat-topped hemispheric knob at the center is seen in the Song Dynasty and onwards, whereas Tang mirrors usually had smaller, hemispheric knobs. The decoration in the outer border is rather crude and uncommon in the Tang era. Now, we see the recycling of old motifs, synthesized with popular styles（the knob, lobed shape）, to create a new aesthetic language in the Ming and Qing bronze mirrors.

111. Ming square erotic mirror 明風月方鏡

Ming Dynasty（1368-1644 AD）   Diameter：length：9.8cm   Width：9.8cm

    This square Ming mirror is in excellent condition and depicts four figural, erotic scenes. Framed within a plain raised rim, a male character, identified by his single, round topknot, engages in sexual positions with four, distinct female companions, each wearing a different hairstyle. The vignettes cover each corner of the mirror, and each pair is cast in three-dimensional, high relief. These four scenes erotic scenes are the only decorations on the object's otherwise plain surface except for a flat, looped knob sits at the center of the mirror.

112. Qing "*hou de rong gui*" inscription mirror 清厚德榮貴鏡

Qing Dynasty（1644-1911 AD）　　Diameter : 5.1cm

　　This Qing mirror looks like a coin, with a brown-gold sheen and four characters surrounding a small lobed, flattened knob. Framed in thick rectangles, the words read, "*hou de rong gui*"（厚德榮貴）, which roughly translates to great virtue or kindness breeds thriving wealth or high rank. Aspirations of wealth, success, and happiness are prevalent inscriptions printed on the Ming and Qing mirrors. A thin ring creates a plain, undecorated border, but on the right side of the piece, we see a possible miscasting where the wax impression did not leave an impression on the bronze mirror's surface. With this as the few last pieces in the collection, we can consider the great stylistic changes undergone from the Warring States to Qing bronze mirror production. From intricate, intertwining serpents, to secular, wishful inscriptions, these utilitarian pieces reflect the trends of their original context, which change by dynasty and even resurface in imitations and adaptations. Most of all, these bronze mirrors recount the lifespan of a single artifact, and its timeless role in Chinese culture.

113. Ming Lan's erotic mirror 明蘭氏風月鏡

Ming Dynasty（1368-1644 AD） Diameter：9.5cm

The remaining embellishments on this piece have deteriorated heavily, leaving few defining stylistic elements. An inscription is printed with the character "Lan"（蘭）, presumably the surname of the mirror's workshop owner. However, it may also serves as a strong hint to associate with the author of the renowned Chinese erotic novel *The Golden Lotus*（金瓶梅）whose name is "The Laughing Scholar from Lanling"（*Lanling Xiao Xiao Sheng* 蘭陵笑笑生）. Lanling is in Shandong province of today. Figures cast in high relief possibly surround the large, round, flattened knob at the mirror's center, and the edge bevels outward to create a wide, raised plain border that frames the piece. From its title, the same motif seen in the previous piece (see mirror 111) could have been transposed and recast onto this circular mirror. A green patina covers its entire surface.

114. Qing "*Si xi*" Four Happiness mirror 清四喜鏡

Qing Dynasty（1644-1911 AD）　　Diameter：5.5cm

　　We have a smaller version of the previous mirror, where we see the same coin-like motif with four characters. This time in each plain square frame, the character, "xi" 喜, a favorable and celebratory term for happiness. The basic four happiness are "Luck"（福）, "Fortune"（祿）, "Longevity"（壽）, and "Joy"（禧）, a more extended meaning of the four happiness is quite poetic in the following:

A good rain after a long drought	久旱逢甘雨
To meet an old friend in a distant land	他鄉遇故知
A wedding festivities night with candles lit	洞房花燭夜
To pass the palace civil examination on top of the list	金榜題名時

　　In this mirror, the character, "xi" is stamped on the four opposite axes in the same place as each character in the previous "*hou de rong gui*" Qing mirror, surrounding a small, central knob. A plain, raised rim also frames this piece.

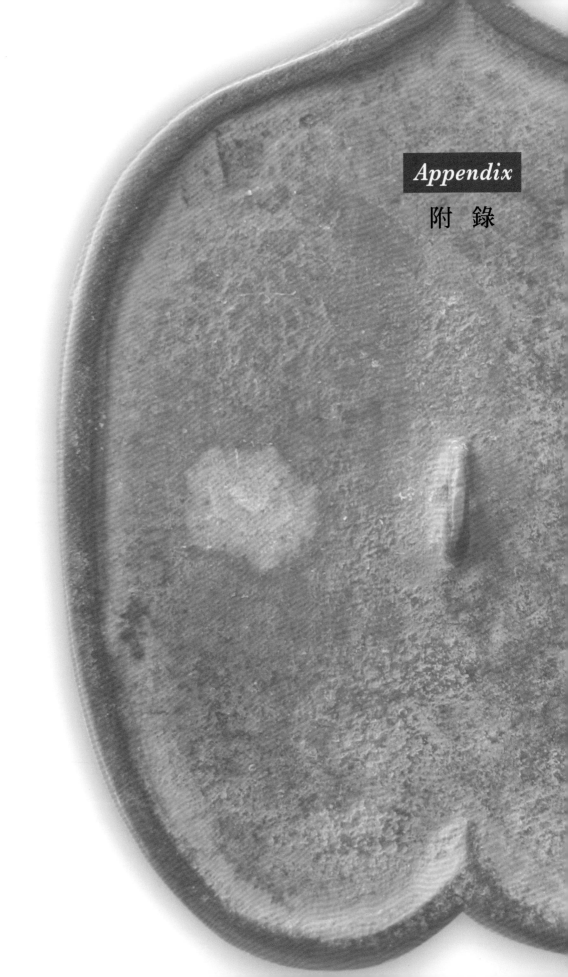

Appendix

附　錄

Selected Bibliography

Books and articles in English:

· Bulling, Anneliesse. *The Decoration of Mirrors of the Han Period: A Chronology*,（Artibus Asiae Supplementum 20）, Ascona: Artibus Asiae Publishers, 1959.

· Cahill, Suzanne, et al. *The Lloyd Cotsen Study Collection of Chinese Bronze Mirrors:* Volume I: Catalogue ; Volume II: Studies（MONUMENTA ARCHAEOLOGICA）, Los Angeles: Cotsen Institute of Archaeology, 2011.

· Cahill, Suzanne, "The Word Made Bronze: Inscriptions on Medieval Chinese Bronze Mirrors." *Archives of Asian Art* 39, 1986, 62-70.

· Chase, W.T. & Ursula Martius Franklin. "Early Chinese Black Mirrors and Pattern-Etched Weapons." *Ars Orientalis* xi, 1979, 215-258.

· Chou, Ju-hsi , *Circles of Reflection : The Carter Collection of Chinese Bronze Mirrors*, Cleveland: Cleveland Museum of Art , 2000.

· Dohrenwend, Doris. "The Early Chinese Mirror" *Artibus Asiae*（later abbreviated as *AA*）27:1/2, 1964, 79-98.

· Graham Jr. Donald H., Nakano Toro et al ed., *Bronze Mirrors from Ancient China: Donald H. Graham Jr. Collection*, Hong Kong : *Orientations* Magazine, 1994

· Hirth, Friedrich. *Chinese Metallic Mirrors ; with Notes on Some Ancient Specimens of the Musee Guimet*（《中國銅鏡》）. Paris. New York: G. E. Stechert, 1907.

· Kargren, Bernard. "Early Chinese Mirror Inscriptions" *Bulletin of the Museum of Far Eastern Antiquities*,（later abbreviated as BMFEA）6, 1934, 9-79.

· Kargren, Bernard. "Early Chinese Mirror Inscriptions" Bulletin of the Museum of Far Eastern Antiquities, "Huai and Han" , *BMFEA*,13, 1941, 1-125.

· Kargren, Bernard. "Early Chinese Mirror Inscriptions" Bulletin of the Museum of Far Eastern Antiquities, "Some Pre-Han Mirrors," *BMFEA* 35, 1963, 161-169.

· Kargren, Bernard. "Early Chinese Mirror Inscriptions" Bulletin of the Museum of Far Eastern Antiquities, "Early Chinese Mirrors: Classifications Scheme Recapitulated." *BMFEA* 40, 1968, 79-95.

· Lawton, Thomas. *Chinese Art of the Warring States Period: Change and Continuity 480-220 B.C.* Washington D.C. : Freer Gallery of Art, Smithsonian Institution, 1982.

· Lawton , Thomas. "Changing Concepts in the Connoisseurship of Chinese Bronze Mirrors" , *Luminous Perfection: Fine Chinese Mirrors from The Robert H. Ellsworth Collection, Christie's catalog*, New York, 22 March, 2012, 8-21.

· Li, Yinde, translated by Harold Mok, "A Han Bronze Mirror" *Orientations*（Oct. 1990）, 74-75.

· Loewe, Michael. "TLV mirrors and their significance" *in Ways to Paradise: The Chinese Quest for Immortality*, London: George Allen & Unwin, 1979, 60-87.

· MacKenzie, Colin. "The Influence of Textile Designs on Bronze, Lacquer and Ceramic Decorative Styles during the Warring States Periods." *Orientations*（Sept. 1999）, 82-91.

· Needham, Joseph. *Science and Civilization in China, vol. IV/1*. Cambridge: Cambridge University Press, 1962.

· Meeks, Nigel. "Patination Phenomenon on Roman and Chinese High-Tin Bronze Mirrors and Other Artefacts" *Metal Plating and Patination: Cultural, Technical, and Historical Developments.* Ed. Susan La Niece and Paul Craddock. Oxford: Butterworth-Heinemann, 1993.

· O' Donoghue, Diane M. *Reflections and Reception: The Origins of the Mirror in Bronze Age China*, Museum of Far Eastern Antiquities, Stockholm Bulletin, v.62, 1990.

· Rupert, Milan. & O.J. Todd. *Chinese Bronze Mirrors*, Peiping, 1935.

· Schuyler, Cammann. "The TLV Pattern on Cosmic Mirror of the Han Dynasty." *Journal of the American Oriental Society* 68（Oct-Dec）, 1948, 159-168.

· Soper Alexander C. "The evolution of the T'eng lion and grapevine mirror. With an addendum The "Jen Shou" mirrors", Ascona Artibus Asiae Publishers, 1967.

· Swallow, R.W. *Ancient Chinese Bronze Mirrors*. Peking: H. Vetch., 1937.

· Thompson, Nancy. *The Evolution of the T'ang Lion and Grapevine Mirror. With an Addendum : The Jen Shou Mirrors by Alexander C. Soper*. Ascona: Artibus Asiae Publishers, 1967.

· Tseng, Lillian Lan-ying. *Picturing Heaven in Early China*（Harvard East Asian Monographs）Harvard University Asia Center, 2011.

· Wong, Yanchung . "Bronze Mirror Art of the Han Dynasty", *Orientations*,（Dec. 1988）42-53.

· Yang, Lien-sheng. "An additional Note on the Ancient Game Liu-bo," *Harvard Journal of Asiatic Studies*, 15, no.1/2 1952, pp.124-139.

Books and articles in Chinese 中文參考書籍及論文：

I. 博物館圖錄：

·上海博物館編，《練形神冶　瑩質良工——上海博物館藏銅鏡精品》，上海：上海書畫出版社，2005。

·國立歷史博物館編輯委員會編，《歷代銅鏡》，臺北市：國立歷史博物館，1996。

·中國青銅器全集編輯委員會編，《中國青銅器全集》，第 16 卷《銅鏡》，北京：文物出版社，1998。

·北京故宮博物院，何林主編，《你應該知道的 200 件銅鏡》，台北：藝術家出版社，2007。

·國立故宮博物院編輯委員會編，《故宮銅鏡特展圖錄》兩冊，台北：國立故宮博物院，1986。

·國立故宮博物院，《故宮銅鏡選萃》，台北：國立故宮博物院，1971.

·吳哲夫，朱仁星，《中華五千年文物集刊：銅鏡篇》上下冊，台北：中華五千年文物集刊編輯委員會，1993。

·上海博物館編，《上海博物館藏青銅鏡》，上海美術出版社，1986。

·日本京都國立博物館，《守屋孝藏蒐集方格規矩四神鏡圖錄》，京都國立博物館，1969。

·旅順博物館，《旅順博物館藏銅鏡》，北京：文物出版社，1997。

·洛陽博物館，《洛陽出土銅鏡》，北京：文物出版社，1988。

·湖南省博物館編，《湖南出土銅鏡圖錄》，北京：文物出版社，1960。

·湖北省博物館，鄂州市博物館編，《鄂城漢三國六朝銅鏡》，北京：文物出版社，1986。

·鄂州市博物館，《鄂州銅鏡》，北京：中國文學出版社，2002。

·洛陽博物館編，《洛陽出土銅鏡》，北京：文物出版社，1988。

II. 著作：

·梁上椿，《岩窟藏鏡》，北京：育華印刷所、大業印刷局，1941。

·梁上椿，《巖窟藏鏡》，台北：國立中央研究院歷史語言研究所，1983，影印本。

·沈從文，《唐宋銅鏡》，北京：中國古典藝術出版社，1958。

·勞幹，〈六博及博局的演變〉，台北《歷史語言研究所集刊》35，1964，15-30。

·阮崇武‧毛增滇，《中國「透光」古銅鏡的奧秘》，上海：上海科學技術出版社，1982。

·孔祥星、劉一曼，《中國古代銅鏡》，北京：文物出版社，1984。

·周世榮編，《銅鏡圖案》。北京：人民美術出版社，1986。

·周世榮編，《銅鏡圖案——湖南出土歷代銅鏡》，長沙：湖南美術出版社，1987。

·王士倫，《浙江出土銅鏡》，北京：文物出版社，1987。

·施翠峰，《中國歷代銅鏡鑑賞》，台北：台灣省立博物館，1990。

·張英，《吉林出土銅鏡》，北京：文物出版社，1990。

·孔祥星、劉一曼，《中國銅鏡圖典》，北京：文物出版社，1992，1994。

·周世榮，《中華歷代銅鏡鑑定》，北京：紫禁城出版社，1993。

·孔祥星、劉一曼，《中國古銅鏡》，台北市：藝術圖書，1994。

·聶世美，《菱花照影——中國鏡文化》，上海：上海古籍出版社，1994。

·李澤奉‧劉如仲，《銅鏡鑒賞與收藏》，長春：吉林科學技術出版社，1994。

·黃茂琳，〈銅鏡、六博局上所謂 TLV/ 規矩紋與博局曲道破譯及相關問題〉，《亞洲文明》第 3 集，安徽教育出版社，1995，97-120。

·李縉雲，《古鏡鑒賞》，桂林：漓江出版社，1995。

·周世榮編繪，《中國銅鏡圖案集》。上海：上海書店，1995。

·裘士京編著，《銅鏡》，合肥：黃山書社，1995。

·郭玉海編著，《故宮藏鏡》，北京：紫禁城出版社，1996。

· 傅舉有，〈論杯文楚鏡·湖南博物館〉，香港《Art of China，中國文物世界》，no.144，August，1997，60-73。

· 傅舉有，〈漢鏡之美燦爛千古〉，台北《歷史文物》月刊，vol.8，no.1，1998，48-55。

· 劉淑娟，《遼代銅鏡研究》，瀋陽：瀋陽社出版，1997。

· 昭明、洪海，《古代銅鏡》，北京：中國書店，1997。

· 趙力光、李文英編著，《中國古代銅鏡》，西安：陝西人民出版社，1997。

· 江蘇廣陵古籍刻印社，影印本《簠齋藏鏡》，據民國劉建叔拓本陳介祺 108 方拓片影印本重印，揚州：江蘇廣陵古籍刻印社，1997。

· 華光普主編，《中國歷代銅鏡目錄》，北京：中國環境科學出版社，1998。

· 馬今洪，《漢鏡》（老古董百科大全·珍賞系列 4），上海：上海科學普及出版社，1998。

· 曾藍瑩，〈尹灣漢墓「博局占」木牘試解〉，《文物》no.8，1999，62-65。

· 董亞巍，《中國古代銅鏡工藝技術研究》，鄂州：自印，1999。

· 何堂坤，《中國古代銅鏡的技術研究》，北京：紫禁城出版社，1999。

· 鄧秋玲，〈戰國山字紋銅鏡析論〉，台北《歷史文物》月刊，no.68，3 月，1999，48-60 頁。

· 游振群，〈漢代六博與博戲之風〉，台北《故宮文物》月刊，vol. 17，no.9，1999，114-133 頁。

· 余繼明編著，《中國銅鏡圖鑑》，杭州：浙江大學出版社，2000。

· 辛冠潔，《陳介祺藏鏡》（線裝本上中下三冊），北京：文物出版社，2001。

· 王度，《淨月澄華 · 息齋藏鏡》，台北：台北國立歷史博物館編輯委員會，2001。

· 沈從文，《花花朵朵 · 壇壇罐罐》，南京：江蘇美術出版社，2002。

· 張錯，〈融舊鑄新，開宗立範——戰國銅鏡的工藝與風格〉，台北《歷史文物》月刊，5 月，no.106，2002，30-39 頁。

· 張錯，〈從昭明到博局——漢代銅鏡的文化藝術〉，台北《歷史文物》月刊，9 月，no.110，2002，8-17 頁。

· 程林泉 · 韓國河，《長安漢鏡》，西安：陝西人民出版社，2002。

· 張金明 · 陸旭春，《中國古銅鏡鑑賞圖錄》，北京：中國民族攝影藝術出版社，2002。

· 孫立謀，《銅鏡珍藏》，瀋陽：遼寧畫報出版社，2002。

· 陳晴，《古鏡——美的觀照》，上海：上海書店出版社，2003。

· 孔祥星、劉一曼，《銅鏡鑑藏》，長春：吉林科學技術出版社，2004。

· 王綱懷，《三槐堂藏鏡》，北京：文物出版社，2004。

· 劉寧編著，《我愛收藏：銅鏡知識 30 講》，北京：榮寶齋出版社，2004。

· 沈從文，《銅鏡史話》。瀋陽市： 萬卷出版公司，2005。

· 管維良，《中國銅鏡史》，重慶：重慶出版社，2006。

· 姚江波，《中國歷代銅鏡賞玩》，長沙：湖南美術出版社，2006。

· 張錯，〈一面銅鏡還是五面銅鏡？唐傳奇〈古鏡記〉視覺文本的探求〉，台北《故宮文物》月刊，4 月，no.277，2006，80-91 頁。

· 張錯，〈素以為絢兮——宋代銘文素鏡風貌〉，台北《故宮文物》月刊，no.295，10 月，2007，68-77 頁 .

· 何富生，《百鏡解讀》，天津：百花文藝出版社，2007。

· 王綱懷 · 孫克讓編著，《唐代銅鏡與唐詩》，上海：上海古籍出版社，2007。

· 曹菁菁 · 盧芳玉，《陳介祺藏古拓本選編銅鏡卷》，浙江古籍出版社，2008。

· 張東，《銅鏡》，上海：上海書畫出版社，2010。

· 丁孟，《古代銅鏡收藏入門不可不知的金律》，濟南：山東美術出版社，2011。

國家圖書館出版品預行編目（CIP）資料

青銅鑑容：「今昔居」青銅藏鏡鑑賞與文化研究 /
張錯著. -- 初版. -- 臺北市：藝術家, 2015.05
256面；26×19公分
中英對照

ISBN 978-986-282-140-4（平裝）

1.銅鏡　2.青銅藝術　3.圖錄

793.61025　　　　　　　　　　103024462

Bronze Luminescence
青銅鑑容

Bronze Mirror Collections from the Present-Past Dwelling
「今昔居」青銅藏鏡鑑賞與文化研究

Dominic Cheung ◎ 張錯 著
With the assistance of Alexandria Yen

© 2015 Dominic Cheung
First published in Taiwan in 2015 by Artist Publishing Co.
6F, No. 147, Sec.1, Chongqing S. Rd., Zhongzheng Didtrict, Taipei City 100,
Taiwan, R. O. C.
Tel: 886-2-23886715　886-2-23719692~3
Fax: 886-2-23896655　886-2-23317096
e-mail: art.books@msa.hinet.net

Publisher
Ho Cheng-kuang

Chief Editor
Wang Ting-mei

Executive Editor
Lin Jung-nien

Art Design
Wang Hsiao-mei

Publishing Office
Artist Publishing Co.
6F, No. 147, Sec.1, Chongqing S. Rd., Zhongzheng Didtrict, Taipei City 100,
Taiwan, R. O. C.
e-mail: art.books@msa.hinet.net

First Edition 2015

發行人　何政廣
總編輯　王庭玫
編輯　　林容年、陳珮藝
美編　　王孝嫩

出版者　藝術家出版社
　　　　台北市重慶南路一段147號6樓
　　　　TEL：（02）23719692~3
　　　　FAX：（02）23317096
　　　　郵政劃撥：01044798
　　　　戶名：藝術家雜誌社

總經銷　時報文化出版企業股份有限公司
　　　　桃園市龜山區萬壽路二段351號
　　　　TEL：（02）23066842

南區代理　台南市西門路一段223巷10弄26號
　　　　　TEL：（06）2617268
　　　　　FAX：（06）2637698

製版印刷　鴻展彩色印刷（股）公司
初版　　　2015年5月
定價　　　新臺幣580元

ISBN　978-986-282-140-4（平裝）

法律顧問　蕭雄淋